1945
ANDREW DURDAN FARM
One Year in the Life of an Illinois Farming Family

Copyright 2007 Jeffrey A. Sparks

Dear Jim,

Thank you for your support of my book. Best Wishes,

Jeff Sparks
6-16-15

Jeff Sparks
06-26-08

Acknowledgements

This book would not have been possible without the help of so many wonderful people.

Thank you to my Mom, Esther (Durdan) Sparks, who provided me with untold stories of her childhood, the family, and the farm. These memories of her childhood, along with Grandpa Durdan's 1945 diary were the foundation for compiling this book. Mom was also the chief editor of this publication.

Thank you to my wife, Wendi, who provided love, encouragement, and support during the months and years it took to write the book. She was behind me 100% all the way.

I want to say thank you to those who willingly shared their knowledge on farming, our family, and life in that era:

Jack Armstrong
Jean Armstrong
Bob Armstrong
Sarah (Armstrong) Diss
Frank Diss
Richard Palaschak, my beloved Uncle (now deceased)
Leland Shields
Kenneth Kollar
Marge Fraser
William Fraser
Sue Fraser
Irene (Durdan) Vercimak
(only living sibling of Andrew Durdan)
Monica (Durdan) Brown
Harold Sparks
Chris (Sparks) Coil
Tony Sparks
Elizabeth Davis
Diane Robinson
Patty (Armstrong) Hayne
R. G. Bluemer
Teresa Italiano Budish

Andy Durdan holding first born, Darlene (circa 1923).
Andy at 27 years of age.

Andrew Durdan

Andrew Durdan was the oldest of 12 brothers and sisters. He stood about six foot two inches tall, and like his brothers, was a little on the hefty side. He was a good father and husband. He and his loving wife of forty years, Mabel, had five girls: Darlene, Gladys, Nancy, Esther, and Joyce. Andy attended school through the seventh grade. As the eldest son, it was best for the family that Andy leave school and help his Dad in the fields. This is where he learned first-hand what was required to run a farm. Like his Father, Andy was very methodical and consistent in everything he did. He maintained his machinery with great care, and kept the house, farmyard, and farm buildings in tip-top shape. He had a wonderful sense of humor and was a very friendly person. In 2005, Jack Armstrong, the son of one of Andy's closest friend Linc Armstrong, said: "Andy never had an unkind word to say about anyone." Every evening before he went to bed, Andy entered his daily activities in his diary. These journals were a gift to his family and gave us a unique insight into this Illinois farming family's life – year after year.

3

TABLE OF CONTENTS

CHAPTER   **PAGE**

JANUARY

I've never needed an alarm clock as nature's morning routine on the farm started long before seven. January 1st, 1945 - the start of a new year to give us hope that God will bring us a better year than last, and that the wars in Europe and the Pacific would soon end.

The wind was beating hard against the windows. Pulling the curtains back revealed it had snowed much of the night. It was not the snow that bothered me as much as the wind, which was drifting the snow that had fallen the previous two days. Looking in the direction of the new garage, one could see how much snow was piled up on the roof to gauge accumulation. Perhaps eight inches on the south side and less on the north side due to the direction of the wind. The northern winds blowing added depth to the drifts against the house, the fences, or anywhere it wished. Good thing the chains were still on the truck – this I had done three days ago. The chains would come in handy today, as chances are that someone would need help if they get stuck in the snow or slid into a ditch. The county's road grader had not yet made it down our road. It wouldn't be surprising if the grader didn't make it down our country road for another day or so. I had cleared the driveway with the Fordson yesterday afternoon, but it was drifted over again, so it would need more attention today.

Morning Chores

Mabel lay peacefully under layers of blankets. She was not fond of these cold mornings. My first chore would be to shovel coal into the furnace in the basement, which will bring the house back to life after the cold air slipped in through the doors and windows throughout the night. Passing through the kitchen on my way to the basement, I noted the temperature outside was 15 above, inside was 56. The cinders from the day before were still burning but needed a boost to heat our old house. I stoked the coals and added ten or so fresh shovels. The huge furnace and coal bin are located in the southwest corner of the basement, with the bin being just below the window where we replenish the supply using the coal chute. It wouldn't be long and it would be above 65 degrees inside. Part of my usual morning routine was to fill the percolator with water and a generous amount of coffee and plug it in. The smell of coffee brewing always makes me feel good and helps me to start a new day.

While the coffee was percolating, I put on my heavy denim coat, my thick wool hat with earflaps, and my trusty winter gloves and headed out the kitchen door. I passed Alfie on my way out - sitting in the pantry. He was usually more than willing to come along with me when doing my chores, but this morning he was a bit reluctant. However, my good friend got up slowly and went outside with me. Alfie was our loyal family dog. He was part collie and part terrier. He was mostly black with white spots on his nose, belly, and legs.

Next in my normal morning routine was to milk the cows. After filling one milk can, I walked outside and placed the can in the horse tank, as the milk truck would not be down today. The horse tank was just outside the barn – it held about 50 gallons of drinking water for the horses and cows. The horse tank kept from freezing by using a submersible electric heater that I purchased from Montgomery Wards. Back in the barn the cows seemed content and warm, looking back at me as if to say "Thanks Andy, can we go outside now?" My next chore was to open the barn doors, and one-by-one, release the cows from their stall clamp - which held them in place while they were milked. The cows slowly made their way outside to a small grazing area south of the barn, and around to the east side of the barn where I put out some feed for them and where they could drink from the horse tank. Later in the morning, I would let the horses out to get their drink of water and feed them oats. With the cows outside, it gave me the opportunity to clean the stalls. Using a pitchfork, I scooped the soiled hay into a wheelbarrow and wheeled the waste out to the pile south of the barn where it was collected over time to be used later on the field as fertilizer. After making a few trips with the wheelbarrow, I cleaned the stall floor, and laid down fresh straw, which was stored in the barn.

Four Horses

We had four horses: Buster, Ginger, Clyde, and Molly. Since we bought the tractors, we relied less and less on them. We learned how to farm using horses, and had a hard time shifting to the tractor. When we worked with the horses, we were a team. Tractors allowed us to farm the land much faster, but I longed for the simpler days. Tractors broke down often and needed lots of preventive maintenance. I always felt that the horses were sad when I rode past them on the tractor. They were being replaced and there was something missing in their step. We still used the horses as much as we could. They came in real handy using the cultivator to pull up the weeds when the corn was just coming up. Also,

9

when the tractors got stuck in real thick mud, or when the tractors or wagons would freeze in the ground, the horses could still get traction and pull the equipment free. There were so many things that the horses could do that the machinery couldn't. We were attached to our horses as much as we are to our family dog.

I remember the time when I was cultivating the small amount of land just east of the pig lot. In small areas, it was much easier to work with horses than with a tractor. However, sometimes the horses made up their minds that they wanted to do something else and would just do it. About half way through cultivating a small plot last year, the horses decided they wanted a drink of water. They moved a little faster and started bolting, breaking the harness, and leaving me, and the cultivator, behind. They trotted toward the barnyard and the horse tank. You could hear their hooves hitting the ground and the harness rattling. This alerted Mabel, and her mother who was visiting at the time, as to what had happened. Mabel's mother, who was in her seventies and all of five foot three, walked up to those large horses as they were slurping the water, and called to them – "whoa...whoa". She then grabbed their bridles, soothed them by talking to them, holding them steady until I got there. Although the horses were mostly tame, I could not believe a woman of her stature could handle those large horses so well.

I could tell that the horses were getting a little hungry as they were getting rambunctious. I had two feeder containers that I have used for years. I filled them half-full with oat feed and hooked it to the horse's bridle. They ate right out of the containers even with the bits in their mouth. The girls loved to watch them, as they would drool, and just kept chomping away. After their feed, they could slurp up a half-bucket of water.

The girls loved the horses, and they always enjoyed their chore to bring the horses back to the barn at dusk. It made me chuckle to hear them yelling and whistling at the horses to try to direct them home. The girls would be giggling and carrying on trying to coerce the horses back. The horses would have their fun with the girls, as they seemed to plot to be difficult, trotting in different directions, being playful. Despite the horses reduced role on the farm, we wouldn't think of selling them, and we treated them with as much love and gratitude as we always had.

The Barn

The barn was approximately 50 feet wide and 50 feet deep. On the north side of the barn there were three doors: one set of double doors on the left, one set of double doors on the right, and a normal-sized service door in the center. The two sets of doors on the left and right were hinged and swung open out toward the barnyard. The doors on the west side was the entrance to the area where we stored the cows, while the doors on the east were for storing the horses. Just above the sliding doors in the center underneath the peak of the roof was a pulley system with ropes and hooks used to hoist the large bails of hay that were harvested from the field. The south side of the barn also had two sets of doors on the left and right, and a large set of sliding doors in the center, which was used for tractors and larger machinery. The service door was nice to have as it allowed us to enter and leave the barn without having to open the larger doors. The hayloft ran the length of the barn on both sides and on the north end, with wooden ladders in place for easy access. There was another pulley system inside the barn to lower the hay bails down inside the barn.

Hay was planted and harvested primarily for bedding the animals. The straw was used for spreading on the barn floor to catch the waste from the animals. Over the years, we have grown three different types of hay: timothy, clover, and alfalfa. The hay would be cut with a sickle bar mower. The odor of new mown hay as you drove through the country was the most beautiful smell! Once the hay was dried and bailed, we would pull the wagon underneath the pulley system and hoist the hay into the loft.

Continuing my chores, I walked back towards the old garage and noticed the light was on in our bedroom. The house would be warmer and Mabel and I could sit down and chat over a cup of coffee.

Mabel took on a very healthy look overall, a little over medium build, and quite a bit shorter than me. She has very thick reddish-colored hair, which always looks nice, no matter how she combs it. Mabel is a strong woman as she helps me from time-to-time in the fields. She spends much time working in her gardens, tending to her canaries, and she diligently performs the normal household chores. She has a pleasant personality and has a way of saying the funniest things at the most unexpected times.

"Good morning," she said with a smile.

"Hello, what's the inside temperature?"

"Fifty-nine and rising," she said, leaning forward to read the mercury. The kitchen was the warmest room in the house. "The girls are all huddled in Nancy's bed, it is the funniest thing to see. Black coffee,

11

sir?"

"Yes, please. Don't think we can make New Year's mass today on account of the drifting," I said.

"Do you think the grader will come down before long?" she asked.

"I'm sure Elmer has his hands full on the township roads today," I replied as I blew the surface of coffee in the cup before taking a sip. Elmer Wallenhaupt was entrusted with clearing our roads and did a fine job. "He is going to have a time clearing the east/west roads since the wind is hard from the north. It may take him a while if the roads keep drifting over."

There were a number of roads between Grand Ridge and Ransom that had to be plowed, and it took a good while. The first roads to get cleared were the major highways - Highways 18 and 23. Highway 18 was the east/west highway that ran through Streator, and Highway 23 was the north/south highway between Streator and Ottawa, and went through Grand Ridge. Unfortunately, we couldn't get to the main highways until our roads were clear – we just had to be patient.

Gladys and her Music

"Do you think Gladys had a good time last night?" Mabel asked while pouring my cereal. I had picked Gladys up from Ottawa High School where she attended a dance.

"Seemed so," I said, "she didn't say too much." Gladys was our second oldest of five daughters. At 17, she was very active in school, and went to many dances. She played the drums for the Ray Bannon Accordion Band. Her band played in a dance sponsored by Ottawa High School, which was 15 miles away. Monica Durdan, John's daughter, plays in the band as well. They once marched together at Soldier's Field in Chicago. For their reward, they were given free passes to Riverview Amusement Park.

It seemed Gladys always had some sort of social engagement. She was very serious about her schoolwork, took tap dance lessons, and we were very pleased at how she regularly attended church and was very devout. Although all farmers would pray for boys, God had blessed me with five wonderful girls.

Darlene and Chicago Bridge & Iron Co.

The oldest, Darlene, is out of the house at 22 living in Seneca with two girlfriends. She works for the Chicago Bridge & Iron Company in Seneca where they build US Navy Surface ships. I had just read recently in the paper that they launched the USS Stentor LST-858, which stands for Landing Ship Tank. These are the large ships that carry tanks and equipment onto land, the exact ships used to carry the equipment needed to invade Normandy France this past June. They launched 78 ships from Seneca shipyards in 1944. We are very proud of Darlene for helping to build these ships and serving our country. About 27,000 people have been working at the Seneca shipyard during the past three years, with more than half being women. Thank God for Rosy the Riveter! At one point this past year, the shipyard produced one LST every four to five days. Once launched and commissioned, these ships steam down the Illinois and Mississippi rivers, into the Gulf of Mexico and out to sea. It is also ironic Darlene is building ships as her boyfriend Sully is fighting overseas while serving in the US Navy. "Sully" is his nickname. His given name is Albert Kollar, and is from a nice family that live near Kangley. Darlene and Sully are hoping to marry as soon as Sully comes home.

We see Darlene every two weeks or so. She and her girlfriends come to spend a Saturday night with us from time-to-time and Mabel and Gladys travel to Seneca to see Darlene. She started working in Seneca in June, 1943, and at times works seven days a week.

Albert "Sully" Kollar – Navy Service

Sully entered the US Navy in November of 1942. He is serving aboard the USS Savannah, CL-42, which is a Light Cruiser. The Savannah was built in a shipyard in Camden, New Jersey, in 1938. She was part of the 1942 North African invasion force called Operation Torch. The Savannah provided gun support to the landing craft carrying troops and tanks. She was also called upon to invade Italy in 1943. It was September 11th, 1943 off the coast of Salerno, Italy, when a German plane bombed the Savannah. The bomb went right through the ship and opened up a large hole in the bottom. The ship was able to get underway despite the bombing, but she lost 197 of its men and another 15 wounded. Nearly 25 percent of her crew had perished. The ship limped back to the Navy shipyard in Philadelphia, and after an 8 month overhaul, was brought back to full service. Sully has been through so much; it will be wonderful to have him home – hopefully soon.

The Three Little Girls

Our youngest, Nancy, Esther, and Joyce – are eight, seven, and five. We waited nine years between Gladys and Nancy, partly due to the depression that started in 1929. Crop prices dropped to an all time low and we were a little hesitant to have more children. Roosevelt got things straight after he was elected in 1933. Roosevelt, taking over after President Hoover, seemed to be able to accomplish whatever needed to be done to get us out of our national depression. Crop prices really turned around after Roosevelt was in office a couple of years. He was now in his fourth term and it seems he will be our President forever. So, after the depression, we decided to add to our family: Nancy in 1936, Esther in 1937, and Joyce in 1939.

After finishing the last spoonful of my cereal and sipping milk from the bowl, I headed downstairs to shave and get ready to paint a few shutters in the basement. Shaving downstairs was part of my normal morning routine. I had my washstand mounted on the wall. I also used the washstand to clean up after working outside, so as not to dirty the sinks upstairs. On the shelf was where I kept my shaving mug with the round-handled brush to dab the soap on my face. The straight razor was kept well out of reach in a medicine cabinet mounted on the wall, and hanging from a nail was the strap to sharpen the razor.

The basement was an area I like to call my "headquarters". During the cold winters, it was very warm downstairs with the furnace going. There was a bench to tinker with different odds and ends, repairs, and it was a good place to paint. When friends came over, we often sat in the basement and talked over a Meister Brau.

The basement was certainly a conglomeration of interest. Around the corner from the washstand was a large table with Mabel's canaries. They were not hanging cages, but designed to sit on a table. There were probably five cages holding a total of approximately twenty birds. It is a lot of work for Mabel to care for them. She feeds them birdseed that we buy in little orange boxes. From time-to-time she feeds them boiled egg yolks all mashed up. Feeding the birds are part of her regular daily chores. We go through many boxes in a month's time, but it is worth it because she truly loves her canaries. Fred Gallup, our gas merchant, and his wife, Olga, have canaries as well. Olga sells the birds at their place in Grand Ridge. She also exchanges canaries if you wanted a different color bird. The markings on the birds are varied: some all yellow, some yellow and black, and some yellow and brown.

The wringer-type washing machine was downstairs with the rinse tubs alongside, and a host of clothesline strung around to dry clothes in the wintertime. The washing machine is so loud that Nancy said she could hear it running while sitting in her classroom at school. It would make her cry because hearing the washing machine made her homesick. Close by we have an area where we store coveralls, coats, hats, boots, snow pants, and gloves. On one wall there are shelves for canned goods of all kinds, paint and anything else that needed storage.

At certain times during the year you may find a little piglet penned up in the corner of the basement. The little piglet was usually the runt of the litter, was neglected by the sow and was cared for by us. So we would hand feed the piglet with a milk bottle until it caught up with the others. The little girls would help out with this chore, as the little piglets were so cute.

It was down here where I would take my breaks, have a cigarette and sit for a while. My brand of cigarette was Pall Mall, and to me they were a way of relaxing. People laugh at me as I usually leave the ashes hang off of the cigarette instead of flicking it off. Since packaged cigarettes are quite expensive, I would try to be thrifty and roll my own.

I pulled a couple of paintbrushes out of my bucket full of linseed oil, which is where I kept my brushes to keep them in good shape. The key to a quality paint job was buying top-dollar paintbrushes and always maintaining them. My father takes great pride in his property and is always painting something, and this rubbed off on me. Now was the time to start painting the shutters. I had pulled the shutters down over two weeks ago and wanted to get them primed, painted and back up before spring.

The girls were up by 8 am. I was always amazed at how much noise they could make in the kitchen. You would think there were 50 people walking around upstairs. It was a good time to take a break and walk upstairs to see my girls. Esther, or my Sweetie Pie, as I called her, was the first to greet me. She always stuck her chin up towards me with a big smile, and I would cup her cute little face in my hand. She would walk along side of me as I cupped her chin. The girls always brought so much life to our farmhouse. They were already talking of making chocolate chip cookies. The cookie tradition came about over the years as a way to lift up our spirits, especially the girls, after having to be cooped inside during snowstorms for sometimes two or three days.

"We have fresh milk to go with those cookies girls," I exclaimed.

"What are you up to down there Andrew?" Mabel asked as she handed me a fresh cup of coffee.

"Painting shutters," I replied, "I've been wanting to get to that for

15

some time now." The girls shuffled off to some adventure in the far room. Nancy in front, and Joyce in the rear.

"Happy New Year!" said Mabel. "I can't believe it's 1945. Where does the time go?"

"I read in the newspaper yesterday that Patton's army pushed the Germans back in Bastogne." I reached for the paper at the end of the table and read aloud, "It says here, 'The military leaders thought the soldiers holding the line might not resist the Germans. But they held them back long enough for Patton and his army to reinforce the line and push the German's back'", I continued, "I think we may win this war soon. We need more guys like General Patton."

"I just pray for Sully and Albert," said Mabel, holding her hand over her heart. We worried night and day for my brother Albert and Sully. Sometimes I feel guilty for not fighting alongside them, but at 48, I was too old to serve.

Most of the day was spent in the basement painting, and by midday I had painted six shutters on both sides with primer. The sky was beginning to clear a bit, the clouds getting thinner, but the wind was still whipping. The footprints I made earlier were already covered over. so it was necessary to clear the driveway again with the Fordson. I was hopeful that tomorrow would be a better day for getting things done.

Just before dinner it was time to feed the pigs. I went outside and made my way to the old garage where the pig feed was stored. I filled the large bucket with the feed, walked just outside the old garage to the hose spigot, and added the right amount of water for the slop and headed for the pigpen. The pigs were all huddled inside which gave me room and time to fill the long troughs without the usual bumping and squealing. They all came running just as I finished pouring. Each pig would fight for position, using their snouts to poke one another in the face trying to make sure they got their share. I rinsed the bucket and put it back into the old garage.

In addition to feeding the pigs, I fed the chickens and provided drinking water for our four sheep. The sheep live and roam in the farmyard and eat hay and grass. They eat grass and graze in areas that the larger livestock cannot get to. We raise the sheep for meat, which is delicious and nutritious. The kids love to play with the little lambs and feed them.

It was already pitch black by quarter to five this time of year. I spent a good amount of time tinkering in the old garage and barn. Inside the

16

kitchen the wonderful smells from tonight's dinner made me feel a bit hungry. Mabel was just pulling chicken potpie out of the oven. We all loved her cooking and she always made plenty. While enjoying a Meister Brau, I sharpened some knives and checked the shutters to see if they were dry. Mabel called and we all sat down for a hot delicious meal. In the evening, the girls were happy to get their chocolate chip cookies, and I had a few myself.

Gabriel Heater

We listened to the six-thirty news on the radio each night that we were home. Mabel always served dinner at six, and by six-thirty I went into the living room where we sat near the radio, a Philco table model, which sat on my desk. We tuned into Gabriel Heater's radio program, which was broadcast out of Chicago on WMAQ, 670 Kilohertz. Gabriel Heater comes on every night at the same time. Just before dinner I would make sure to turn on the radio to give the electric tubes time to warm up, as without some time to warm, the radio programs from Chicago would not come in as well. Gabriel Heater had a voice you could trust, and he would always start the broadcast with, "Ah, there's good news tonight!" No matter how bad things were during this terrible war, Mr. Heater always found positive things to say and pass along to us. The girls knew to keep quiet during the broadcast so we would not miss anything. They usually went upstairs just after dinner out of habit knowing that one little peep would quickly get them shushed. This evening's broadcast was especially good news from the war in Europe.

Battle of Bastogne

General Patton, commander of the Third Army, along with the 101st Airborne were successfully defending and pushing back at the German offensive in Bastogne. Bastogne was a town in Belgium where Germany, France, Luxemburg, and Belgium come together. Since the Normandy invasion in early June of 1944, the allied forces had pushed their way through France from the north to the south. The British and the Canadians fought alongside the Americans to make up the allied forces, which were being led by General Dwight Eisenhower. The allied forces landed at different areas in France near Normandy and pushed the Germans back, but not after many casualties. The allied forces all joined in mid-June 1944 to form a line to march south and regain France. The allied forces recaptured Paris at the end of August 1944 with many German surrenders. As the winter months came, the allied offensive stalled due to lack of supplies. The Germans mounted an assault on Belgium from the German border and broke through the allied lines and went deep behind the lines causing a bulge. The German advance stopped at Bastogne. According to the radio report, the Germans had asked for our surrender at Bastogne. Thanks to General Patton's Third Army who relieved the soldiers at Bastogne, and help from the British under the command of General Montgomery, German advance was halted. The Germans retreated one day after Christmas 1944.

There was also good news from the war in the pacific. Between General MacArthur and Admiral Nimitz, they were fighting to take back the islands in the central and southwest pacific including taking back the Philippines. In one battle in October of 1944, the Americans sunk or damaged over 50 Japanese warships. The island chains leading back to Japan were key to provide the airfields needed to launch our bombers against mainland Japan.

After the news, around seven, Fibber McGee and Molly came on the air and the girls were called to come downstairs. They sat on the floor, listened and laughed. There were other programs throughout the week that we would listen to like Edgar Bergen and Charlie McCarthy, Amos and Andy. Later in the evenings we could listen to Bob Hope, Jack Benny, and Burns and Allen. I much preferred listening to the news. Sometimes when we had company we would listen to Bob Hope or Jack Benny for a good laugh.

My desk was the place where I kept my diary, and it was usually in the evening before going to bed that I would make my brief diary entries, noting weather conditions, market prices, jotting down my accomplishments for the day, and noting special events.

The Koetz's

Tuesday morning brought a warmer temperature and some sunshine - it was 28 above. Sometime between dinner and bedtime last night, Elmer had made it down our road with the grader. I cleared any remaining snow off the driveway and pulled the truck out of the old garage in order to take Gladys down to Bill Koetz's place. Gladys spent a lot of time over at the Koetz's place with their oldest daughter, Betty. Mabel also likes spending time with Bill's wife, Carrie. The Koetz's were in our square mile, just to our southeast - we shared property lines. The Koetz's had three girls and three boys. When I arrived, Bill was busy clearing his driveway. When he saw us he waved, stopped his tractor and met us half way to the front door. Bill and I were good friends, and he was part of our farming gang, a hard working man who was always willing to help me.

"Good morning, Bill," I said taking off my glove to shake my friends hand. "I'll pick you up after dinner Gladys." Gladys ran up the walk into the house.

"Andy, can you give me a hand with the Plymouth?" Bill asked, sighing. "She's dead again." He led us to the garage where we pushed the Plymouth out onto the driveway. Bill attached a rope to the hitch of my truck. We gave it a pull and she started.

"You really need a new battery Bill," I said feeling a bit guilty for being so blunt. He seemed to know I was going to say that.

"You know, I've been meaning to pick up a new battery, but just haven't gotten to it. Do you have a spare Andy?"

"You betcha Bill, I have a spare that I keep charged. Let me bring it down later today when I pick up Gladys. You can keep it until you get a new one," I said, motioning with my arm as if it was no bother.

He replied, "Thanks Andy, it won't be too long, I'll be getting a new one here real soon".

"See you later," I said. I waved and headed back towards home. I got home just before 8:30 am and the girls were up and about. School was still out for the holidays. Nancy and Esther attended the country school; a one-room building that was located on the northwest corner of our property, less than a quarter-mile up the road. Both Mabel and I were active in happenings at the school. I performed all the necessary maintenance at the school, including cutting the grass. Joyce was still too young and stayed home with Mabel during the day. They were excited to have one more day off. I thought it would be a good day to take the girls sleigh riding.

Having spent most of the morning painting the shutters, I was able to put a coat of white paint on the six that were primed yesterday, and then primed six more. We had a total of ten sets of shutters around the perimeter of the house. People thought I was a bit too fussy painting so much, but we took pride in our house, and we enjoyed it when the buildings looked freshly painted and the yard neat and trim.

Sleigh Riding

I went upstairs and found the girls bored to tears.

"Who wants to go sleigh riding?" I asked the girls, knowing well that they would be in their warm coats and mittens in ten seconds flat. Oh the simple pleasures of life - I loved to see them happy.

19

We ate chicken salad sandwiches, went to the old garage to fetch the sleds and tossed them in the back of the old truck. Mabel stayed behind, as she wanted to get some sewing done. Taking the old truck, equipped with tire chains, we would be sure to make it through the snowdrifts. The two older girls sat in the back with the sleds and Joyce sat in front with me. We made our way north up the road apiece to a safe little spot about one mile away where there was a good-sized hill that led down to Shapland's creek. This was not the official name for the creek – we just gave it that name because it ran through Minnie Shapland's property. The creek was very shallow and mostly frozen near the edges, but you could still hear the trickling of the current. The three girls shared two sleds, which were made by my father. The new sleds that we had seen at Montgomery Wards looked cheap to me, and these were sturdy and built to last a good while. The girls must have gone down the hill 15 times or more. Joyce was a bit adventurous and wandered down by the creek and got her feet wet. Fearing Joyce would catch cold, the four of us jumped back into the truck and headed for home. Mabel greeted us at the door with hot chocolate, and she quickly ran and got a towel to dry and warm Joycie's feet.

Taking into consideration their age, Nancy is quite a bit taller than Esther and Joyce. I guess Nancy gets her height from me. They all have brown hair, Joyce having the naturally curly hair. They all have brown eyes and high cheek bones, which makes their faces look slender. Joyce has a litter flatter nose that makes her look so cute. Nancy is fussy about her clothes and is always asking Mother for something new to wear. The other two are just satisfied with hand-me-downs or something homemade.

I was able to prime four more shutters and felt pretty good about my progress for the day. After dinner and my evening chores, I took a half-hour nap and then listened to the radio before logging my diary entry and going to bed.

Mabel and the Dentist

Wednesday things got busy again, with a temperature in the morning being 30 above with only a mild wind. We took Nancy and Esther to school and Mabel, Joyce, and I headed into Streator to take Mabel to the dentist. Mabel had finally made the decision to make a dentist appointment, have her teeth extracted and have dentures made. This was something that she was dreading. Streator was around twelve miles from our farm, about a twenty-minute drive. The roads were still a bit slushy, but not too bad. Streator was full of life that day, a town of about 13,000 people.

"You can just drop me off," suggested Mabel as we pulled up in the parking spot in front of the dentist office.

"We'll take you inside," I told her, "I need to talk to Dr. Kozlowski about the bill anyway."

Mabel checked in with the receptionist and I asked to have a word with Dr. Kozlowski.

After about five minutes Dr. Kozlowski poked his head out and asked, "Hello Andy, hello Mabel, and who is this cute little girl?"

"This is our youngest, Joyce," said Mabel proudly.

"I think you should get a sucker for helping your mom today. What do you think?" Dr. Kozlowski asked Joyce and pulled a sucker from a jar that sat on the reception desk and handed it to her.

Joyce reached up with a smile, accepted the gift and said, "Thank you sir."

"Can I have a word with you doc, about the billing arrangements?" I said.

"Sure, Andy", he replied making a hand gesture towards the door that led to the examining rooms and his office. I passed a few small rooms with dentist chairs, one chair with a large woman who did not seem very comfortable. The office had a small desk and college diplomas on the wall. I didn't want to keep the doc away from his work too long, especially if it meant keeping that woman in that chair waiting with her mouth propped open and stuffed with cotton balls. Once inside the doc's office, he turned around with a concerned look on his face.

"What is it Andy?" he asked.

"Well, as you know it took me a long time to convince Mabel to get new teeth, way too long," I continued, "no matter what she says, I want you to give her whatever she needs and give her a good set of choppers. You know what I mean doc? She doesn't like to spend a lot of money, especially on things like this. She wants not the best, just something she can get by with. Something reasonable in price. But you just go ahead and set her up good and send me the bill whatever it is."

"Ok Andy, I know what you mean. Don't you worry, we'll take good care of her and her dentures will be solid, comfortable, and will last a long time. We've really come a long way with these new composites, and the prices aren't too bad." He smiled and gave me the assurance I needed.

"All right then doc, we'll be back in a couple hours to fetch her. Thank you," I said as I headed back out to the reception area. I gave the woman in the dentist chair a nod and smile as if letting her know that the doc will be back soon to resume working on her teeth.

Downtown Streator

After wishing Mabel good luck, Joyce and I went for a stroll to the five-and-dime to look around. We continued our walk down Main Street, stopping at clothing stores, gift shops, and the bakery where I bought each of us a donut, a hot chocolate for Joyce and a cup of coffee for me. The local merchants were busy clearing the sidewalks to let customers know that they were ready for business.

Streator was a major railroad town, which connected the Santa Fe, Chicago Burlington & Quincy (CB&Q), and Illinois Valley and Northern lines. You couldn't go too far without going over a set of railroad tracks. Passenger trains, freight, livestock, grain and coal cars passed through Streator everyday. Darlene was a graduate of Streator High School, and Gladys is a soon-to-be-graduate. Streator has the nicer restaurants, department stores, and a movie theater. They have a large Montgomery Wards store where I get many of my tools, tires, and other necessities. Mabel and the girls look forward to our trips to Streator on Saturday night. Most generally they go to the movies, while I spend time at Shab's tavern playing euchre with friends.

After our stroll, Joyce and I got back into the car and decided to go down to the Santa Fe train station to see if there were any troop trains passing through today. We parked and walked through the train station to the depot where quite a few women were busy setting up for the arrival of a troop train from Chicago.

"When are the boys coming through today?" I asked one of the canteen organizers.

"Train should be here around noon," she said and continued, "not sure how many we'll have, but we'll be ready."

The Santa Fe carried troops from Chicago through Streator on their way out west – probably California. Canteen volunteers came from local companies, churches, and many other organizations. It all started back in 1943 when three women, Streator locals, started using a food cart to serve to troops passing through. Since then it has grown into quite an operation.

"Is there anything I can do?" I asked one of the ladies.

She hesitated seeing Joyce was with me, then responded, "You

22

know, they need someone out front to carry in boxes of produce that just arrived. If you care to help, I'll watch the little one here." The shipments of meat, milk, and produce came from local farmers and businesses.

"You betcha," I replied. "Joycie you stay with the nice lady, okay."

I went through the station to the front and saw a grain truck, very much like mine, with boxes of local produce stacked on the back. I helped the truck driver carry the boxes inside into a well-organized central hub of canteen activities. We had donated many fruits and vegetables to the canteen through Mabel's involvement with the Home Bureau volunteer activities, but I had never seen this very efficient operation up close. He and I made four or five trips to get everything inside. He thanked me. I went back to the depot to find Joyce helping the nice lady prepare for the servicemen. We said our goodbyes and headed back.

After nearly two hours, Joyce and I arrived at the dentist office to find that Mabel had not yet completed her appointment, so we sat down in the reception area. Joyce wasted no time picking up a crayon and started a game of connect-the-dots in a children's magazine. Mabel came out looking a bit pale with a mouth full of cotton. Before heading home, we stopped at the pharmacy to fill a prescription to help with the pain. The ride home was quiet, with Joyce nodding off to sleep in the back seat. Mabel kept quiet and still, surely in pain. She wasn't one to complain. All she managed to say was "Four today and four next week."

"Bill will be at the house at two to butcher one of his cows", I said as I swung the family car into our drive.

Butchering a Cow

Bill arrived on time pulling the trailer with his cow to be slaughtered. I never quite got used to the process of butchering an animal. It was a necessary evil in farm life. It was something I learned from my father. We used pretty much the same process as he did, but from time-to-time, would adjust our routine to make things easier. The necessary tools include a sharp knife for cutting through the hide, skinning knife, 22-caliber rifle, meat saw, gambrel, and a come-along to hoist the animal. I preferred to slaughter the animals in the machine shed. I kept all the necessary tools there and had an area in one corner of the building where I set up a drainage system to catch all of the fluids.

Slaughtering was a messy business. We needed to butcher livestock in the winter months when the temperature was freezing. The lower temperature allowed for hanging the meat without fear of it becoming spoiled, and there were no flies at this time of year. It is always best to not feed the animals 24 hours prior to butchering as to make the job a bit easier. The best way to kill the cow is by shooting them between the eyes with a 22-cal. You then use your sharp knife to cut through the hide at the neck to allow the blood to drain. The most difficult part was skinning the animal. We would use the come-along and a gambrel to hoist the animal as we removed the skin. Once the meat is skinned we cut it into quarters and hung the meat for some time to make it tender. We rented a meat locker in Streator to store the meat. The cost for the locker was only $13 a month. Either Mabel or I would stop in and pick up a few packages while we were in town doing other errands. Once the meat was hung, we spent an hour or so cleaning up the place and discarding the remains that we could not eat.

Bill was about ready to leave for home when Mabel came outside to tell Bill that his daughter, Dorothy, was on the phone inside. Dorothy moved to Cleveland, Ohio last year and called from time-to-time to talk to her parents. The Koetz's did not have a phone and we were happy to let them use ours. Most of the time Bill would set up a planned time for Dorothy to call and make sure he and his wife, Carrie, were here to receive the call. Bill talked for five minutes or so, sent his love to his daughter's family and left to head back home.

The remainder of the week was uneventful. I continued priming and painting the shutters. I decided to get all of the shutters primed before painting the final coat. Bill Koetz came by Friday to take the hanging meat down that we butchered on Wednesday. As Bill usually does, he cut off a couple good-sized slices of the top round for our family as a complimentary gesture.

(19 Jan 45) Friday evening after dinner I took Mabel and the girls to Marseilles to see her Mother and have dinner. I left for home around eight pm, leaving Mabel and girls. Mabel was heading off to Chicago tomorrow by train with two of her cousins to do some shopping. She would leave the girls with her mother, or "Ma" as we affectionately called her. All that was left in the farmhouse was Gladys and I. The two of us played solitaire before we turned in for the evening.

Ma lived on Clark Street in Marseilles, and Mabel's sister Anna lived two houses away. The girls could run back and forth to play as long as they weren't banging doors, running in and out, or coming in with dirty shoes. Usually they ate at their grandma's. The biggest adventure for the kids was they were allowed to go for penny candy at the little store on the corner of Clark and Pulaski Street. They were told to be ever so careful crossing the street.

Back at home, Gladys and I spent some time talking about her boy friend Dick Palaschak. The two were in their final grade at Streator High School. They knew of each other, but really got to know each other while visiting Uncle Pete's one evening. Dick's parents would go play euchre at Pete's and we happened to bring Gladys, and Dick came along with his parents. The two really hit if off and have been dating ever since.

Selling Hogs – Provance Trucking

(20 Jan 45) Saturday I finished painting all of the shutters and put them in the old garage where they would sit until time availed itself to hang them. Lloyd Provance, owner and operator of Provance Trucking, came by around 2:30 pm to collect six hogs to take to the market. I would sell anywhere from 10 to 15 hogs per year. Provance would send out a truck to pick up the hogs and cattle when requested. Lloyd would schedule a number of farms in our area for the same day, and he would make his rounds and pick up the livestock and haul them off to the Chicago stockyards for sale. Lloyd would handle all of the paperwork and send a check with an itemized list of number of hogs or cows, that were sold and total weight. The receipts were kept for the purpose of income tax filings. In addition to those hogs sold, we would also butcher a hog or two to store in our locker in town. Some would be cured in the smokehouse. It was best to avoid the hogs reaching the 250 pound mark, with the ideal weight being around 200 pounds. If the hogs got too big, it just meant more fat. The income from the hogs sold today should come to approximately $300.

Lloyd backed his rather large truck into the driveway with ease. His rig was not much to look at, but he kept it in tip-top shape.

"That should do it Lloyd, right there," I yelled to Lloyd. He shifted his eyes from his left side mirror to the right and backed up another three or four feet and stopped just one foot from the step loader. He didn't need to take directions from me, I thought.

"Okay, that's good," I said.

Lloyd jumped out of the cab of the truck with a big smile. "You weren't worried about me hitting your loader were you Andy?" he asked.

"No, just trying to give you a little help that's all."

The step loader was positioned just in front of the entrance gate to the hog pen. The loader was a rectangular wooden box open on both ends, which served as a funnel to guide the hogs which were to be sold from the hog pen into the truck. Lloyd used his prod to persuade the hogs selected for sale into the loader. The prod was a long piece of iron electrically charged by a battery. The point of the prod would let off a charge when it came into contact with the hogs skin. Those hogs would really get to squealing loud. There was one hog that Lloyd prodded into the truck that I was very happy to see go. He was a mean old bugger, and would terrorize the other animals to no end. There were some hogs that we became attached too and we were sorry to see go. The girls would play special attention to the runts that they nursed as babies. We would watch them grow and give them special names. There were some hogs that I purposely avoided selling because they were like our pets.

"I'll settle up and send you a check within a few days. And thanks for your business, Andy," he said as he walked away, jumped up into the cab, and waved goodbye.

"Drive safe Lloyd," I said waving back. Lloyd was very efficient and wasted no time with small talk. He drove off to his next customer.

Saturday evening was snowy and cold, and it was a good night to stay home and listen to the Lawrence Welk Show.

(21 Jan 45) On Sunday morning, we woke up to another six inches of snow. I spent a good part of the morning on chores, plowing the snow, and was unable to make it to church. I put the chains on the family car and headed to Marseilles around noon to pick up Mabel and the kids. Gladys stayed home and prepared the top round for our dinner. We spent an hour or so with Ma and family, and then headed back home by four pm. When we walked in the kitchen, Gladys had the table set for dinner.

"Dinner is served," she proclaimed with self-satisfaction and a smile on her face. We all sat down and ate; thankful everyone was home safe and sound.

FEBRUARY

February on the farm was much like January as far as weather and chores go. We had higher than average snowfall so far this year, and a lot of wind. February is one month closer to the spring planting, when things really start to get busy. It truly pays to be a good planner – to start thinking about farm machinery maintenance and other items that needed attention.

Farming is a year-round business; but some months were slower than others. February is a slower month on the farm and I like to take advantage of the extra time to get the farm machinery up to snuff. There are always maintenance items that needed to be done as the result of a long harvest. Most of this knowledge came from years of watching and learning from my father.

Peter Durdan Sr. and Mary Zec Durdan

My father, Peter Durdan, was born in Slovakia on July 21, 1874. Slovakia is in central Europe, where the land has rugged mountains, with vast forests and pastures. Since Dad came to America, Slovakia joined the Czechs after World War I, in1918, to form the new joint state of Czechoslovakia. Dad complained that Hitler had disgraced his homeland when the Germans occupied Czechoslovakia in 1939. He was always so thankful to be in America, away from all of the chaos in Europe. He came to America with his mother, two brothers and three sisters when he was ten years old. His father stayed behind in Slovakia until he could make enough money to follow, but he died in Slovakia before he could join them. Dad worked as a hired hand for a man not far from our farm, helping to support his mother and family.

My mother, Mary Zec, was born in Slovakia also, in the town of Presola, in 1876. Mother came to America when she was only 14 to be with my Aunt Barbara and brother-in-law, Mike Bosko, who at the time lived in Virden, Illinois, which is 150 miles south of Grand Ridge. After arriving in New York City, my mother realized that she had lost her passport and was nearly sent back to Slovakia, but a Jewish couple in New York City took her in as a hired girl in a dairy. My Aunt Barbara growing weary waiting for my mother to arrive, advertised in a New York City newspaper that she was looking for her sister. A Slovak speaking man working at the dairy informed my mother, who was unable to speak or read English, of the advertisement and helped her contact Aunt Barbara. They were reunited. My mother moved with her sister and brother-in-law to Nakomis and eventually my mother went out on her own and moved to Streator. She took a job as a hired girl for the Amos Johnson family farm on Richard's road. My mother and father met shortly thereafter, and they were married on November 12, 1894.

Coal Mining – Cherry Mine Disaster

My father worked for the Kangley Coal Mine for two years. They lived in a small house built by the coal company. I was born in Kangley on March 21st, 1896. We moved to Streator to work where Dad worked in the number two mine for another two years. My brother Peter came along in March of 1897, and mom was carrying my brother John when Dad decided to start farming.

Life as a coal miner was extremely difficult for Dad and our family. Dad always spoke of the underground work being very dangerous, dirty, and damp. Working in the underground tunnels is hard, even for a short man, and especially hard for my Dad, who was tall and could not stand straight most of the day on account of the low tunnel ceilings. He picked and shoveled the coal for ten hours a day, loaded it on small cars, and pushed them to an area where mules would pull them to the cage to be hauled to the surface. He breathed stale dusty air all day long. Back then, the mine owners did not provide a safe work environment for the miners.

Today the United Mine Workers of America, a labor union, look out for the miners. I never knew much about Dad's work in the mines until the great Cherry Mine Disaster of 1909, where over 250 men and boys lost their lives when a small fire erupted in the inner recesses of the mine shaft, and soon burned out of control. Dad told me that one of those men who died in the Cherry mine was his brother, Andrew, whom was my namesake. He had told me how the family traveled to Cherry to attempt to recover his remains, which were never found. It was so sad for my Uncle to have lost his life so young, and so tragically. Dad told me all about the dreadful conditions in the mines and how he wanted better for his sons.

Our First Farm – Ed Kuhn Place

As a family, we started out farming the Isaac Mason farm, then onto a farm south of Blackstone, and settled on the Ed Kuhn farm for seventeen years. This is where I progressed from youth to finally reaching manhood. Having to work side-by-side with Dad and brothers, I was only able to complete the seventh grade. Dad was a great teacher and a very hard worker. He taught me everything I know about farming. Mabel and I were married on February 25, 1922 and started farming on our own. In 1930, my Mom, Dad and family moved to a farm north and west of Grand Ridge, where my Dad lives to this day. My Mother was a strong, confident woman and a wonderful mother. They had 13 children of their own and one "adopted" son. Rafel (Ray) Wilson was not legally adopted, but Mom and Dad took him in after his parents were killed. Ray has a brother, Albert, who was taken in by my brother Pete, and his wife, Mary.

There were eight boys and five girls that spanned 21 years. I was 26 years old when Mabel and I were married. At that time my youngest sister, Irene, was only five years old. One brother, Thomas, died when he was only six months old. My mother died in June 1941.

I am the oldest at 48, then there is Pete Junior who is 47, and John is 45. Mary is the oldest girl at 44, is married to Milt Inks and living in Michigan. Mary was the first of us brothers and sisters to get married, back in 1921 – I was Milt's best man. Then there was Anna at 42, Steve at 41, and Clara at 40, which are all married. George is 3 years younger than Clara at 37, and Margaret is 5 years younger than George at 32.

There are only three brothers not married: Albert at 30, Ray at 28, and Edward, also 28. Albert and Ray are both overseas serving in the US Army. Edward and Irene, the youngest sister at 27, are living at home with Dad. Irene married Michael Vercimak last year while he was home on furlough. She is anxiously awaiting his return.

My Father encouraged each of us boys to go into farming as opposed to mining. When we were first married we rented the Graham property near Kangley. This is where we lived when Darlene and Gladys were born. As a young man going into farming, you needed more than knowledge to secure a farm of your own. Buying your own land required a substantial down payment, and at the same time, purchasing farm equipment and horses. So in those days you worked as a hired hand, then rented, and eventually bought your own land. A farmer could make a good living on a 200 acre farm. The proprietors were discreet in letting us work and manage our rental property for the most part. As long as we paid our rent all was well. One time while we were renting, John Miller and I traded farms while the owner was away. We both rented from the same person. We had a larger family than John Miller, and needed the bigger house that the other farm could provide.

Our Farm – Purchased 1940

We bought this farm in 1940, which comprises 240 acres. We had purchased the farm in February of that year, just prior to the planting season. I felt it was best for us to stay at the Graham farmhouse while we farmed both the Graham property and our new 240 acres near Grand Ridge. However, not long after we purchased the new property, Mr. Graham had found new tenants for the rented farm, so we decided to go ahead and move. That was a very busy spring, but also very exciting. We have come a long way since then and really take a lot of pride in our own farm. What a blessing to have our own land and property. All my girls and I couldn't be happier. It is in our long-term plan to buy a second farm as soon as we save enough money, with the intention of renting the farm out to a young farming family. It is hard to find land close by – hopefully we will achieve our goal. With the extra income we may be able to expand even more. My brothers Steve, George, John, and Pete all own farms nearby. We share farm machinery, knowledge, and have helped each other immensely over the years. There was no problem that we could not solve together. Dad served as our model to follow, and he helped us boys by encouraging us to invest in good land and machinery.

Friday morning I spent a couple of hours after chores putting up a mirror in the bathroom. I repaired the wood frame, which broke in one corner after it fell to the floor. I then gave it a nice paint job and had it back in service. Gladys had been asking for the past three days about the mirror.

"Dad, when is the mirror going to be back up?" Gladys had been asking anxiously.

"I'll have it up soon, sweetie. What do you need a mirror for anyway?" I teased her knowing full well that Gladys spent more time in front of a mirror than any of us, as most girls her age do.

I was a bit tired and feeling rotten this morning. We got to bed late after picking Gladys up at the Eagles in Streator. She played her drums at a dance there. While Gladys was playing, I had gone to the late show and saw a western starring John Wayne. By the time I picked her up and got home it was past one am.

Linc Armstrong and Family

As I walked outside to return the tools to the old garage, I saw Linc

Armstrong driving up in his truck with Bill Koetz in the passenger seat. Linc, short for Lincoln, was my best and closest friend. I considered him just like a brother. Linc worked hard, was a very smart man, was always fun to be around, and his laughing was contagious. Linc, his wife Mary, and their four children lived just one mile to the east of us. They had two boys: Jack and Bob; and two girls: Sarah and Patty. Linc's boys were so polite, helpful, and always fine young gentlemen. The girls would play with our girls all the time. And of course, Mabel and Mary liked to spend time together, and help each other out with driving the kids to town or to each other's farms.

The Headquarters

I invited them, Linc and Bill, down to the basement headquarters.

"Coffee boys?" I asked knowing they would say yes. I headed upstairs and returned with the pot - we had just enough for three cups.

"I got one for you Andy," Linc blurted as he prepared for his first joke.

"A skeleton walks into a bar and says, 'Barkeep, give me a pitcher of beer'," he hesitated, looked at both of us to signal that the punch line was coming quick and we better get ready. "And a mop!" He gave us half a second to let it sink in and then belted out his deep, loud, laugh that I have come to love. Bill and I followed in heavy laughter as it finally hit us.

"Get it? A skeleton, and a mop," Linc explained to make sure we really understood how funny his joke was.

After the laughter died down and he felt it was proper time for the next joke, Bill was ready with one of his jokes.

"A farmer was working on his broken-down tractor when one of his neighbor's cows came up to the fence on the border of their properties and said 'It's probably the magneto'".

Bill continued, "The farmer was so distraught that he ran all the way to the neighbor's house and knocked on the door. The neighbor came to the door and asked 'What is it?'".

"The startled farmer said 'One of your cows just talked to me, and he said that the problem with my tractor is that it has a bad magneto.'"

"The neighbor asked, 'Was it a big brown cow with a black spot on his head?'"

"'Yes, yes,' said the farmer, 'That's him.'"

"The neighbor shook his head and said, 'Don't listen to that cow, he doesn't know anything about tractors.'"

Both of us had heard it before but we laughed as if we had heard it for the first time. We didn't have much time to recover from his first joke and Bill hit us with the other barrel.

"A farmer was in his barn milking one of his cows and a fly flew round and round his head and flew directly into the cow's ear." Bill paused a bit then continued. I was pleased because I had not heard this one before, so he got my attention. "The farmer didn't think much of it until the fly squirted out into the milk bucket." Another pause. "Then the farmer thought, well, in one ear and out the udder."

We all continued laughing holding our stomachs, spitting out coffee. Bill was very pleased with himself. While laughing I could tell that Linc was trying hard to come back with another joke that could keep us going a bit longer.

"Where do the Polish put their armies?" Linc asked almost yelling to get above the laughter. "In their sleevies!" Linc roared.

We all kept right on laughing, and finally, as all joke telling times must end, we sat there smiling and sipping our coffee. Our joke-telling sessions had become famous, especially to Darlene. For years Darlene had written down our best jokes and captured them in a "joke book". Whether we were telling jokes at the kitchen table, in the barn, or in the basement, Darlene would run for her joke book and make an entry. If I heard a good one, I would make it a point to tell her.

Russians Push into Germany

(3 Feb 45) I sat down after dinner to listen to Gabriel Heater's six-thirty radio news program. In Europe, the Russian Red Army was smashing their way into Germany after many long months of pushing the Germans out of Romania, Bulgaria, Hungary, and Poland. There was also news of massive allied bombing campaigns in Berlin. The Americans and British were using these new firebombs that would set whole cities ablaze killing tens of thousands of people. I hated to hear of such horror, but I was all for getting the war over as quick as possible.

"I just can't imagine what it must be like in some of those cities over in Europe," Mabel said with a look of confusion, "it's so hard to imagine."

"Some of those cities have been reduced to rubble," I replied.

"Why don't those Germans just realize that they can't defeat all of us – the Russians, the British, and us."

"That Hitler really thinks he can conquer the world, but it sounds like we are hitting him from all sides."

We have been listening to these radio war reports for so long now. It's really hard to take in all of the news and understand just how awful things are over there. I couldn't imagine what it would be like to be bombed here in the United States. We have had the black out drills, but never heard planes overhead. Thinking of it gives me the chills.

The Cistern

(5 Feb 45) Mabel served my favorite breakfast - shredded wheat with ice-cold milk, and coffee.

"The cistern is nearly empty, Andrew." Mabel's first words of the day were straight to the point.

"Baths last night?" I asked as I pushed my shredded wheat into the milk. It needed to soak a bit, but not too long.

"Yes," she answered, "I would have woke you up, but you looked so peaceful." I normally took my bath after the girls, but I took a longer nap than usual after dinner. Mabel sometimes overused the water, but I bit my lip knowing that I would put the cistern at the top of my list without any further discussion.

The cistern was a 40-gallon tank that was just outside our kitchen window submerged in the ground. Most farms relied on a cistern to hold water for household use. Our water source was a deep well that was located north and west of the old garage. There was a concrete foundation with the well in the center and a 40 foot tower above that held a windmill connected to a long shaft that extended into the well, and connected to a well pump. There was also a handle for hand-pumping small amounts of water into pails. In order to fill the cistern or the horse tank, the windmill was used, or if their was no wind, I could hook up the tractor.

After drinking my last half-cup of coffee, I headed out the kitchen door. I walked around to the side of the house and wiped the snow off the wooden cistern cover, lifted it, and slid it off to one side, and looked down. There was enough daylight to see that the water level was below the pipe that was connected to the pump in the kitchen. The cistern was never actually empty as the inlet pipe was a few inches above the bottom of the cistern. I then headed toward the machine shed to fetch the one-inch pipe that was used to get the water from the well to the cistern. Pipe couplings were used to piece together the ten or fifteen six foot pieces needed to reach the cistern. I threw the pipes in the truck and drove over to the well, pieced everything together, and connected the windmill shaft. After a few minutes of trickling, the water finally started to flow at a decent rate. I would keep my eye on the flow rate from the pipe, as well as the level in the cistern, for the next three or four hours.

(14 Feb 45) I sat down for the six-thirty radio news to listen to Gabriel Heater's Chicago broadcast. The allied fire bombing of Germany continued, this time in the town of Dresden, another large city. There were reports of as many as 35,000 to maybe even 100,000 Germans dead. The news reports lately made you feel that we were coming close to victory over the Germans and Adolf Hitler.

I had mixed feelings after tonight's radio report. Of the 100,000 Germans dead, was this all military? Or were many of these civilians in the city. I feared that the fire bombs were also killing women and children.

(17 Feb 45) Mabel and the other Moms had established a ritual on Saturdays while the kids were attending Catechism, to meet at Bid Kuhn's for coffee, rolls, sharing of new recipes, and partake in some neighborhood gossip. Bid was Mary Armstrong's mother. Mabel had asked me to go along for a visit, and I decided it would be nice to socialize for a bit.

Since Bid Kuhn's place was so close to the church, we dropped the girls off and waited at Bid's for catechism to let out, then the girls walked to Bid's. We met Linc and Mary Armstrong at Bid's place and drank coffee and ate pastries. Linc livened up the party by passing around a pint of bourbon that he pulled out of Bid's cupboard.

"Just a little taste for the coffee?" Linc offered to the ladies. We laughed and joked for about a half an hour when the sky opened up and the heavy snow started.

"Should we go get the kids Linc?" Mary said worriedly, "it's really coming down. Remember that I have to take the Nuns back to Streator today."

It was well known by all that Mary did not like to drive in bad weather. She was a real trooper and the most reliable driver, filling in for others who couldn't go on their scheduled day, but she did not want to drive in the snow.

"Relax Mary, everything will be fine," Linc responded making light of Mary's concern.

Linc and I carried on joking and just about finished the pint of bourbon before Mary became more agitated and really concerned about the snow. I glanced outside and realized that the snow was accumulating quickly.

"Why don't you call Mr. McCormick." Mabel suggested to Mary. "Perhaps he can take the Nuns back to Streator. You drove for him two weeks ago when he had to go out of town."

"Why can't one of those Nuns study up and get a driver's license? There's nothing against Nuns driving is there Andy?" Linc stated the question followed by a roar of laughter as he reached into Bid's ice box. "To early for a beer Andy?"

I reached my hand out for the beer. Why not, I thought. It wasn't often when a special get-together occurs like today. Linc and I laughed and carried on about why Nuns should be able to drive. Mabel was giving us stern looks like we shouldn't be talking about the Nuns that way.

Mary insisted that a decision be made immediately as to how the Nuns would get home.

"I vote for Mr. McCormick," Linc suggested, who was happy to leave the driving to someone else and stay put in the warm house watching the snow fall, and drinking beer.

Mabel reached Mr. McCormick on the phone and asked him if he could substitute for Nun duty. He spoke with such a loud voice that I could hear him clear across the room reply, "Why of course I can do that. Tell Mary not to worry about it."

Mary with great relief, exhaled and said, "Oh, he is a good old soul, that Mr. McCormick."

"Here's to Mr. McCormick," said Linc as he raised his beer in a toast. "And may the Nuns reach the convent safely."

(18 Feb 45) We received a nice long letter from Darlene today. She is fine and getting along in spite of the many hours working at the Prairie Shipyard. I would imagine it was hard work as well. She really doesn't come home all that often considering the gas shortage and Seneca being quite a few miles away. She did mention in her letter she was coming home this weekend. It seems there was an accident at the shipyard and a co-worker was electrocuted. She stated that she was quite distraught over that.

Admiral Nimitz Pushes Towards Japan

(25 Feb 45) The familiar voice of Gabriel Heater reported that Admiral Nimitz was pushing closer and closer to the Japanese mainland.

Nimitz had already taken Saipan, Guam, and other important islands. The islands at Guam were within 1200 miles of Tokyo Japan, which was in range for the mighty B-29 bombers. These bombers were such amazing pieces of machinery built by American hands, and mostly wives of the men serving, women like our Darlene helping to build ships in Seneca. The reporter also stated that Nimitz had sent the Fifth Marine Corps to invade another island, Iwo Jima, within the past week and that the Japs were defending this small island, five and a half miles long and two and a half miles wide.

I had never heard of these islands. I guess we are just taking one island at a time and heading for Japan. So many have lost their lives on these islands. Admiral Nimitz seems to be a great leader and I trust that this is the only way to win the war.

"Well enough about the war Andy, Happy Anniversary," said Mabel.

Boy, did I slip up, I thought - forgot all about it.

Mabel continued, "Twenty-three years already – doesn't seem like we have been married that long."

Not knowing what else to say I added, "I've enjoyed all these years with you Mabel. In another two years it'll be our 25th – then we can throw a real shivaree."

Losing Buster

The sun was beginning to set and it was best to get the horses into the barn before it got too dark. I whistled for Nancy and Esther to give me a hand with gathering the horses, which they were always willing to do. The girls loved the horses.

During my morning chores, it was standard routine to chase the horses and cows out of the barn, down the pathway about one hundred yards that led to the pasture. The pasture was rectangular and approximately four acres. We let the cows and horses run free in the pasture each day, unless there was bad weather. Near dusk we would rustle all of the animals back into the barn. Most of the time, the horses would be near the gate that led from the pasture back into the path leading to the barnyard. Sometimes we would have to go run one or two of them down. That seemed to be the case today, as only three horses were ready to come in.

"Dad, I'm going to find Buster," Esther yelled out. Nancy opened the gate to the pathway and led the three horses in single file down the path to another gate to enter the barnyard, then finally into the barn and into their stalls. Nancy secured the three horses in the barn and ran down the path and into the pasture. The energy the girls had was amazing. Chasing down those horses was a chore I was glad to give to them. After ten minutes or so, it seemed that the girls were not having any luck finding Buster. He made a habit of being stubborn, finding ways to get outside of the pasture and wander about. There were spots in the fence vulnerable to breakouts that needed mending.

I was on my way out to the pasture, when Esther and Nancy came running back, without Buster.

"Got out again?" I asked.

"Yep, Buster's not out there, but the other three are in their stalls," Nancy replied. The girls ran back down the path, through the barnyard and into the house. Their work was done and it was time for play.

I jumped in the truck and headed north to see if I could find Buster. No horse, so I turned around and headed back, past the farm, and toward the south property line and that is where I found him. He was on his side wedged under some barbed wire near a hedge post. He must have tried to get through and got caught, and probably the more he struggled, the more damage the barbed wire did to his flesh. Unable to get free, he fell over, and eventually bled to death.

Emotion doesn't normally get the best of me, but seeing Buster there, that big, beautiful animal, made me choke up and I cried. He must have suffered greatly, slowly bleeding, with no one to help. I wished that someone had driven up or down the road and warned us, as he was clearly visible from the road. We had Buster for over six years. Not knowing exactly how old he was, the auctioneer where we purchased him said he was at least 15, maybe 20 years old. Knowing some horses were known to have lived to be 30 or 40 years old, it was sad to think poor old Buster hadn't quite reached middle age.

Leaving Buster where he was, I headed back to the house and called Steve and Linc to give me a hand, and also called the Kollar's rendering service to have them come out and pick up the remains.

"Hello, Jake here." Jake Kollar at the rendering service answered with little enthusiasm. The service the Kollar's provided was to pick up and dispose of dead animals. It was no easy task to move a 500 pound animal.

"Jake, Andy Durdan here, one of my horses just passed. Can you send somebody out to pick it up?" I asked talking softly as not to let the kids or Mabel know the bad news just yet.

"It's late Andy, won't be until the morning," he replied.

"All right then. If that's all you can do – hopefully in the morning?" I pressed.

"In the morning... sure, let's say ten o'clock. Is the horse stiff yet?"

"Yeah he is kind of stiff, not sure how long he's been there," I grimaced thinking about his lifeless body.

"Rigor mortis has probably set in. Do the best you can to get him in an open area near the road so we can get to him. Where is he now?" Jake gave instructions and asked questions like he has done this ten thousand times. There was not much emotion in his voice, which was understandable in the business he was in.

"He actually bled to death while getting caught in a barb wire fence on my south property line. He's only 30 feet or so from the road. Steve, my brother, and Linc Armstrong are on their way to help me clear him from the fence and move him closer to the road."

"Okay Andy. Hey I'm sorry about your horse." His voice sounded sympathetic.

"Thanks Jake. Bye now." It felt good to know that help was on the way, as these types of things are hard to handle on your own. Linc was kicking up dust along the north road by the time I stepped outside, and Steve arrived shortly thereafter. The three of us clipped away the barbed wire, used a combination of straps and ropes to harness and pull the horse using the Fordson. It was Steve's idea to cover Buster with a tarp so as not to startle people passing by.

As with any animal dying, it was tough to tell Mabel and the kids. They all seemed to take it well, for the moment anyway. I'm sure it will be difficult the next time the girls bring in the horses. Plus we all know that horses go to heaven, and the girls smiled knowing Buster would be okay up there.

MARCH

As March came along, it was still very cold, but the thought of spring being just around the corner made me very happy. The major task at hand for this month is putting up a new fence around the pasture. Losing Buster was a big loss for us, and the fence needed to be replaced. There was also some fencing on the north side of the barnyard that needed replacing. The farm was in very good shape overall. Of the 240 acres, the farmhouse and buildings sat on just under 6 acres.

Location of Farm

Our farm was six miles east and two miles south of Grand Ridge, Illinois; and six miles east and five miles north of Streator. The farmland in LaSalle County, like most counties in the state, was split up into sections of one square mile. One hundred sixty of our two hundred forty acres of our farmland was situated on the northwest corner of our square mile, with an additional eighty acres on the square mile immediately to the west, and right across the road from our house. We shared our square mile with two other farms: The Rinker's, who owned the northeast corner, and the Koetz's, who farmed the south section. The Armstrong's farm was one square mile to the east of us.

Farm Buildings

Our farm consists of eleven buildings, from largest to smallest: barn, corncrib, house, machine shed, old garage, new garage, hog house, chicken coup, feed house, pump house, and brooder house. The front of our house faces west and is 50 or so feet in from the road. The house is two stories, with our bedroom downstairs, and four bedrooms upstairs. There are three entrances into the house: one entrance through the front porch, one into the kitchen on the north side, and one on the east side through the pantry.

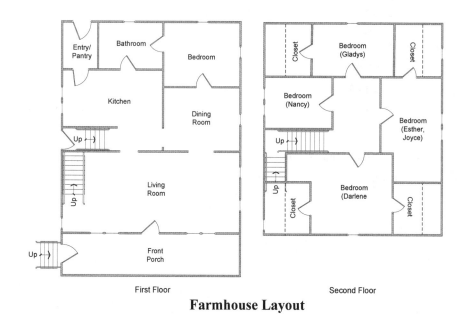

First Floor

Second Floor

Farmhouse Layout

There were a number of trees here when we bought the place, and we have planted many more since. We have maples, elms, oaks, poplar, evergreen, and fruit trees: apple, cherry, and pear. We also have grape vines along the fence near the road, and a large garden where we grow tomatoes, potatoes, watermelon, beans, cucumbers, and a few other vegetables. There are no trees around the corncrib or barn as to not interfere with the animals or farm machinery. Electric power is connected to our farm from a power pole on the far side of the road. The wires run from the pole on the road to another power pole in the middle of our barnyard. From there, the electric power is metered, and passed along on separate power lines to the house, the new garage, the old garage, barn, and brooder house. With the exception of the electric wiring to the new garage, all of the electric wiring was completed before we bought the farm. We have gravel for a driveway, with the main entrance just north of the house and just south of the corncrib. There are larger entrances along the fence line for getting large machinery in and out, one north of the corncrib and another south of the house. The machine shed is the building furthest from the house, positioned just north of the corncrib. The old garage sits on the edge of the barnyard across from the barn. The place where I spend most of my time tinkering and fixing things is either in the new garage or the machine shed.

Just to the east of the old garage there are four huge elm trees, which provide nice shade. There is also some storage space for machinery - like the disc and other large items that I cannot store inside elsewhere.

Gas Tanks – Darlene and the Frozen Pump

Next to the old garage there are two gas storage tanks. We have a 150 gallon tank used for the tractors, and a small 50 gallon tank for the trucks and cars. The gas for the tractors, or yellow gas, is around 15 cents per gallon. The gas for the trucks and cars, or white gas, is around 19 cents per gallon. Both tanks are based on separate homemade wooden structures that also house the pumps and hoses. From time-to-time I call Fred Gallup from Grand Ridge and he comes out in his fuel truck and fills the tanks through threaded fittings on the top of the tanks. Whoever has the misfortune of getting into an auto that registered "E" for empty, or close to it, needs to refill from the smaller tank. The girls pay me whatever the rate for gas was at the time – they usually leave money and a note on my desk if I am not around.

One time last year, Darlene was pumping gas early in the morning. I was just getting out of bed when I heard Darlene yelling "Gladys, Gladys, hurry up get Dad, I can't stop the pump!" Before Gladys even knocked on our bedroom door I was headed out through the kitchen with nothing on but my underwear and undershirt. It had happened to me a few times before - the cold weather sometimes made the pump mechanism freeze in place.

"Put your hand over the nozzle Darlene, hold it tight." I gave the instructions clearly and calmly so as not to startle her any more than she already was. She hesitated a second, then cupped the palm of her hand over the nozzle and sure enough, the pump stopped automatically due to overpressure, but not soon enough as she had gas all over her slacks and shoes.

"I'm sorry Dad, look at the mess I made," said Darlene, drooping her shoulders looking at her slacks and shoes soaked with gas. Gladys followed me out and I heard her chuckling behind me. I turned around to see Gladys with her hands over her mouth. Then Darlene and I both belted out a hearty laugh, looking at each other. We were quite a sight with Darlene covered in gas, and me in my long underwear. As my thoughts drifted back, it made me chuckle again.

1938 Chevy Grain Truck

We had built the new garage a few years after we moved in. This is where we kept the family car, as the new garage was close to the house, so it would be a short walk when it was cold outside. My real treasure and the piece of machinery I use the most on the farm is my 1938 Chevy Grain Truck. The truck is equipped with a 236 cubic-inch engine, 4-speed manual transmission, with a load capacity of 1.5 tons. It has much more power and is much more versatile than the other trucks I have owned. It has four sturdy wooden panels that form a box, which is eight feet wide and ten feet long. These panels are easily removable to have the option of converting to a flat bed. Most of the time I keep the panels on. There is a hoist on the back used to pick up heavy loads. There was room for three people in the front, and I often let the girls ride in the back if we weren't going to far. I purchased the truck at an auction when it was only three years old, and it has been a real gem as far as maintenance. The truck is quite a bit longer than my previous trucks, but it fits nicely in the old garage, and still left me plenty of room to get around. On account of the fact that the law required it, I painted my name on the door in square letters "AND DURDAN". Somehow I forgot the "Y" at the end of my name, and just left it. Friends tease me about that all the time. The cab of the truck is just right as it has lots of headroom.

Like most of my brothers, I am over six foot tall. I have to admit, my brown hair is graying a little bit on the ends. Some of my brothers are shorter than me, but all of us have big hands. In spite of my masculinity, I am not awkward, and am pretty adept. Mabel said I can set the mousetraps with bait better than she. I wear a pretty good sized cap, and have a round face. Half the time my face is two tone, as you can just see where my cap shades my face.

Nearly half of the farm is taken up by the barnyard, which is situated north of the barn. This is where the brooder house, chicken coup, feed shed, and pump house are located. The only building left to mention is the hog house, which is situated between the corncrib and the old garage.

Battle of Iwo Jima

(1 Mar 45) The ever-faithful Mr. Heater reported on the fighting on the small island of Iwo Jima. The U.S. Marines were having trouble clearing the Japanese out of caves and tunnels that were reinforced with steel. The B-29 bombers were having little effect against the caves and

the only way to get them out was by using tanks, flame throwers, and our soldiers fighting to get into the caves. This type of warfare was hard on our soldiers, with initial reports that as many as 10,000 marines may have lost their lives since landing on the island in the middle of February.

We had been hearing a lot about the warfare on this island. The marines seemed bound and determined to root out every last Japanese. I thought about what it must be like to walk into one of those caves looking for the enemy, not knowing when and if you were going to be shot at. Sometimes I feel guilty for being here safe and sound on our farm in the United States while so many of our boys were over there in harms way. All we can do is pray for each and every one of our boys fighting over there, and thank them for their service when they come home.

(5 Mar 45) On Monday morning, I did my chores and headed into Streator in the family car for a 9 am dentist appointment, and then to the service station to have a tire repaired on the car and have all of the tires inspected. It was particularly sunny this morning, the air was crisp and the sky was blue. Spring was just around the corner. The fields still had a few inches of snow lying atop the corn stubs left behind from the year before. It is such a pleasant feeling to ride down the country roads looking at the land that we work so hard to maintain. I would compare our land and farm to those I passed, always noticing the smallest of details - like newly painted fences or shutters, or new barn siding. You find that most of the farmers did a good job keeping their places up, but there were those who let things go.

Main Street was busy as usual, but I was lucky to find a spot right in front of Dr. Kozlowski's office. The dentist was pleased with my teeth overall, gave me a good cleaning, and told me he was keeping an eye on one of my molars that may need some work next time. I tried to see the dentist once per year.

Tires and the WWII Rationing Program

After paying the dental receptionist by check, I headed to the service station. Charley, my auto mechanic of choice, has been my maintenance man for nearly ten years.

"Well Andy, three of the four tires look good, but you really should replace the front left soon. I patched up the one tire and put it on the front right, and put the spare back in the trunk. Monkey Wards is having a tire sale, you might want to have a look-see." Charley twisted his cap on top of his head, his way of letting you know that he is ready to move on to the next customer.

"All right then Charley, I'll head on over and get one on order. Thanks," I replied. I paid the nice lady at the customer service desk with a check and headed to Montgomery Wards, which was right downtown. As I approached the counter, I was greeted by a very busy young lady who seemed to be doing three things at once with a smile on her face.

"Hello miss," I said politely, "I would like to apply for a new tire."

"One minute, sir." With another smile she gave the back of the counter a shove with her legs like she was pushing off the side of a swimming pool and rolled backwards on a rolling chair. She snatched a form out of a bin before she came to a stop, twisted in the chair, with both feet landing squarely on the wall on the other side of the room, made another shove which sent her back my way. I had to chuckle at that little maneuver.

"Here you go, Mr. Durdan. How many tires are you applying for?" I was impressed that she remembered my name. I had seen her once or twice before, but I did not remember her name. I looked down and noticed her nameplate on the desk was "June".

"Just one car tire, June," she smiled at my reply. She asked for the size of the tire, and jotted it down, printing neatly.

"Please fill out the rest of this form and sign," she said handing me a fountain pen. I was not fond of these forms, but I was used to the rationing process. Ever since the start of the war in late 1941, the United States was on a rationing program, and tires were one of the items rationed. I had to fill out a Tire Certificate form, an impressive looking government form with "Tire Certificate (R-2A)" in bold across the top. I did not check the box that asked "Is this for farm equipment?", since this was the family car. I checked "No" to the question whether or not I had purchased tires this year.

"I think that will do it, June," I said, handing the form to her. She tore off a carbon copy and handed it to me, and set the remaining sheets in a bin marked "For mailing", which to me meant the transaction was completed and I could be on my way.

"Thank you, Mr. Durdan. You should hear from us in two to three weeks."

"You're welcome, see you soon then." I gave her my best smile in return, but was unable to top hers.

Montgomery Wards would take my request form and submit it to a local ration board, which met at city hall once per week. This was all part of the ration certificate program. The local ration board kept detailed records of purchased rationed items in order to determine who was eligible to make certain purchases. They kept folks honest. Once the local board approved my request, I would receive a certificate in the mail allowing me to go back to Montgomery Wards and make my purchase. The certificate program was also used for automobiles, typewriters, bicycles, rubber footwear and stoves. There was also a program for coupon or stamp-type program that was administered by the Streator National Bank. Everyone was entitled to the stamp program, which allowed you to buy certain foods, fuel oil, gasoline and shoes. Sugar was the most coveted food of all during time of war. To buy food items the government sent out war ration books through the public school system and through the US Mail service. Mabel was not very fond of the books, but it made you plan ahead and we did not waste anything. Each member of our family had their own ration book, which made sense, so a larger family could get more food. Besides sugar - butter and coffee were other especially scarce and highly valued items.

The government literature we received urged all families to do home canning of vegetables and planting of "victory gardens". While gardening and canning was something that we were accustomed to doing, the food ration stamps were a challenge for the first year or so to adjust to. Misplaced ration books became a source of frustration for Mabel – we had seven to manage. By 1945 we were old pros.

(8 Mar 45) Mabel turned 44 years old today. The three little kids and I sang happy birthday to her before breakfast. Each of the kids made her a little card of construction paper, crayons, and little flowers attached with Elmer's glue. I surprised her with a potted plant for her flower garden.

Headed to Grand Ridge this morning to buy some hedge for the pasture fence. I would need to split the hedge into fence posts. The hedgerows that you see around the farms here were all planted by settlers many years ago. The hedgerow's woven stems and underbrush provided a very thick and sturdy border that pigs, horses, cows, nor bulls could penetrate. Before the advent of barbed wire, wooden or metal fences were very expensive. The hedge plants could be purchased in nurseries and were very inexpensive. Once full grown in about five years, they stood four to five feet tall. They did have to be trimmed or they would get overgrown. Most of the hedgerows in this area are gone. We still have some in the southern part of our property, but they have become too large. Many farmers slowly took them out because they took up valuable planting space. Barbed wire became more popular than hedgerows after the turn of the century. However, farmers still use the wood from the hedge for fence posts because it is the most durable wood for both weather and disease.

After getting home I wanted to start splitting the hedge into posts. The pasture was nearly four acres. I need enough posts for only three sides, as one side was replaced two years ago. The pasture was 200 feet by 800 feet. I needed one post every rod, or roughly 16 feet apart. My calculations showed I will need about 100 fence posts. The fence posts need to be between six-and-a-half to seven feet tall, as two feet are imbedded into the ground. I knew that the amount of hedge I purchased would only be good for about one-third of the posts I would need. So, with an axe, wood splitter, and saw, I started the task. By supper time I had split enough hedge for 15 posts. I realized that I had not had a good workout in a good long time.

(9 Mar 45) Spent all morning splitting hedge. Didn't quite finish with the hedge I had on hand by lunch, but was able to finish by two pm. I figured I would get these posts in the ground before I went to Grand Ridge for more hedge. I loaded the hedge posts into the truck and cleaned up my tools.

Stung By Bees

(12 Mar 45) Now that I had completed splitting my hedge posts for the new fence around the pasture, I was ready to start drilling the holes for the posts. My post-hole digger mount for the John Deere tractor is in storage outside on the east side of the old garage. I started clearing away weeds that had grown over the digger so I could pull it out. In the process of jockeying the digger out from under an elm tree branch that was hanging down, out of the corner of my eye I saw what looked like a huge moving black mass, which turned out to be a very large bee's nest. About the time I had realized what it was, I saw the bees coming at my face and attaching to my arms and hands. I never knew a 48 year old man could run so fast and swat so many bees as I did. I ran around the front of the old garage and towards the house slapping my face, neck, arms, and even started taking off my shirt thinking that the bees would get inside my clothes. I tripped over something and fell down, but

snapped right back up and kept moving. After a bit, I started to calm down and started to feel the pain from the stings. I could see where the little buggers had stung me. There were eight or ten places on my arms and hands, and I could also feel a couple stings on my neck.

I went inside and Mabel put ice packs on the stings, which made it feel much better.

"Where did they come from?" Mabel asked.

"The nest was somehow attached to a tree branch back where I store the machinery next to the old garage. I looked right down the barrel of that nest, and they weren't too happy. I never knew I could run so fast. Boy, were they mad - holy smokes!" I was still stunned.

"Just be still while the ice cools down your skin and you'll feel better. How are you going to kill those bees? We can't have the girls getting stung." Mabel was already thinking of the next attack.

"Linc has some pesticide spray that will kill them - he has helped me before." The ice was helping. It was a good time to take a nap; I would tackle the bee's nest later.

After supper and evening chores, I stopped by Linc's to get the pesticide to take care of the bees. I gave them a good spray from about 20 feet away. I'll show them who's boss, I thought. Just before dark I was able to get the post-hole digger positioned, without disturbing any bees that survived the pesticide, so I could pull it out with the Fordson. Tomorrow morning I would take the plow off the John Deere and replace it with the post-hole digger.

(13 Mar 45) By mid-morning I had the digger on the John Deere and heading to the pasture to start digging the post holes. I drilled the holes about three feet away from the existing fence. This will give me room to work and I could put the new fence up around the old one. Once the new fence was up I will get rid of the existing one. Drilling holes goes pretty fast as long as everything works okay. It took me two hours to drill 500 feet worth of holes. I drove back to the barn to get the truck and the hedge posts.

The posts are set by hand. The auger drill on the post-hole digger makes a nice neat pile of dirt around the hole. I first set the pole in the ground and fill in dirt as needed so the pole is at the right height, and then fill and pack it around the post. By 5:00 pm, I set all the posts that I had split into the ground, 35 in all.

(16 Mar 45) By Friday afternoon, I had made two more trips to Grand Ridge for the necessary amount of hedge to make enough posts to complete the three sides of the pasture, dug the holes, and set the posts. I would have been done yesterday if it had not been for the post-hole digger mount malfunctioning and needing repair.

Today was a very warm day. I started the day with a long-sleeved shirt under my coveralls. By the end of the day I was working in my undershirt. It seems like spring will start a bit earlier this year.

Next week I will reinforce my corner posts and run the wire. Then I will have to spend some time building three entrance gates, which is quite a bit of detailed work.

Nancy Falls Out of Moving Car

(17 Mar 45) St. Patrick's Day today – didn't really plan to celebrate much. After morning chores I pulled the disc and drags out of the machine shed and attempted to put the combine in the shed. It would not go, so I tried to put it in the south end of the crib, but it would not go there either. So I decided to leave it outside for now. Took the bad front tire off the Fordson in preparation to take it into town to get it repaired.

I was getting a bit frustrated as the morning was not going that well and I did not get much done this week as I wanted, and here it is Saturday already.

Darlene called from Seneca and asked if it was okay for her and her girlfriends to spend the night.

"Sure Darlene. That would be fine," I gladly agreed. It was always fun to have Darlene and her friends here. "What time do you think you will be getting in?"

"Oh, I'd say around five-thirty. Would that be okay?" asked Darlene with hesitation, knowing it would mean extra for dinner.

"Your Mother was kind of hoping you'd make it home for St. Patty's day. We have plenty in the freezer. So, we'll look forward to seeing you."

Mabel was happy to hear we were to have company and pulled some meat out of the freezer for dinner.

Mabel and I decided to run a few errands this morning. Sent the rascals to bed early last night, but Mabel still had to go upstairs a second time to hustle them out of bed. We planned to make a quick stop at the bank to deposit the bean check, stop at the Co-op to buy supplies I had to pick up for the baby chicks we had on order, and Mabel wanted to drop off some canaries at Olga Gallup's place. She lived only a couple of blocks from downtown Grand Ridge.

To my utter amazement, just before the Grand Ridge road on our way to town, I heard some commotion and some screaming.

Mabel turned around to look in the back seat and screamed, "Good heavens, Nancy fell out of the car."

I slammed on the breaks and it seemed forever before I stopped the car. I ran as fast as I could toward Nancy. By the time I reached her she had started to pick herself up. She was not crying as she was so startled.

I gently touched her hands and arms and legs to check for any breaks or bleeding.

"Nancy, are you okay?" Mabel asked as she reached her only a few seconds after me.

Finally realizing what had happened, Nancy started to cry. Mabel reached down, picked her up, and held her in her arms. She had scrapes on her arms and legs, she was bleeding a bit, and gravel clinging to her skin.

I struggled to get myself calmed down. Thank God that she did not go under one of the tires. I followed closely behind Mabel as she helped Nancy to the car, all the time inspecting her arms, legs, and head. I was relieved to find that she was okay.

It had always been hard for Mabel to handle a bad situation. She put Nancy in the car and just stood there in tears.

I approached her and spoke softly. "She'll be fine. Let's get home and have her lie down for awhile." I helped Mabel into the car, turned around and headed back home to wash Nancy up a little and make sure that she did not need a doctor's attention.

The canaries weren't going to make it to the Gallup's today – maybe tomorrow. The birds were chirping away as we carried them back in the house in their cages.

Nancy hated to see the bottle of iodine – she knew it would sting. After applying the iodine, we just wrapped her arm and leg with some bandages. I thanked God for sending His guardian angel to watch over Nancy today.

Darlene and her friends arrived safely at around 5 pm. We had dinner and talked for a good while. The shipyard was busy as ever, and the shipyard girls were ready to let off a little steam. We drank a few beers and played cards. We turned on the record player and danced in the living room. Mabel and I went to bed around 11:30 pm, but Darlene and her friends stayed up much later I'm sure.

Tokyo Firebombing

(18 Mar 45) Gabriel Heater's report spoke of more allied B-29 firebombing of Tokyo. This is the same tactic we were using on the Germans. A total of 279 B-29s dropped nearly 2000 tons of firebombs on Tokyo killing tens upon tens of thousands of people. Reports from Tokyo claimed that Tokyo was on fire, the entire city in flames.

I could not imagine the horror of these bombs. I think of Chicago or St. Louis being attacked by Germans. This bombing affected mostly civilians. German and Japanese children being killed sickened me, but I felt more compassion for our boys fighting and dying every day.

(20 Mar 45) Started running barbed wire at my corner posts. The first wire was about eight to ten inches off the ground. I had to buy special fasteners to connect the wire to the posts. I then ran three more wires twelve inches apart for a total of four strands of wire from top to bottom. The downside to barbed wire is that the livestock can cut their hide on the barbs. You want them to stay away from the wire if possible. Making the wire electric can keep them away and prevent them, especially the horses, from trying to get out. The shock will send them back away and they learn over time not to get close. When the electric fences first came out, they were expensive, but are now quite reasonable.

Shelling Corn

(21 Mar 45) Almost forgot what day it was when Mabel greeted me with a "Happy Birthday, Andy" when I came inside from my morning chores. I turn 49 today.

"What can I make you special for your birthday supper, Andy?" Mabel asked.

"Oh, don't go making a big fuss on my birthday," I replied, "but if you don't have anything else planned, I have a craving for a steak."

"I can pull a couple out of the freezer."

"Good, I will be looking forward to that."

After breakfast I got the truck ready for shelling corn. I planned to meet my Dad and Pete at the Hagie place to shell. The corn that we picked last fall was stored in the crib. Farming is a good solid business, and we wanted to get top-dollar for our crops. We watched the market prices daily, and my theory was to never sell on a down market. If the price of grain fell a nickel, more or less, the price usually would creep up again. The corn was at a pretty good price now at a dollar and a quarter per bushel, so we decided to sell some.

Prior to shelling, we would contact the grain elevator, either in Grand Ridge or Ransom, to inquire on the current price. If I wanted to sell, the buyer at the grain elevator would give me a quote over the phone – this would be the sales agreement. If the price was not right, I would arrange for the corn to be stored to be sold at a later date. The grain elevator would sample my crop by testing for moisture content, provide a report, and a receipt of current holdings.

In years past, farmers had hand-turned shellers, where you would feed the corn into one end and turn the hand crank. The spikes inside the mill would rub the corn off the cob. The corn would drop out the bottom and shoot the cob out the side.

Through the years, the shellers were mechanized, bigger and faster. Dad has a larger sheller that is on wheels that he would take from farm-to-farm. With this sheller, I would use the grain truck to catch the corn from a conveyer chute and haul a full load to the grain elevator.

The cobs were saved and stored in the basement, and were used in place of coal to save money in the winter. The cobs burned much faster than coal, but if you ran short of coal, the cobs could heat the house. As the mechanized shellers operated faster, we had more cobs than could be used at one time. We fed many of them to the pigs, and hauled what we could not use away as garbage.

For even bigger jobs, we would engage a larger sheller from a company doing this type of work. You paid quite a bit for the service, but you could really get a lot done in a short time. These shellers could shell up to 1500 bushels per hour. You would pay the shellers to haul it away as well, in much bigger trucks. Even when engaging a sheller you need at least two men feeding the corn into the machine. The last thing you want is to pay for the service and not run it efficiently as possible, so we made sure we had enough manpower. It was a pretty big operation. Normally, three or four of us would pitch in to engage the sheller for an entire day. The sheller would go from farm-to-farm and haul loads all day until we all were finished. When we engaged a sheller, we would shell one entire side of the crib – which held about 2500 bushels.

My Dad was happy using his smaller mechanized sheller. We could shell whenever and wherever we wanted to. We were quite a bit slower than the larger outfits, but we didn't mind. So for our operation today on the Hagie place, we positioned the sheller at the end of the corn crib. There was a drag in the middle of the crib that would pick the corn and drag into the mouth of the sheller. The output chute of the sheller dumped the corn into the grain truck. One of us would make sure the corn was spread out in order to get a full load. It would take a pretty good while to fill up the whole truck. I hauled the grain into town, and while I was gone Pete and Dad made sure there was plenty of corn ready to be dragged out and shelled for our next load. By the time I was back, Dad and Pete were ready to start shelling the next load.

We were able to get four loads done today. We finished up around 2 pm. We agreed that we would shell again within a week.

(23 Mar 45) I finished the pasture fence today and started dismantling the old fence. I used the Fordson to pull out the old posts. Some of the old posts were badly rotted, many were old and brittle, but there were a few worth saving for different applications. I still had some adjusting to do to the corner posts braces and to the gates, but I could pretty much put this job behind me.

Introduction to Hay

(24 Mar 45) Left early morning to go to Geiger's in Grand Ridge to buy hay seed. I have bought my white clover and other seeds from Geiger's for years. This year I will plant clover, hay, and timothy on 40 acres across the road. Hay is used primarily for feeding and bedding for the animals: cows, horses, pigs, and chickens. Clover is also essential for improving the soil. It is my normal practice to cycle crops around to improve the soil. For example, if I plant oats on 40 acres this year - then hay the next year - then corn the third year - my crop yields will be much higher. You can really tell the difference in the soil after clover has been grown and plowed back under. The texture of the soil is much improved, having a deep rich black color, and more fertile. Hay grows real well even in poor, dry soil. I have made it a habit to sow the seeds in early to mid April. I look back in previous diaries to see when I planted a certain crop the year before, or the year before that. The hay that you plant this year, is not cut until the next year. For the harvest, there are usually three cuts if you have a good crop. A good cutting is when the hay is 20 to 30 inches high before the bloom buds appear.

We use a sickle bar mower pulled behind a tractor to cut the hay. Once it is cut, we let it dry in the field a few days, then we use a side delivery rake to put it in a windrow and get it ready for the hay loader. The hay loader went behind the hay rack, or hay wagon. The hay loader is about ten feet long and gathers hay from the ground using fingers and works it to the top of the rack on the wagon. We normally have one or two guys tapping down the hay rack. We fill the hay rack and head back to the barn to unload it. Once we get all of the hay back to the barn, we call the baling company, who come to the farm and bail all of your hay in a pretty short time. We would then hoist the hay bails up into the barn for storage. Sometimes we put the hay up in the barn loose.

Using the hay loader and hay rack sure beats the way we did it in the old days. I remember spending all day tossing loose hay from the ground to the top of a wagon with pitchforks. That was a grueling job.

If I want to keep the hay for a second year, I leave about eight to twelve inches. If I want to turn the soil the next year and rotate crops, I will cut it as short as possible.

Allied Forces Take Iwo Jima

(25 Mar 45)   An unfamiliar voice, not Gabriel Heater's, had important news from the front lines of Iwo Jima that the U.S. Marines have taken the island, eventually forcing all of the Japanese to surrender or be killed in their caves. Most of the Japanese died defending and would not surrender. U.S. Marines killed in action was estimated at nearly 7,000, while we killed nearly 21,000 Japanese. The way the Japanese defended this island worried the military leaders and the soldiers as to what lay ahead in mainland Japan.

"Well, we finally took that island," I said to Mabel, "what an unbelievable task that was."

"How many soldiers did he say died there?" she asked astonished.

"Seven thousand, if you can believe it."

"Good Heavens." That was all Mabel could say.

"But the island is ours now, and I'm sure the Japanese are shaking in their boots, because we are breathing right down their necks."

(26 Mar 45)   It was time to take care of a few maintenance items with the John Deere tractor before I starting sowing the oats across the road. I had purchased some new lug nuts and put those on just after breakfast. That was a job that I had wanted to do for a month or two. It wasn't easy, as I had to jack up one side of the John Deere using a hydraulic unit borrowed from Linc. It took me a little over three hours to get it all done. And I thought to myself "that wasn't so bad."

My John Deere was a 1937 Model A. I had bought it when it was only two years old. It has been a very dependable tractor – she hasn't given me much trouble at all.

Mending Fences

(27 Mar 45) This morning I was to meet Dad and brothers Ed and Steve at the Hagie place to mend some fencing. Dad had bought the property a few years back, and the farm was only a few miles from us - as the crow files. Dad was still in pretty good health at age 71, and still did a quite a bit of work. He had help at home and in his fields with Ed still living there and all. Irene took up all of the cooking, washing, and other household tasks after Mom died. Mom passed on just four years ago at age 65. After caring for her husband and raising all the kids she was probably just plain tuckered out. Irene spent many long winter nights knitting and sewing, thus adding to her hope chest. When her husband returned from the war they hoped to get a place of their own.

We spent a good part of the morning replacing about 15 old posts and nailed on some new wire. Dad worked right along with us. He's always been a hard worker, and wanted us to know he was still the foreman.

"It seems I remember replacing these posts myself at one time," Dad remarked. "Must be too much water standing here, wouldn't you say Andy?"

"Well, these posts here seem like they've been here for a good while. Not sure if you replaced these posts, but you're certainly right about the posts getting too wet." I replied.

"They all look the same to me after a while," Ed chimed in, "how do you figure you can remember when you replaced posts?"

"I remember these." Dad repeated.

After securing wire to the new posts in one location, we moved the equipment down another 100 feet or so where the fence dipped again. We inspected a few posts and decided they needed replacing. Using the John Deere with the post-hole digger attachment, we dug a new hole, slid in a new post, and covered it over with dirt. Dad was getting a little tired by noon, so we headed back to Dad's place for lunch. We decided that we had done enough for today and made plans to do a little more next week. I was to start sowing oats tomorrow, so I would be busy for the rest of the week.

Patton Crosses the Rhine River in Germany

(29 Mar 45) The same unfamiliar news reporter came on at six-thirty – I hope Mr. Heater is okay. General Patton and his Third Army had crossed the Rhine River, the greatest natural barrier in Western

Germany. The allied forces were on the move to take Germany. The Russian Red Army was moving in from the east as we moved in from the west. The allied forces had taken as many as 300,000 German prisoners on their march to the Rhine River. Hitler would not retreat and paid dearly.

Mabel looked at me and waited for the report to finish and asked, "Now Andy, if we run into the Red Army over there, are they going to be friendly? Are they on our side?"

It was a question I had asked myself a number of times. But now it seemed that we would meet up with them somewhere in Germany.

"I'm pretty sure that we are friendly," was my reply, but I didn't sound very reassuring. "They would have to be because we are both fighting Germany."

"Sometimes I feel like a complete imbecile listening to these reports," she said, "I'm not sure where any of these places are."

"Oh, Mabel, you are no such thing. I'm sure that most people don't know where these places are."

Make Time for Family

(30 Mar 45) "Andy, don't forget that we are going to Steve's." Mabel had come outside to the old garage to remind me of our plans to go to my brother's place for dinner, as we did quite often. We would have supper there, and then play euchre for a couple of hours.

After straightening things up in the old garage, I headed inside to our bedroom to change into some clean clothes. Mabel was in the kitchen writing a letter, most likely a letter to Darlene.

"Are the girls just about ready?" I asked Mabel.

"They are out back playing. They don't seem too keen on going to Uncle Steve's".

"Is that right." I walked outside and signaled the girls to come in.

"Let's get ready to go girls."

"Where?" responded Nancy. She knew darn well where we were going – playing games.

"We are going to Uncle Steve's for dinner, now let's get going."

"Do we have to go?" said Nancy, and Esther chimed in "Dad, do we have to go tonight?"

Joyce was silent, but they were banding together like the three musketeers. After giving them a good stare, I admonished them. "Do you mean to tell me that you don't have time or that you don't want to visit your Uncle Steve and his family?"

The girls looked a bit stunned, except for Joyce, who was a bit young to grasp the seriousness of the situation. Nancy started heading for the house, with Esther and Joyce right behind. I followed behind them and watched them bounce up the stairs to change their clothes.

"What did you say to change their minds?" Mabel asked.

"They just needed few words about family, that's all."

We had a good time at Steve's, playing four or five games of euchre, boys against the girls.

Baby Chicks

(31 Mar 45) Mabel went into town this morning to purchase baby chickens at Ott's Mill and Hatchery. She arrived back around 10:30 am with 50 to 75 little bitty chicks in a box. The brooder house was waiting for them. I had purchased the brooder house a month ago and had it wired for heating. It was a small house with a heater and light in the center which kept the little chicks warm.

"I just think they are so adorable. Don't you think so Andy?" Mabel looked down at her little treasures.

"They surely are cute. They look really lively and healthy," I replied. The chicks had nice fluffy fur and were moving quickly around in the box.

We carried the chicks, still in the box, and put them in their new home. We would check on them periodically. The girls enjoyed sitting in the brooder house and playing with them. As they get bigger, we will move them over into the chicken coop.

APRIL

(1 Apr 45) Today was a day I enjoyed – a day for some fun – April Fool's Day. I love to catch the girls off guard. Nancy came down the steps first into the kitchen.

"Why do you have one blue sock on and one black one?" I asked.

She looked down at her feet and I said loudly, "April fools!" I couldn't stop laughing. I enjoyed the joke much more than Nancy did. She just moved along figuring that old Dad is up to his jokes again.

A little later Gladys came into the kitchen in a hurry, as usual.

"Your slip is showing," I said

She looked down and once again I said, "April fools," laughing again.

The girls would eventually all start laughing, and playing April Fools on each other.

"All right Andrew, that's enough," Mabel said snickering all the time she was reprimanding me.

"Wait until I get to school – I am going to play April Fool's with Mary Lou," Nancy proclaimed.

Every year I was able to catch the girls off guard. April fools is a day I always enjoyed because of the fun and laughter.

Oats and Threshing

Late March or early April is the time to start sowing oats. Oats are primarily used for feeding horses. The demand for oats has decreased since the dawn of the tractor age, which meant the horse's roll has diminished. Fewer and fewer acres are used for oats these days.

Like hay, oats are easy to plant and harvest. Oats also improve the soil when rotated with other crops. We plant the hay seeds (clover, alfalfa, and timothy) and the oats at the same time, using a seeder wagon, which had seed hoppers inside. There is a large hopper for the oats and a smaller hopper for the hay seeds. Chains connected to the wheels of the seeder wagon spins the little rotator between the hoppers and flings the seeds out.

After planting the oats, we then have to disc, then drag the soil. The disc also mounts to the tractor and there are a number of large circular discs working together to break up the soil to a fine texture.

After discing, you come over the same dirt with a drag. You want to

57

drag the seeds in within three days of planting. Early on we used horses to drag – but nowadays we use tractors. We use a rake, or spike harrow, for the dragging. Rakes are made of steel and wood with metal spikes that dig into the ground. The depth the spikes go into the ground can be adjusted. The purpose of dragging is to kick up the dirt, pull up any weed seeds ready to sprout, works the hay and oat seeds into the soil and covers them with dirt.

The oats come up first and grew much faster than the hay. In August, the oats are ready for binding and threshing. The hay is growing down below the oats. The hay has to sit a full year before it is cut.

I use a binder for cutting the oats. The binder cuts the oats and they fall into a canvas. The canvas wraps around the cut oats to make them into a bundle. Whenever the bundle gets to be the right size, the binder trips, and a knife would go down and wrap twine around the bundle. When the twine is wrapped around the bundle, the binder kicks the bundle out into the bundle carrier over the side. When there is about five bundles, the binder lets them down using mechanical fingers onto the ground to unload them. This is all one machine that initially was pulled by horses, but nowadays is pulled by tractor.

The process of stacking the bundles is called "shocking". It takes a couple of guys to go behind the binder and shock the oats. The men put five to seven bundles together; standing them up on the butt of the straw and the head facing towards the sky. The bundles are leaned against each other so they stay in place. Then one bundle is placed on top. This is called the cap. The cap keeps the water out and allows the bundles to dry. Darlene and Gladys have helped with shocking, but it is work really meant for a man. Carrying the shocks and propping them up is very hard work. Once dried, we haul the shocks to the thresher by hayrack.

Threshing is done in the late summer or early fall. The steam-operated thresher separates the grain from the stalk. The threshing machine can be setup just about anywhere. Bill Koetz owns the threshing machine that we use. Our "threshing gang" includes me, Koetz, Connors, Long, Bedeker, Kates, and Hanusik. Bill pulls the thresher to a location on the back of a big trailer. The trailer is pulled by a tractor with big steel wheels. He uses the same trailer for hauling big tractors. We set up the thresher in the yard at the end of the barn.

The shock bundles are fed into the thresher. The stalks are separated from the grain, then directed through a chute and blown into the barn rafters. The stocks are used for bedding. When the rafters along the upper east end of the barn were full, we could blow the stalks into the barnyard. This made a windbreak for the cows, and a nice bed for the cows to lay in.

Since threshing machines are very expensive, it is normal practice to rely on one thresher for all members of the threshing gang. For the past three years we used Bill's machine. We all pitch in for spare parts, if needed, and we all had our special ways for repaying Bill for his generosity. We go to one man's farm, thresh there for three or four days, and then move on to the next farm. We moved from farm-to-farm until all of the threshing work was completed.

The first day of threshing is always very exciting and required good planning. Each man has a specific job in the threshing gang. One man is needed to keep the steam engine fed with fresh coal to keep the steam going. Two to three men are responsible for throwing the shocks of grain into the hayracks to be pulled by horses, or tractor, to the threshing machine. Another two or three men are needed to take the shock bundles and throw them into the thresher, where the thresher does its job to remove the kernels of grain from the stalk. This is a difficult, tiring, and dirty job, especially near the thresher, with the hot steam and the straw chaff blowing everywhere. We rotate to different stations to make it a bit easier.

The going rate for a bushel of oats is 66 1/2 cents. The oats are stored in a bin, and hauled into town later. The oats are stored in the upper part of the corn crib. We use the elevator to raise them up and into the bin. The crib holds corn on the sides and the oats are up above in the center. If you walk into the corn crib and look up – that is the oats bin. When it is time to haul oats to town, I pull the grain truck into the corn crib, pull out a little slide and the oats run out into the grain truck, ready to take to the elevator at market price. Although the horses consume most of our oat stock, we also feed the younger calves and chickens some.

Windrower and Combine

The windrower and combine will eventually replace the binder and thresher for harvesting oats. Using the windrower and combine is a whole new ballgame. The binder can be modified to be made into a windrower. The top part of the binder that makes up the bundle is eliminated. I wanted to keep the binder as is, so I purchased a second binder at a farm sale, and modified it to make my windrower. When the oats are cut using the windrower, the oats lay on the ground. Instead of being bundled, the oats come to one side of the windrower and laid down in a neat row on the ground. Instead of bundles being dropped down five or six at a time, the result is a constant row of oats with the head of the stalk pointing away from the windrower. We let the oats lay and dry for a bit.

Once dry, the combine comes along and picks up that row of oats by the head. The combine I own is an Allis Chalmers. It is called a tractor combine – meaning you pull it with a tractor. It picks the oat head up onto the combine's canvas first and pulls the head off and separates it from the straw. The combine rips off the straw, shreds it up a little bit, and then shoots it out the side. We either leave the straw there on the ground, or shoot it into a truck riding alongside. The grain goes through the combine and collects in an onboard bin.

For this year, and probably the next few years, I will use both the binder/thresher and the windrower/combine methods. Switching from the binder to the windrower has to be gradual. This is very similar to changing from horses to tractors. The benefits of the windrower/combine method were pretty good. We are able to do away with the threshing machine, which is difficult to use and expensive to maintain. The combine separates the grain from the straw just the same and loads it nice and neatly into an onboard bin as you drove along. I would still need help to drive the truck next to the combine to collect the straw. Unfortunately the truck filled up rather quickly requiring multiple trips to the barn to unload. The thresher could blow the straw directly into the barn. With the windrower/combine, there was no more need for shocking. So, there were good and bad with both methods, but in the long run, it is easier to use the windrower/combine.

Started plowing the north forty this morning. Mabel had mentioned she wanted to go to Streator to pick up some clothing she had ordered from Sears, and to pick up some meat at the locker. As I finished plowing the field, decided I would go in the house for a quick lunch – sardines, some crackers, and a glass of ice tea sounded real good right about now.

Mabel Spins Through Kernan

Upon returning from plowing the north forty, I noticed some spots of tar on the fender and tires of our car. Mabel must have drove over some fresh tar. I picked at it with my fingers and removed most of it with gasoline. It was hard to remove and I knew the girls would not be able to get it off when they washed the car this weekend. Washing the family car was one of their chores, and they did it without having to be told.

Alfie was at the back door wanting in, so I opened the door for him, and we both went into the house. I could tell Mabel was a little upset. She started to explain the incident about how the tar got on the car.

"Oh, Andy, as I was going through Kernan this morning on the way to Streator, they must have just laid tar on the Main Street through town. I was intending to slow down, but it all happened so fast. I could feel the car start to slide, and before I knew it, I had made a complete circle right in the middle of the street."

Astounded, I said, "Then what happened? Did you get out of the car or what?"

"No, I ended up going in the right direction towards Streator, so I just kept right on going," was her calm reply.

"Well ain't that a fine Howdy Doo!"

Sometimes Mabel just floored me. The thought of her spinning around on Main Street for everyone to see, and the fact that she kept right on going made me chuckle inside. Mabel didn't want to make any more fuss about it, so we moved on.

To get off the subject Mabel asked, "Oh, by the way, did you check on the furnace at the school?" The furnace had been acting up and I mentioned to her during breakfast that I had to check on it.

"Yes, I think it finally gave up the ghost. I'm going to give Fred a call and let him know that we need to replace it before next fall." Fred Johnson is our school superintendent and would authorize the purchase.

"Well, I'm sure he will understand. I know you have brought this up to him in the past. We can't let the children catch cold in that school," replied Mabel.

"Well, he said that he was going to budget for it. I'll just make sure I remind him. I'll call him this evening. Well, better get back to work. See you in a while." I kissed her on the cheek to let her know in a silent way that I was glad she was okay, then walked out the kitchen door.

As I walked past the car on the way to the north forty to continue plowing, I thought about Mabel's incident in Kernan. She could have gotten hurt hitting a tree or colliding into another auto. What's a little tar, I was just happy that she is all right. Thank God she is a very good driver.

I was bouncing along on the tractor and I glanced over towards the cow pasture and thought I saw some movement near the teepee. The "teepee" was an area where I reinforced the corner of the cow pasture with tall fence posts and guy wire. The hedge grew all around it and it looked just like a teepee. This was the same area where a number of foxes had lived for awhile last summer. We had noticed that we were missing chickens one-by-one over a two-week period. We figured that these foxes were our chicken thieves. So, what I did was watch from the barnyard after dark to see if the foxes came lurking. Sure enough, two or three of the foxes came right up to the chicken coup. When they saw me they scurried off. I asked Linc – the expert hunter – to see if he could take care of the problem for me. Linc and I drove out near the teepee the next day and Linc shot and killed one of them. The others ran away and I hadn't seem them since.

On the way home from the field, I drove a little closer to the teepee. I didn't see anything, but I would surely keep my eye out for them.

Battle of Okinawa Begins

(5 Apr 45) We were pleased to hear, "Ah, there's good news tonight" for the six-thirty radio report as Gabriel Heater, back in his radio seat, spoke of the continuing war in the Pacific as we fought for the islands that led to mainland Japan. The Tenth Army landed on the island of Okinawa with 172,000 soldiers and marines. This island is only 330 miles from the mainland, 67 miles long and 18 miles wide. This island would be the launching point for the attack on Japan sometime in the near future. This island is much like Iwo Jima, caves and tunnels of reinforced steel. Our experience in Iwo Jima should prove to be valuable in this battle. There were two large airfields and a valuable seaport.

We are getting closer and closer to the Japanese mainland. Hopefully this island will fall to the Allied Forces a lot faster than Iwo Jima did. I wondered if there were any troops from Illinois that landed on Okinawa, or maybe even from Streator or Ottawa.

Farm Sale

(6 Apr 45) Found time today to go to a farm sale at Wade's farm near Grand Ridge. I called my brother John, whom I often went to farm sales with, asked if he would like to come along, and he accepted. It started at nine am and we arrived shortly after ten. It was a chilly day, so the auction was held in one of the machine sheds. The Wades were retiring after many years of farming and intended on renting the farm. They raised two daughters here on the farm, Judy and Amy, I think their names were. The two daughters, who were now married with families, acknowledged our presence by saying hello. I was happy that they

remembered who we were. We also said hello to their mother who was serving sandwiches. She offered one to John and I.

"Don't mind if I do, thank you," I said selecting one off the pile.

The family collie dog stopped by to see if we would give her a pet - which we did. She sniffed my hand hoping I would give her a taste – which I did. The collie made her way around the crowd having a good time with all of the company.

Quite a few farmers had shown up for the sale. We saw familiar faces that frequented farm sales. Many of the older folks declined to purchase. They just liked the company and free sandwiches. Good turnout, but not many earnest buyers. There were many small hand tools sold by the box full. Sadly enough, many of the big machinery items sold dirt-cheap. They did have a lot of wear and tear on them.

Mr. Wade had a lot of equipment to sell, so the auction lasted well past three pm. Like most auctions, the item you are interested in buying might not come up for quite awhile; consequently, the crowd remained.

I was the only bidder on a box full of woodworking tools: block planes, chisels, hand drills, and saws. I bought a few more items – it seemed like I brought home a lot for what little money I spent. Five dollars for a box of picks, a crosscut saw in good condition, small sawhorse, pickax, and two sickles. John won the bid on a very nice sickle bar mower.

Farm sales were always a bit sad to me. It symbolized a closure of one phase of life. Some folks were happy to retire, and some were very sad. I sensed that the Wades were a little upset to see everything go. I know that I would be distraught to see my tractors and tools all of sudden gone. Slowly, everyone ambled off to their vehicles, loaded up their treasures and drove away. I dropped John off at his place and visited a bit with Anna and family before heading home.

When I pulled into the driveway, the girls were feeding the lamb that was given to us by the Smith family who lived in Ransom. It was a friendly little thing. We'd only had it a few days and it looked like it gained weight already with Nancy feeding it milk from the bottle every few hours. We just put a small pen in the front yard near the garage, and found an old wine barrel in the machine shed that she could fit into for now.

Spring Cleaning – Mabel Falls Through Floor

In the spring, along with caring for the baby chicks, tending to her flowers, and a sundry of other things that needed tending to this time of year, Mabel was set on a complete house cleaning – or as much as she could get done. She would feverishly start washing walls, curtains, and windows. Some of the rooms would need painting as well. Her Mother would come out to help in this endeavor.

"I think this year I should clean out that big register between the living room and dining room. It hasn't been done for a long time." I said to Mabel as she was headed out the door to bring the curtains from the clothesline. She thought that was a good idea – the more cleaning we could do the better. The register was easily removed with a screw driver, which I pulled out of my pocket. No time like the present, I thought. I took the register downstairs for a thorough cleaning.

I heard a strange-sounding thud on the floor and Mabel calling for help.

"Oh Pa! Somebody come and help me."

I rushed up the stairs realizing half-way what may have happened and said, "Goodness gracious, the register," as I realized that I had removed it without thinking of Mabel.

When I reached Mabel she was flailing her arms about trying to pick herself up out of the void in the floor where the register was supposed to be. She had intended to go into the dining room to place her freshly washed and dried curtains on the table, and with her hands full she could not see ahead of her, and fell right into the void. Her coat was swirled around the opening and I could not tell how far down she actually was. I struggled to pick her out of the hole feeling really bad that I had not given her fair warning. She held on to me very tight and I was able to lift her out, help her into the kitchen, reaching for the closest chair.

"Oh Mabel, I am so sorry. I should have told you I had removed the register." I said comforting her and searched for injuries or possible broken bones. I could see that she was a bit shaken, only had a few scratches and I was certainly relieved.

"With my arms full of the curtains, I didn't notice it was missing," she replied, referring to the register, with frustration in her voice. "What kept me from going straight through Andy? Thank heavens I didn't fall clear through to the basement."

Mabel was looking at me and could tell that I didn't know how to respond. The frustrated look on her face slowly changed to a grin and she startled to chuckle thinking of how it all happened.

Then I said, "You gotta watch that first step, Mabel, it's a doozy."

She started to laugh.

"We could sell this to Laurel and Hardy, huh Mabel?" I said as I laughed along with her. We both joked around a good while, the nervousness giving way to relief that she was okay.

"Why don't you get up and make sure you didn't break anything," I suggested.

Mabel got up and walked around. I helped her pick up all of the curtains that she dropped near the register. I gave Mabel a warning to be careful not to fall in the floor again, and quickly finished the register and put it back in place. Mabel's guardian angel has been busy lately - with the near-miss in Kernan the other day in the car, and now the register.

Jewish Prison Camp Liberated in Germany

(10 Apr 45) During the radio report at six-thirty we learned that the allied forces had liberated another Jewish prison camp in Germany. Over 30,000 Jews had been murdered there and over 1,000 Jews were living in barns meant for 80 horses. There were over 20,000 prisoners found alive, many near death. Camps like these were found in Poland where Jews were victims of mass murder. It was undetermined how many Jews Adolf Hitler and his generals had killed. In the Pacific, the battle over the Japanese island of Okinawa had turned to heavy fighting as the US troops ran into the first large Japanese defensive positions on the island.

These radio reports were getting more and more alarming. Mabel and I were both speechless at the awful news. The thought of our forces finding these camps where so many people have been killed made me quiver. The further our Allied Forces advanced into Germany, more brutality and mass murder carried out by Hitler and his armies was exposed throughout the world. I guess we need to thank God that there were still some people alive that could be set free.

(11 Apr 45) Couldn't help but notice how many birds, mostly robins, were flying around the barnyard this morning. All the rain we had last evening made the ground ripe for night crawlers. It was a beautiful morning, a bit on the windy side, but the sky was very clear.

Took a trip to Grand Ridge and picked up a load of gravel for the machine shed floor. I backed the truck up close to the sliding door on the east end. Out came a skunk as I opened the door.

"What in the deuce!" I yelled. "How did you get in there you little bugger!"

The skunk scampered away slowly without spraying me, luckily.

But one step inside the shed revealed that he had sprayed in there somewhere. The odor inside was pretty bad. I aired out the shed for a little over an hour before backing the truck up and shoveling the gravel inside so that I could spread it around where needed.

Start Sowing Oats and Clover

I pulled the John Deere tractor around and hitched up Linc's seeder wagon. This was the special seeder that sows oats and hay at the same time. I got the seeder hitched up and pulled it across the road to sow 20 acres, and was making good progress on sowing the seeds with no difficulty. I thought it would be best to put off finishing the clover until tomorrow while I disc the oats for the second time where Mylem had hauled the limestone near the schoolhouse. Stopped off at the house to have a quick lunch - chicken salad sandwich and a glass of milk. I changed out the seeder for the disc and headed to the north section where I spent an hour and a half in that field spreading limestone.

LaSalle County Home Bureau

We had supper a little early tonight to allow for Mabel to clear the table and get ready for the LaSalle County Home Bureau meeting. During World War II, Mabel and other ladies from our area joined in forming a local Home Bureau. The Home Bureau was a National organization of country housewives that grew out of the local County Farm Bureaus, the group that gives advice and help to farmers by providing new ways to grow crops, such as soil testing, and the use of the new seed corn. The Home Bureau was heavily promoted leading up to, and during the Second World War. The purpose of the Home Bureau was to bind all women together through a common interest, the business of homemaking, and to share ideas and help each other. These meetings helped greatly in our understanding of the rationing program. They spent much time talking of ways to stretch the dollar in tough times. And of course they could laugh and socialize. Mabel always enjoyed her meetings, and was very proud to host from time-to-time. Twelve ladies showed up tonight and it seemed they wanted to get right down to business. So after saying hello I excused myself to do my evening chores.

After my chores, I gave the disc a good cleaning and greasing. By the time I was done working on the disc, the Home Bureau ladies were just about done with their meeting. I turned the cows inside the barn and headed towards the house pretty tuckered out after a long day. The wind was finally starting to die down, and I was hoping for another nice day tomorrow to allow me to get the clover done and the seeder back to Linc.

Carrie Koetz and Mabel were talking at the kitchen table when I walked in.

"How was your meeting ladies?" I blurted out, not meaning to interrupt their conversation like I did.

"Oh just fine Andy," Carrie replied. "How was your day? Looks like you have been busy."

"Yep, but having good luck lately," I said reaching for a glass out of the cupboard for a good drink of water. "Say hello to Bill, and tell him that we are planning to engage shelling over at Ray Bedeker's within the next few days."

"Sure will Andy. Well I should get going. Thanks for having us Mabel, the cookies were delicious."

"Oh take some home with you," said Mabel while wrapping a few cookies in a napkin and placing them in a small paper sack, "maybe Bill would like a late night snack tonight."

Carrie left and Mabel cleaned up the kitchen. I made my diary entries and headed for bed.

(12 Apr 45) With a full head of steam after my morning chores, I hooked up the seeder wagon to the John Deere and worked sowing the oats and clover across the road all morning and finished by lunchtime. After lunch I continued with the seeder wagon in the field by Rinker's place and finished there by 4:30 pm. I got the seeder wagon back to Linc just after dinner. I gave it a good cleaning and greasing before returning it. Sat with Linc for a while and we had a couple of beers together.

As I got up to leave, I wanted to thank Linc for his help. "Well Linc, I can't thank you enough for the use of the seeder wagon. I don't know how I would have gotten the oats and clover done without your help."

"Don't worry, I'm sure I'll be needing your help soon enough. Maybe you can come by in the next couple of days and help me fix the elevator on the combine?" he asked apprehensively, not wanting to ask for a favor in return so quickly. I knew he really needed to get that fixed.

"You betcha. Just let me know when you want to tackle that one and I'll give you a hand," I replied as I made my way to the truck to head home for dinner. As I drove out I could see the girls playing in our yard across the way. It wouldn't be long and the corn would be coming up and then only the tops of the buildings would be visible.

Tonight Mabel served sauerkraut that my brother Steve had made from their homegrown cabbage, and sausage – and it was delicious.

President Roosevelt Dies

The news report tonight was the most shocking news I heard in a while. President Roosevelt died at his Georgia retreat home. Cause of death was a massive brain hemorrhage. Vice President Harry S. Truman, from the state of Missouri, had been sworn in as our 32nd president of the United States. With so much good news on winning the war in Europe and the Pacific, it was very discouraging to be losing our president at such a crucial time in history.

"I can't believe what I just heard," said Mabel clearly astonished.

"Well, I don't know how we're going to get over this," I said after a moment of silence, "nothing you can really do."

"Do you think this Truman is up to the job, Andy?"

"I suppose so. Roosevelt wouldn't have picked him as a vice president if he didn't think he could do the job."

"What about the war?" Mabel stood looking at me with her hands on her hips, then continued. "We need our leadership."

"Remember that it's the generals and admirals directing this war. They know what they are doing."

"I suppose you're right," she agreed.

We both stared at the floor for a bit thinking about our fallen president. I gave Mabel a smile and headed out the pantry door to do my evening chores.

(13 Apr 45) It rained real hard last night. I just tinked around most of the morning. Fixed the tire on the bike, and got the truck ready for shelling corn. Mabel called me inside to tell me that Sully was home on leave, and that Darlene would be coming tonight to greet him here.

"How long will he be home on leave?" I asked Mabel while preparing myself a cup of coffee.

"Not sure, didn't ask that. Molly didn't say," said Mabel referring to Sully's Mother. She continued, "Sully is going to come for dinner tomorrow and he and Darlene plan to go to Chicago for a few days vacation. Darlene is hoping to get a few days away from work. They have been promising her time off. For heaven's sake, that poor girl is working her fingers to the bone at that shipyard."

"Well isn't that nice. I imagine you want to go with them." I said snickering knowing that Mabel loved to shop in Chicago.

"You go ahead and laugh, but I'm thinking on meeting them either Sunday or Monday in Chicago."

Darlene arrived home by 9 pm. I took her over to the Kollar's in Kangley. Sully looked really great. He had been stateside for a few months, he said, and they were feeding him pretty good. I left Darlene in Sully's care and headed back home.

Sunday Church at Ransom

(15 Apr 45) We woke up to a beautiful Sunday morning. It seemed as if spring had finally had its way after our long winter. The sun was shining and even though it was a bit on the windy side, I could tell that it was going to be a beautiful day. Gladys, Nancy, Esther, Joyce and I headed towards Ransom in the family car for ten-thirty church. The car was nice and clean as Esther and Nancy did a fine job washing it yesterday morning. You could see the fields coming to life on the country roads that led to Ransom. Dick Palaschak met us near the door and escorted Gladys inside. The girls and I took our normal station on the right side of the church.

The happiness that this day brought was mixed with a deep sadness for the loss of our great president. Many came to worship – the parking lot was near full and the pews were filling up fast. After the readings and gospel, Father Eagan spent a good amount of time talking to us about how much President Roosevelt meant to our nation, and that we should pray for the first lady and the new President, Harry Truman. I looked down at the girls to see how they were responding. Nancy seemed to understand and was listening intently, and looking up at me to see how I was responding to the Father's monologue. Esther was attending to Joyce who was fidgeting with the hymnal, neither seeming to comprehend the gravity of the situation. Better off them not knowing, I thought.

After visiting with a few friends after church, we were headed back home. Gladys gave me a peck on the cheek and let me know that she was going to Dick's place for lunch, and they walked off holding hands. When we arrived, Mabel was, as usual, making our Sunday lunch. Today she made fried chicken, potato salad, and one of my very favorite desserts - Mabel's delicious tapioca pudding. The three girls had gone upstairs and changed into play clothes, and came rustling back down the stairs.

Lilac Grove

"Dad, we're just going to walk down by the lilac grove for a little while," said Nancy, "Is that okay?"

"Mother, is there time?" I asked Mabel, as I did not want to upset the lunch schedule.

"That's fine, Nancy, but make sure you get back in just a little while, we are eating in about an hour, okay?" she replied.

"Okay Mom, we won't be long," Nancy said, speaking for the girls, as she was the leader of the pack.

"Don't touch the electric fence girls, it'll getcha," I added as they slipped out the back door.

Down the road apiece, south of our house on the other side of the road, and up a small lane, there is a grove of lilac bushes. Who knows how they got there – probably twelve large bushes all together. The lilacs seemed to welcome us into spring. The girls just love to take a stroll to the grove to sit and talk, and giggle. I don't suppose at their age they thought that much about heaven, but when I am in that grove, I imagine this is what heaven must be like. The grove is a very quiet and serene place where you can enjoy the beautiful aroma of the lilacs, and talk to God and thank him for all His blessings. Darlene often talked about wanting to have fresh lilacs adorn the alter at St Patrick's church when her and Sully get married.

Forty-five minutes had passed and I thought I would take a walk to the grove and escort the girls back. Alfie decided to go with me. As we walked up the lane I heard Esther counting "three, two, one, ready or not hear I come." Hide and go seek was being played and they had lost all track of time. I sat on a log from a distance and watched Esther going from one bush to the next looking for Nancy and Joyce. It was very quiet and then there was a scream and laughter as Joyce was found. She came running into the lane and saw me, and ran to me for protection. I guess she felt if she made it to me before being caught by Esther that she would be free. Esther had just about caught her when Nancy saved her sister at the last minute by distracting Esther away and running in the other direction between two lilac trees. Alfie got in on the fun and was darting around and barking.

By the time we got back, an hour and ten minutes had gone by – how time flies when you are in heaven. The table was set and the food smelled delicious. We thanked God for such a beautiful day and for His bountiful blessings.

(16 Apr 45) Mabel had decided to head to Chicago early this morning to meet Sully and Darlene to go shopping and spend the day together. I sent Nancy and Esther to school and dropped Joyce off at Pete's where Mary would watch her for a few hours while I ran to Grand Ridge.

I pulled the grain truck into the crib below the oats bin and filled up a pretty good-sized load, and hauled it to Grand Ridge by 10:30 am. Bought some corn and chick feed to haul back home. We got a good rain on the way home.

After I ate, I headed to Pete's to pick up Joyce. She was busy playing in the front yard when I drove up. Pete came outside and wanted to play some catch.

"How's that arm feeling, Andy," asked Pete as he tossed me a mit.

"Oh, I'll let you know after I throw a few." It felt good to throw the ball again. The Durdan brothers, along with nephews and cousins, had a baseball team. We played in a league in Grand Ridge.

"If this rain would ever let up we could start practicing," said Pete pointing to puddles in the driveway.

We must have thrown the ball for 15 minutes before we both decided that we better stop before we overdo it and wake up tomorrow morning with sore shoulders.

Joyce and I headed home and the rain continued. Joyce got sleepy, so we both laid down and took a two-hour nap.

(23 Apr 45) Mabel and I called Darlene this evening to wish her a happy birthday – she turned 22. After hanging up the phone Mabel stood there staring at me.

"What is it, Mabel?" I asked.

"Well," she said, "I can't believe that she is 22. It just seems like yesterday that she graduated high school."

"She certainly grew up fast."

Russians in Berlin

(25 Apr 45) Mr. Heater sounded happy and excited to report there was good news from Europe as two and a half million Russian soldiers attacked one million German soldiers in and around Berlin, Germany just a few days ago. The fighting was fierce, but the Russian assault was taking its toll on the German city. The Russians had all but conquered Berlin and there were rumors that Adolf Hitler was either dying or dead.

The German's defense of Berlin had been failing and the leader had been wounded. In the Pacific, US soldiers and marines continued fighting for the island of Okinawa. The fighting has lasted over a month trying to penetrate the Japanese defenses around the town of Shuri. The US losses were estimated to be near 5,000 dead, and 25,000 injured.

There was so much news tonight it was hard to take it all in.

"Well, it seems the Red Army may have killed Hitler," Mabel said optimistically.

"Sounds like his goose is cooked," I replied, "and it looks like the Red Army and the US Army haven't met up yet."

"Are we friends with them, Andy?"

"Yeah, I think so." It only made sense that we both had the same idea in mind, to take out Hitler and his army.

The Phone System

We were just about finished with dinner when Bill and Carrie Koetz pulled into the driveway.

"Oh, I almost forgot, I told Bill and Carrie that it is okay to give Dorothy a call in Cleveland," said Mabel.

"That's just fine, no sense having a phone if we don't make good use of it," I replied. I got up from the kitchen table, went outside and met Bill and Carrie in the driveway.

"Don't you both look spiffy?" I commented as I let them in.

"Thank you Andy," replied Carrie with a smile, "Bill took me to a nice dinner in Streator." She continued, "thanks for the use of the phone, we really appreciate it."

"Oh, you're always welcome Carrie, you know that. Besides it would be nice to hear how things are going for Dorothy."

Only one of three farms in our area has a phone. We were lucky as the phone line was already installed when we bought this farm. Each telephone subscriber is connected to the nearest central exchange office. Our exchange is "Grand Ridge", our phone number is 6724, and we are connected to the central office, in Streator. This office was simply called "Central", which is needed to make all calls outside of our exchange and out of town calls. We share a party line with several of our neighbors. When using it, you have to be careful what you say, because you never knew who is listening. Sometimes we have to wait quite awhile before we could make our phone call.

Making local calls is much easier than long distance. A local call is considered a manual exchange if you called someone within the Grand

Ridge area. Calling long distance to Cleveland takes a bit longer. The central phone office is needed for all out-of-town calls. Long distance calls required operator assistance, and if the calls were going very far, a chain of operators would be involved. You give her the city and state, the exchange or central office name, and the phone number. It is supposed to get easier to call long distance once they assign special numbers to each area within the state, and country for that matter.

After about five minutes of multiple connections, and a few sighs of frustration from Bill, he was finally able to get through to Dorothy. Bill and Carrie each talked about five minutes. Everything seemed to be going well for Dorothy and family. Bill and Carrie stayed and had coffee with us, filled us in on how Dorothy was doing, and then headed back home.

MAY

During the month of May while the oats and clover are growing, it is time to turn my attention to corn. Last year I started May 18th, two years ago it was May 29th, and three years ago it was May 8th. The way things are going, it will probably be sometime in the third week of May this year. Planting the corn normally takes me about two weeks time, as long as there are no major problems.

Introduction to Corn

First thing I need to do is run the plow through the fields and turn the dirt real well. Then I go over it again and plow the furrows shut. The furrows are 12 inch-wide channels made by the plow. The soil is now ready for the disc. Just as I did earlier in the spring for the oats, discing breaks up the soil into little pieces and prepares the soil for planting.

Plowing and discing are relatively easy compared to planting. With plowing, I could simply mount the plow or disc to the tractor and circle the fields. Planting was a whole new ballgame and required more starting and stopping, moving the wire, and refilling the planters. Planting by wire has been around for quite a few years. My planter can plant four rows at a time. I bolted two, two-row International Harvester planters side-by-side. This method is practiced by many other farmers, which cut planting time in half. The wire is staked at one end and strung out across the field. The spool of wire is 80 rods long and has knots in it every 40 inches. A rod is a unit measurement system used by farmers. Where 80 rods equals one-quarter mile, 40 rods equals one-eighth of a mile, 20 rods equals one-sixteenth mile, and so on. The wire is fed through the arm of the planter and the knot engages the planter to drop four or five seeds into the ground. A small runner on the front of the planter makes a small furrow where the seeds drop into, and then a scraper covers the seeds as you drive along. Only one wire is needed for multiple rows, as the knots trip seeds for all four rows simultaneously. The seeds are planted 40 inches apart. So in the end you have 40-inch separation north-south and east-west – like a checkerboard. This allows for cross cultivating. In order to know where to start the next pass after four rows were complete, a boom extended out and a small disc marks a line 40 inches away from the fourth row.

There are some newer, more advanced corn planters where you don't need a wire, but they are not good at evenly spaced rows in both directions. As tedious as the wire is, it still makes a lot of sense. To plant corn efficiently, it is best to have two men. I could do it myself, but it would take a lot longer. Walter Budach, my brother-in-law, is going to help me plant corn this year. While one person is driving the tractor pulling the planter along, the second person is moving the wire across the field or discing to prepare the soil for planting. It is also handy to have help to make sure that you don't replant a row or miss anything.

Once the planting is complete you need to drag the field with a rake to work the seeds in and pull up any weed seeds starting up. Normally, I plant a field and then drag within a day or two. That's why it is a good idea to have two tractors. One tractor to do your planting and the other to pull the rake. It is nice not to have to change out the machinery. That is why I have my eye on that F30 Farmall tractor. There is going to be a sale this Thursday in Marseilles and I'm hoping to buy it. I could use the John Deere for doing most of the plowing and raking, then use the Farmall for planting and picking.

Once the dragging is done I pull out the roller. The roller has three roller sections that stagger and overlap each other a bit. I like to pull the roller with a four-horse team. The roller packs the ground to conserve the moisture. Like plowing, discing, and dragging, the rolling went pretty quick – I can roll all the acres planted in one or two days.

Two to three weeks after you put the first corn seed in the ground it is time to cultivate. By that time the corn plants start popping out of the ground and you can see the rows forming. The weeds start popping up and need to be plowed under. The first time I cultivate north-to-south. The second time is a cross-cultivate, or east-to-west. Then the third time is north-to-south. By the third cultivation, the corn is knee high (by the fourth of July) and should be free of weeds.

Four months after cultivating it will be time to pick. Between now and then we watch, wait, and pray for rain. A few times during the fall before it is time to pick, I will husk a jag for the pigs. "Husk a jag" was a saying I picked up from my Dad. We go out and pick the ears by hand – enough to feed the pigs. They would gobble the corn husk and all. Husking a jag also gives us an opportunity to see what kind of shape the corn is in.

Crop Rotation

Through trial and error, and picking up tips from my father, it is best to rotate your crops. We have 240 acres, of which approximately 200 is used for planting. The other 40 acres is our farmhouse area, the fields for the livestock, some land taken up by the schoolhouse, and other land that is either rocky or drainage areas. I split up the tillable acreage into smaller planting areas, with each area ranging from five to forty acres in size. It is best to plant something different in each area every year. The normal rotation was oats, hay, then corn. Although it doesn't always work out this way - this is the plan.

Since corn and beans are row crops, and oats and hay are cover crops, there was more work to be done in the fields to make the transition. In the fall, where hay or oats were planted would be plowed under to prepare the soil for corn the next year. When transitioning from row crops to oats or hay, the challenge was knocking down the rows and knocking the ridges down.

Hitler Reported Dead

(2 May 45) The six-thirty news reported a German radio broadcast announcing Adolf Hitler had died in the fight to save Berlin. The British Foreign Services demanded Hilter's body be given as evidence and stated that it is only rumor until proven that it's true. The British also reported that Hitler might have died of his own hand, committing suicide. The newly appointed German head of state offered to make peace with the allied forces if they together would fight the Russians for Germany. Of course, President Truman would do no such thing and demanded surrender on all fronts.

"Well it looks like they really did get him, Mabel," I said.

"I think so, or maybe he took his own life like they said," Mabel replied.

"This is going to make a big difference with him out of the picture. I bet their army folds now."

"Boy, I sure hope so."

Purchase F-30 Farmall Tractor

(3 May 45) I was the highest bidder at a farm sale in Grand Ridge today and purchased the 1939 F-30 Farmall tractor. It sure made me happy to get such a nice one. It was tough to put the money down, but I'm sure it will pay for itself in just a few years. This is an extremely versatile tractor that allowed me to do just about anything I want it to do:

plant, drag, cultivate, pull the binder – you name it.

The seller and I worked out a deal for the tractor to be delivered in two days. That will give us time to work out the details with the paperwork.

I stepped into the kitchen and Mabel could tell by the smile on my face that I bought the tractor.

"Did you get it, Andy?" Mabel asked.

"You betcha!" I replied. "She'll be here Saturday, or Monday at the latest. We need to work out a few details with the payment , but she's ours alright."

"Well that's just wonderful," said Mabel very pleased. She knew how much this tractor meant to me.

"Well, I guess I better get to fixing that yard gate. It's wide open again. I need to fix that post."

I removed the gate from the post, dug up the post to find that it was rotted out about six inches down. I had a spare post in the barn as a replacement. I set it in there good, and attached the gate to the new post. Good as new.

Garnet Goes Into Labor

(5 May 45) During morning chores in the barn, I noticed that Garnet, one of our four-year-old heifers, started birthing. A heifer is a young female cow that has never had a calf. Some heifers have no trouble with their first, but this is not the first time there has been trouble with a heifer giving birth, and I didn't want to take any chances. I thought it best to keep an eye on her as she was breathing heavy and seemed to be having a difficult time. After checking back at seven and nine, not much had changed. I felt that it was time to call the veterinarian for help. Doc Curtis ran a small clinic in Ransom and would also travel to aid the farmers in some cases.

Mabel was making cookies as I came in the house to use the phone. I clicked the receiver twice to signal the operator.

"Operator, how I may direct your call?" said a woman's voice at the exchange.

"Hello, yes, Ransom 4728, Doc Curtis' please." The operator could probably have connected me by just saying "Doc Curtis", but it seemed that the operator's job was getting harder every day with more and more phone connections. We had a handy list of phone numbers near the phone. It seemed it was getting less and less personal on the phone these days. When we first got the phone, the operator seemed to know who everybody was. But now, there seemed to be many new operators we did not know.

Doc Curtis answered and said that he would be out within the hour.

"That would be fine," I said. He suggested that I try to get the heifer to lie down and keep the other cows away if possible. So I did the best I could to keep her comfortable and gave her some extra room in hopes she would lay down. I left the other cows in the small field the rest of the morning and waited for Doc to show up.

"Is she going to be okay, Andy?" Mabel asked with concern and offered me a warm chocolate chip cookie on the end of her spatula.

"I hope so. Don't want to lose her like we lost the one two years back."

"Well, it's good you called Doc Curtis, he'll take care of her." Mabel was always positive, giving me encouraging words when I needed them.

Our Faith

"Are you going to get the nuns?" I asked.

"Yes. I'm just finishing up with these cookies, and I will be on my way," Mabel replied.

The two nuns came out from Streator to teach catechism at St. Mary's church on the Grand Ridge road. The parish families provided transportation on a rotating basis, so it was not really a burden on one family. Typically the girls did not like catechism class, but took it seriously. I believe they were truly frightened of the nuns because of the way they dressed – black long robes, head piece and shoes that laced all the way up to the ankle, with a cross hanging from their waist. They were not used to that, and I do think they were a little strict, much more so than the teachers they were used to. Esther would be receiving her first communion this year. She was already talking about getting her white dress, veil and shoes.

Mabel and I were married in a catholic church, but she found the mass hard to follow, as at that time the mass was in Latin. She always felt her first obligation on Sunday was to have a nice meal on the table a little after the noon hour, and quite a few Sundays we would have company over for dinner. The girls would get up and go to church with me and would help their mother with setting the table or mashing potatoes when we got home. Mabel dearly loved her Presbyterian church in Brookfield Township, and occasionally on Sunday would attend. She knew a lot of parishioners at the church including her brother Howard, his wife Alma, and their family.

Ole Olsen and Kate Looft Olsen

Mabel was half Norwegian and half German, and her maiden name was Olsen. Her father, Ole Olsen, was born in Norway in 1862 and came to the United States when he was near twenty years of age. Ole settled in Brookfield Township, bought a farm and built a large house on his land. Mabel's Mother, Kate Looft, was born in Germany in 1862, and came to the United States with her parents when she was only two years old. Ole's parents, Burnt and Christine Olsen had nine children, all born in Norway: Ole, Thor, Martin, Christian, Anna, John, Bert, Martha, and Minnie. Ole was the first to leave Norway for the United States. He eventually sent for the rest of his family, and all of them came to the United States and settled in the Seneca/Marseilles area, with one exception, which was Minnie who came to this country with her husband, John Gulbronson, and settled in Albert Lea, Minnesota. Thousands upon thousands of Norwegians settled in Illinois and the Midwest, and most of the Norwegian settlers were farmers.

It was in the Marseilles area that Ole and Kate met, and were soon married in 1885. Ole loved how hard Kate worked on the farm and how much she helped working in the fields. Ma told us many times that she once left a sleeping baby with another of their children at the end of a row of crops when Ole needed help. They had four children: Anna, Howard, Emma, and Mabel. Anna was the oldest, born in 1886, and Mabel was the youngest, born in 1901. Ole and Kate celebrated their twenty-fifth wedding anniversary, four years before Ole died of tuberculosis in 1914. Ole's funeral was on Christmas Eve at Brookfield Presbyterian Church, and he was buried in the Marseilles Riverview Cemetery.

Ma is doing very well and living in Marseilles. She makes the best apple jelly and apple pie, and most of the apples from our trees end up in Marseilles for her to make her specialties. She also makes the best fried potatoes I have ever had. Ma has lived many years as a widow but she does very well and keeps very busy. She has made every one of her children beautiful quilts. Mabel has picked up many of Ma's wonderful traits, including being a wonderful helper around the farm, a handy seamstress making clothes and beautiful dresses for our girls, and a great mom. Mabel goes to Marseilles at least once a week to see Ma and Anna. Anna married Charles Schank in 1905, and they had six children. Howard married Alma Wergin and had four children. Emma married

John Sweeden and had four children.

Mabel and her Cemetery Visits

Mabel was a loyal visitor to the Riverview Cemetery to visit her Father's grave and those of other family members. She would usually pick up her sister Annie (even though her name was Anna, we called her Annie) and Ma with our girls and nieces in tow. By Decoration Day, May 30th, or any other time during the summer, Mabel could go to her flower garden and pick huge beautiful bouquets. In early spring, it was peonies, daisies, iris, columbine, and phlox. The girls hated to hold the peonies while in transit, as they were full of ants.

Her cemetery visits were usually on a Saturday. She loved to visit with her Mom, sisters and nieces. By the time Mabel got home later on Saturday afternoon, she would really have to hustle to get supper on the table, get cleaned up and ready for our Saturday night into town or dance night at the Moose lodge in Marseilles. I often wondered why she tried to do everything in one day, but that was Mabel. Often times she would bring home a new plant for her garden and ask, "Andy, do you think you could…". "You betcha," I would say as I went to get the spade and a bucket of water, then waited for her to decide where she wanted it.

Garnet Gives Birth

As promised, Doc Curtis arrived within the hour. He did what good vets do, and gave her a thorough once-over. He then gave her a shot from a large syringe that he produced from his bag. "Andy, this will help her calm down, and it will help her through this," Doc Curtis said pushing the syringe into Garnet's hide and squeezing the giant plunger with both of his thumbs until it was empty. He continued, "She is having a rough time. There is not much more I can do right now. The fetus position of the calf is fine. Keep a good eye on her, and you will probably have to help her with this one. She is going to give birth in the next six or eight hours from what I can see. I know that you know what you're doing. Call me if you need any more help."

"Much obliged, Doc. I just wanted to make sure everything was okay."

"Please say hello to Mabel for me. I'm pretty sure I passed her on the way here with a couple of nuns in the car." He ended his sentence as if it was a more of a question.

"Yep, that was her. It's her turn to get the nuns from Streator for catechism this morning."

"Isn't that nice of her," he responded, "well I should be on my way. Please let me know how things turn out for your heifer. Perhaps I could be of help later if you'd like."

"Okay Doc, I'll give you a call." I handed him a check for the standard fee of a vet tending to an animal on a country visit. He gave me a nod and off he went.

I checked on Garnet once every hour, and it was on my trip to the barn just after eleven in the evening that she was laying on her side and I could see the hooves coming out. I ran back in to get Mabel. We gently pulled on the legs, helping Garnet just a bit, but not too much. Soon we saw the head and shoulders. We continued gently pulling and Garnet seemed to be doing surprisingly well. Whatever Doc Curtis had given her seemed to be helping. Not long after the head and shoulders were out, the back hips came out quickly and all of a sudden a cute little calf was laying on the straw. We cleared it's nostrils and then tickled the calf's nostrils with a few pieces of hay. This is something we had learned over the years to help the calf to breathe. The calf started breathing after a brief moment and let out a little whale. Garnet's motherly instincts took over and we left her alone to take care of her newborn. Our new calf was a female, and we would come up with a name together, as a family, tomorrow.

Allied Forces Meet Red Army in Germany

(5 May 45) At six-thirty, Gabriel reported that the allied forces and the Russian Red Army were converging at the Elbe River in the heart of Germany. Since July 1943, the Red Army had pushed back the Germans out of Leningrad, out of Russia completely, and out of Poland into Germany. The Allied Forces came from the west while the Russians came from the east. The two forces met at the river and celebrated their victory. The meeting of these two great armies was orchestrated by the allied commander, General Eisenhower, and Stalin. A cable sent from Eisenhower to Stalin urged advanced coordination of the armies to meet and finish off the Germans. Eisenhower wrote, "If we are to complete the destruction of the German armies without delay, I regard it as essential that we coordinate our actions and make every effort to perfect the liaison between our advancing forces."

"Well, there is your answer Mabel," I pointed out, "the Russian Army and US Forces are friends."

"Isn't that wonderful," she said, "that must have been quite a gathering."

"I'm sure it was."

I thought of three armies, the Russians, Germans, and US Forces, all in the same area, it must have been hard to distinguish who was who. Couldn't help but think it probably took some time to sort it all out.

(6 May 45) Didn't do much this morning on account of all the rain that we had gotten the previous two days. Spent a few minutes looking over the crib and noticed that it was about time I do some painting. I made a mental note to paint at least one side within the next few weeks if weather conditions permit.

Went over to Elmer Kates' place around 10 am to help him shell. We finished two full loads before they hauled away the machine. Elmer and I had a cup of coffee in the barn. After a bit of a rest, I headed back to our place and decided, despite all the soggy ground, to start spreading manure.

In early spring before planting corn and beans, I would load up the manure spreader cleaning up the pile that had accumulated over the winter. Using the tractor to pull the spreader over the field, I tried to cover as much ground as I could. There was no better fertilizer to work into the soil than from our livestock. It got pretty messy handling the manure, and it didn't help matters with the ground being so saturated. I cleaned up the best I could by spraying my boots with the hose and then washing my hands in the sink downstairs. I figured I would go in for a late lunch.

I can always tell when Mabel is mad just by looking at her eyes. When she was mad, she would close her eyes and take deep breaths. When she finally opened her eyes, after a few long seconds, she would tuck her hand under her chin, and begin fluttering her eyelids kind of slow. She wore glasses, but I could still see her eyelids kind of flitting open and closed. She didn't talk in a loud voice like some women do, or pace, or walk out the door – just closed her eyes.

"Andrew, please turn around and go back outside. I will bring your lunch out," she said sharply.

"Sorry. I thought I had cleaned up pretty good." I guess I was accustomed to my own smell. Don't know why we grow too soon old and too late smart.

She would get a little upset when I came in after working on a really dirty job. Sometimes I would get my coveralls all smudged with linseed oil, black coal, turpentine, or pig slop. This time it was cow manure and mud. And as you can imagine, I didn't smell like a bouquet of roses either. My boots may have been cleaned up, but my coveralls were a whole different story – they were a disgusting mess. I didn't say a word, turned around and just went outside, moseyed around a bit waiting for Mabel to bring my lunch. She came out with two beef tongue sandwiches and a glass of cold milk.

"Thank you Mabel," I said and gave her a smile.

She smiled back and gave me a friendly warning, "Those coveralls aren't coming upstairs today. Please leave them downstairs and I will soak them."

I nodded without argument, ate my sandwiches, and drank my milk. Beef tongue wasn't my favorite, but it was pretty good if cooked right. Mabel would boil the tongue for hours, then served cold and sliced, with mustard.

With a full house, three young daughters, and me to clean up after, Mabel did have quite a lot of washing to do. We do our best to conserve water and learned to wear garments two or three times before tossing them into the hamper. Mabel uses the old wringer-type washing machine in the basement, hauling the clothes up and out the door to the back yard where the clotheslines were. In the winter, she hangs clothes on lines in the basement, as well as outside, and sometimes draped over chairs in the dining room. Nancy and Esther would bring the frozen clothes in from the outside clothesline in the 30-degree weather – stiff as boards.

When we bought the house, there was a narrow door in the dining room where an ironing board was installed and could be folded out for ironing. We always raved about such a wonderful invention. Of course we had to show all of our visitors this wonderful contraption. Mabel taught the girls how to iron. She taught our older girls one of her ironing secrets. She would sit a bowl of water on the ironing board and dip her hands in and sprinkle droplets of water on shirts and blouses to help get the wrinkles out. Darlene and Gladys eventually learned to replace the bowl of water with a sprinkling device that fit on the end of a ketchup or soda bottle. Then along came the steam iron and Mabel had to purchase one immediately. Boy how times are changing. After a couple of years of folding the ironing board up and down and up and down – we just decided to leave it out all of the time, unless we had company.

Germany Surrenders

(8 May 45) The first words out of Gabriel Heater's mouth at the evening radio report were "Germany surrenders, I say again, Germany

surrenders." The Germans had surrendered to western allies and the Soviet Union at the headquarters of the supreme allied commander, General Eisenhower. The war in Europe lasted 5 years, 8 months, and 6 days. Truman made the announcement on his 61st birthday.

I was sitting alone in the living room when I heard the news of the Germans surrendering. The news reports over the past week made it seem pretty clear the Germans were doomed, but just to think they had surrendered was so wonderful to hear. I called for Mabel but she did not answer. I found her outside putting laundry on the clothesline.

"Mabel, the Germans surrendered!" I yelled as soon as I stepped outside.

"What was that, Andy?" She either didn't hear me because of a slight breeze or she couldn't quite believe what I just said.

"Gabriel Heater just reported that the war is over in Europe." She stared at me in disbelief, "The Germans have surrendered to the Allied Forces."

"That is wonderful," she said, dropping her laundry basket to the ground and giving me a big hug.

"Maybe that means Albert will be coming home."

"We can only hope."

The evening was extra special. We listened to the live radio reports coming out of Chicago. People were celebrating in the streets and tomorrow they were planning a ticker tape parade downtown Chicago. The reporter spoke of how this country was still trying to recover from the loss of President Roosevelt, and that this celebration was in his honor. We listened to the radio until after midnight. It was so exciting to listen to the celebrations.

(10 May 45) I heard a vehicle approaching from the south as I was putting some equipment away in the machine shed. There was never a lot of traffic on our country road, which was okay with Mabel. She disliked the dust that was stirred up on the gravel road as a vehicle went by. It filtered through the screens and created dust throughout the house. Mabel would oft times run to the living room to close the windows if a tractor was making its way down our road.

The pickup truck turned into our driveway – it was Myrtle and George Hallett who lived about three miles down the road from us. They stopped in often for a few good laughs, and we leisurely conversed to catch up on the latest news. Some would call it gossip. George was a tall man, even a little too tall for his vehicle. The top of his cap touched the ceiling as he drove, and he had to duck his head to get out. Myrtle and George's favorite thing to do was visit, talk and have fun.

With a big smile on his face and his hand held out for a shake, George said, "Put her there Andy."

"Hello George. Hello Myrtle. And what do we owe the pleasure?" I replied while giving George a firm return handshake and a pat on the back.

George and Myrtle's daughter, Marilyn, crawled over her Mother's lap and out the door of the truck, running to beat the band toward the house. "I want to play paper dolls with Nancy, Esther, and Joyce," she yelled. She did not want to waste any time.

"We got some coats for Mabel, and we promised we'd bring them over," said Myrtle pointing to the bed of the pickup where a number of old winter coats laid in a big pile. Mabel coordinated the collection of winter coats to make rugs. When enough coats were collected, we boxed them up and shipped them off to the Olsen Rug Company in Chicago where they were made into rugs. We would call Olsen's in advance for an estimate of the cost and send a check with the coats. It only took a few weeks from the time we sent the coats off until we received our rugs. They may not have matched the decor, but they served the purpose and kept the floors warm in the winter.

Mabel was making her way to meet us in the drive and looked into the truck. "My oh my, Myrtle, where did you ever come up with so many coats?"

Myrtle was happy to tell the story behind the coats. "My sister-in-law has been saving these old coats for years in her basement. I mentioned that you have these rugs made, and she just said to take them. They weren't doing her any good anymore."

"Well, isn't that generous of her," said Mabel with delight, "I can surely have two good-sized rugs from this many coats. I will be sure to get one of the rugs back to her."

"Oh, Mabel, she doesn't expect anything."

"We'll see when we get them back. I'm so excited."

Simple pleasures for Mabel, I thought. She really got a kick out of salvaging those old coats. They were good conversation pieces for our guests. They would look at the floor and say, "My, oh my, look at this new rug. It certainly is colorful." I would reply teasing, "Beautiful, isn't it?"

Satisfied with my accomplishments for the day, I was ready for a little break.

"How about a cold beer George?" I asked.

George accepted. I went to the pump house and pulled a few beers from the cold tub. I was half expecting Linc and Bill later this afternoon, so I was prepared.

The four of us sat outside talking for quite awhile. The Hallet's sure didn't worry about things too much. They enjoyed their life and were very carefree. Mabel and I truly enjoyed their company. We spoke a good portion of their visit about the war coming to an end in Europe.

"Albert was in Europe, wasn't he Andy?" George asked.

"Yes. He is still there as far as I know," I replied.

"I imagine he might come home soon now that the major fighting is done over there?"

"Dad seems to think that it will take time to get things straightened out before they send our boys home. But we are sure praying for him to come home real soon."

"Have you heard from him?" George hesitantly asked.

"Well, Dad received a letter from him not long ago. Maybe a month or so, and he was doing fine. Hopefully we will hear from him real soon." I paused then continued, "The war sure looks like it's coming to an end with Germany surrendering and all - don't you think, George."

"Sure looks that way, Andy. It's been a long hard battle, that's for sure. Our servicemen will be so happy to be coming home – back to the good ol' USA." George took a sip of his beer and then continued, "You know our Della has been writing to her fella, Wayne Finch all along – still is as far as I know. He is in Europe somewhere and she tells us he'll be discharged next January, if not sooner."

"You don't say. Do you suppose you will have a wedding coming up her real quick? Our Darlene is planning her wedding as soon as Sully is discharged."

"Don't know," he replied, "you never know what these young people have on their minds." After a pause he continued, "Wayne's twin brother, Duane, was killed in Germany right before the Battle of the Bulge last year. A tragedy for their parents to be sure, having two serving, twins and all, and then to have one killed."

"You're right, George, some of our people here in the U.S. have really suffered through this war."

Everyone was still celebrating the end of the war in Europe. Our servicemen and women would be coming back home and they will get a hero's welcome. Albert has been gone nearly three and a half years.

Before George and Myrtle left, we made plans to see them at the Box Social and dance in Kernan Saturday evening. Gladys would be playing in the band, and more than likely I would be calling a few square dances. The Box Social is when girls or women make a box lunch. Inside the box would be a sandwich and side fixings – maybe a pickle and some pudding. The guys would bid on the box and dance with the girl who prepared it. The dance was a way for young people to meet. If a young fellow knew who made the box lunch and really wanted to sit with her, he would bid high. Eventually they would sit down and eat the lunch together.

May Baskets with the Armstrongs

(15 May 45) Mabel and the girls had spent the better part of the past two nights preparing May baskets. May, to our kids, meant May baskets, and the girls spent a lot of time making them. They asked for construction paper and glue, and then shaped the construction paper like a cone with a handle at the top. They then filled it with tissue paper, dandelions, wild flowers, and whatnot.

When I walked in from outside around six o'clock, Nancy was hoping to go May basketing.

"Dad, can we go hang May baskets tonight at the Armstrong's?" she asked.

"You betcha we can honey. Do you girls have everything ready to go? I know you have been working hard on them."

"Yes we have, but we have to wait until it's almost dark, right?" Nancy knew that it would have to be dark or pretty close to dark so the Armstrong's would not see us coming.

"Let's go about eight o'clock okay? Make sure you are all ready to go then," I said. That would give me time to tinker with a few things.

I went out to the old garage and greased the old truck. Also cleaned up the bench, putting away nuts and bolts that were lying around. I had been wanting to get things more organized so I made a few wooden boxes up to hold more nuts and bolts. It had been a good day to work inside as it rained most of the day. I was hoping that it would stop drizzling by eight so the girls could do their May basketing without getting wet.

By the time we left for the Armstrong's, the drizzling had stopped and the girls were very excited to be going. We all piled into the car and headed towards the Armstrong's place, but we stopped well before their driveway and out of sight. This way the girls could surprise them. The girls got out of the car and ran the rest of the way, up their driveway, and quietly hung the baskets on the door. They knocked and then ran in separate directions to hide. Then the fun would begin. No matter that they might fall and get hurt, no matter how dark it got, seven kids would be out there running, hiding, and having fun. We would worry about Joyce being so little and participating, but the older kids always watched the younger ones. Mabel and I made our way up the driveway to join in the fun and watch the kids play.

"Hello Andy, Mabel, come on inside," Linc said laughing. "Here it is the fifteenth of May and they're still at it." The official May basket day was the first of May, but the kids would keep returning the favor. It continued for many nights. From the looks of how much fun they were having, it may continue, and the Armstrong children would come surprise our girls in the next day or so.

Linc, Mary, Mabel, and I sat around the kitchen table and had a nice chat about the happenings and what was new in our farm neighborhood. It started to sprinkle again a little after nine, so we said our goodbyes and walked back down the driveway and up the road apiece to our car and headed home.

(22 May 45) I greased the disc first thing after breakfast to get ready to start discing the field across the road in preparations for planting corn. I wanted to use my new Farmall, but realized that I was missing a part needed to hitch up the disc. So rather than wait, I just used the John Deere.

Everything was going pretty good across the road for a little over an hour, but I ran out of gas. When switching from using the Farmall to the John Deere I failed to check the gas level. So, I walked back to the farm and filled up two five-gallon cans with gas and looked for Mabel. She was in the basement feeding her birds.

"I ran out of gas. Would you mind driving me back to the tractor?" I asked a bit frustrated. I didn't want to pull Mabel away from her chores but did not want to leave the truck in the field, and didn't want to waste time walking back and forth.

"That would be fine," Mabel agreed, "just let me finish feeding my little birdies and I'll take you out there."

"Vy do ve zo soon get old." I said.

"And so late schmart," said Mabel finishing my rhyme. We both laughed. I had written this old adage on my chalk board in the new garage some time ago and had never erased it. The other funny proverb from the chalk board is:

> So jo dede go, touson buses in a row
> No jo dem ere trucks, som mit cows in,
> Som mit duks

I still laugh every time I read those old sayings.

So, Mabel drove me out to the John Deere. I was able to work another hour before Mabel made her way back to the field in the truck waving me down.

"Paul called and was hoping you could help Mrs. Broadus," shouted Mabel from the truck window.

"What's happened?" I assumed she meant Paul Rinker.

"Paul said that her car is broke down and she needs help."

"All right, lets go see if we can help." I climbed down from the tractor and jumped into the passenger seat of the truck. I sure didn't want to leave Mrs. Broadus stranded, but I sure wasn't making much progress with running out of gas and now - Mrs. Broadus.

We saw her and Paul looking inside the hood of the car just past Paul's place.

After inspecting the car and trying to start it a few times it seemed apparent that either the starter was bad or the battery was dead. We decided amongst the four of us that we should tow the car into the service station in Grand Ridge and drop Mrs. Broadus off at her home. She thanked Mabel and I for our time. By the time we got home, it was time for supper. I decided to call it a day and get a fresh start in the morning.

(23 May 45) I was able to finish discing across the road by 10 am. I then moved the tractor and disced across the road and completed the small piece of land by the schoolhouse by noontime. After lunch I went to Missel's to buy the part I need to hitch the Farmall to the disc and planter. I will need two tractors: one for planting, and the other for discing.

Missel's had the part I needed, and when I got home, I got the Farmall hitched up to the disc. Started discing the big field near the house. It was exciting to be using the Farmall for the first time on our farm. I noticed that she handled much better than the John Deere. I was able to get a few rounds completed before it got dark, then headed in.

Start Planting Corn

(24 May 45) Today was a big day, as it was the day to start planting corn. I had the four-row corn planter ready to go for some time, and got it hooked up to the John Deere by seven-thirty am. The first field to plant corn was the 20 acre piece across the road.

Walt arrived at 8 am to help me with planting.

"I like your new tractor, Andy," said Walt as he stood admiring the F-30.

"Yeah, she handles real nice. I got her at the Grand Ridge farm sale I told you about."

"Well, whataya say we get started?" Walt said with enthusiasm.

"Have you had a coffee yet this morning?"

"Maybe I'll have another cup, thank you."

We sat a few minutes and planned out our day. We had 20 acres across the road, and the small piece by the schoolhouse that was ready for planting.

"Why don't I get you started with the wire across the road and I'll finish discing the big field here," suggested Walt, pointing toward the new tractor. "I'll keep an eye on you across the road to see when you are ready to go up to the schoolhouse."

"Okay Walt, sounds like a good plan."

"Besides, this will give me a chance to try out the Farmall."

Across the road, Walt staked the wire and connected the 80-rod wire spool loaded on the John Deere. I drove the tractor 80 rods to unspool the wire and connected it to another stake that Walt had pounded into the ground.

"That should get you started Andy," said Walt. He headed back across the road to start discing the big field near the house.

The first four rows went in the ground without much trouble – a good sign. I disconnected the wire from the planter, turned the tractor around, moved my stake over four rows, re-connected the wire to the planter, and off I went.

As I rode along, I could see that Walt was making good progress on the discing. I was at it a good hour-and-a-half when he came across the road with the truck and some jugs of water from Mabel.

Walt filled up the planters with seed and headed back to the big field.

We both had good success and worked until 1:00 pm before stopping. We filled up on ham salad sandwiches for lunch. Walt offered to plant, but I said that I'd rather keep going. He agreed. We finished up our fields at about the same time, by 4:30 pm. We were both satisfied with the progress on our first day.

Back at the house we each had an ice tea and sat in the chairs under our shade tree in the front of the house.

"Do you want to get started the same time tomorrow?" Walt asked as he finished his tea and stood up to leave.

"Okay," I replied, "we'll see you here in the morning."

(25 May 45) Walt arrived at 8 am sharp, ready to go. I took the John Deere and planter up the road north to plant the small piece by the schoolhouse. Walt needed to run the disc in the big field by the house just a bit more before moving the Farmall and disc to the north forty. By noon I was able to complete the piece by the schoolhouse and brought the planter down to start the big field by the house.

Mabel came outside with our lunch.

"Why don't you take lunch out to Walt, Andy?" Mabel handed me a white cooking pot with mason jars inside filled with cold water, a sack of sandwiches, and pickles.

I parked the truck near Rinker's place and walked out to meet Walt.

"How's it coming along?" I asked.

"Okay, I guess. Seems a little dry in spots," he replied and took a drink of water and continued, "I'll probably be out here the rest of the day. I hope I can finish. We'll see."

"We're doing just fine Walt."

By the end of the day, I was able to complete planting one-third of the field by the house, and Walt disced the entire North field. This makes 55 acres of corn planted in only two days – we are clipping right along. Walt informed me that he could not help this weekend, but would come back Monday morning to help with the bean field.

Gladys Graduates from High School

When I went inside, Mabel reminded me that I had better get ready for the graduation. We needed to be at the high school by 6:30 pm.

"Where's Gladys?" I asked.

"She left with her friends," she replied, "they have to be there in advance to prepare for the ceremony."

"How about the kids?"

"They are upstairs getting ready now."

"Well, I guess I better get a movin' then."

"Yes," was her reply, "I set some clothes out for you on the bed."

We were able to get there five minutes early despite all of the worrying about being late. The ceremony was outside in the football stadium. It had been a beautiful day, with very few clouds. Overall, a picture perfect evening for a graduation.

Dick's parents were there, as it was Dick's graduation as well. The ceremony lasted a little over an hour-and-a-half. Mabel got choked up during the graduation song that they play at all of the graduations that I have ever been to. I was very proud of Gladys. She seemed more mature than most of the kids graduating that day. She was very confident when she crossed the stage to receive her diploma.

After graduation, we went to the Palaschak's for a little graduation celebration. Gladys and Dick left after a little while to go attend a graduation party with their classmates.

LaVerne Schank Lands Plane in Corn Field

(26 May 45) Continued planting corn in the big field by the house. I wanted to get back to the house by two pm in order to get ready for Mabel's nephew, LaVerne Schank, to land his plane in our field. We had received a call mid-week from LaVerne asking if Saturday was a good day to stop in and visit. Not a visit by car, but by air!

"You want to land your plane?" Mabel belted out loudly to LaVerne, with a big smile on her face. "Well let me ask Andy." She was very excited.

I had told him that the south field had just been disced to prepare for planting and would be nice and smooth for his landing. His timing was perfect as I had just started planting corn in that field today, and would be done in the next couple of days.

LaVerne keeps his plane in Marseilles. He had said that he planned to leave Marseilles around two pm, and it was just about two-thirty when we started looking intently in the sky for his plane. It was Nancy who spotted it first. She screamed, yelled, and pointed. Mabel, who was busy in the kitchen, had asked the girls to let her know when the plane was spotted. When she heard the commotion, she came out the back door trotting toward the south field. LaVerne made a large circle around the farm property, showing off his beautiful two-prop plane. The girls were waving and yelling "hello up there". They were so excited they could hardly believe their eyes. They had seen planes before at the Streator airport, but never flying in the air so close to the house. After his circle, LaVerne made his final approach from the east and made a nice smooth landing just south of the house. I had been a bit concerned that it might be too bumpy, but the plane was very sturdy and it's heavy weight allowed the wheels to cut right through the earth. He made a slight turn and sat for a while to allow the engines to stop. LaVerne climbed out of the cockpit with a big smile on his face.

We gave him a hero's welcome. Mabel hugged him, he patted the girls on the head, and we shook hands.

"So what do you think, Andy?" he asked pointing to the plane.

"Some plane LaVerne. And you landed it real nice," I said as I patted him on the shoulder, "thanks for dropping in."

"Oh, my pleasure. I know that we have been talking about this for a while, you and me. You got her disced up real good – I had no problem in your field here."

"Well, like I was telling you on the phone, I've already started planting this field, and this here section should be done before too long, so you timed it perfectly." LaVerne seemed real pleased with himself, and we were certainly proud of having a relative that could fly a plane.

LaVerne took time to point out his favorite features on the plane. He spoke about the security in having two engines in case the other went out while in flight. One engine could get him home if need be. LaVerne explained that although he had been flying over ten years, this is only the second year at flying his own plane. Prior to owning, he had to rent. He also said all pilots had to build up flight hours and get all the necessary training in order to get fully certified.

"How far can you fly this plane LaVerne?" asked Mabel curiously.

"Well, the furthest I have flown was from Marseilles to Milwaukee, Wisconsin," he replied proudly, "but she'll go as far as a full tank of gas will take her." You could tell that LaVerne was proud that he earned his license, and that he loved flying.

Mabel made a quick lunch for us after discussing all of his experiences as a pilot, and in no time he was bidding farewell. He started the engine, made a half circle in the field, and pointed his plane back toward the East. He gave us a wave goodbye, and pressed the lever forward and the plane took off. I was impressed with the power of the machine. After his wheels left the ground he made a pretty steep incline, and banked North as he headed home toward Marseilles. We all waved goodbye as the plane flew out of sight. Mabel and I agreed that it was a very unusual event – a visitor from out of the blue.

"Just between you and me and the gate post," I said to Mabel, "I think landing in the field like that is risky business."

After LaVerne left I decided to call it a day for planting and do my evening chores a bit early. Mabel and the kids went to Marseilles to go to a baby shower for one of the Olsen nieces. I headed into town to play euchre at Shab's.

(27 May 45) Went to 8:30 am church and stayed home the rest of the day. Got a good hard rain in the afternoon. I thought of Walt's comment about the north forty being dry the other day and was happy to see the rain coming down. During my evening chores, I discovered that one of the sheep had died. It was laying near the trees behind the old garage. It smelled pretty bad. It must have died late last night or very early this morning, as I know I had seen all four sheep last evening. I looked the sheep over good to make sure that those pesky foxes that Linc and I chased off last month didn't attack it. I didn't see any bite marks or blood anywhere, so I assumed it died from some disease. Rather than salvaging the meat and the risk it was spoiled, I buried the sheep.

(28 May 45) Walt and I got a fresh start this morning. I continued planting in the field near the house and Walt ran the disc over the North field once again as we both felt it needed it before planting. After lunch, Walt helped me move the wire in the big field and we were able to get about three-quarters of the field completed by quitting time.

Walt had to go to the courthouse on business tomorrow. I told him I could certainly finish up myself.

"Thanks so much for all your help, Walt," I said extending my hand, "I really appreciate it. Anytime you need anything let me know."

"You are welcome Andy," Walt shook my hand and patted me on the shoulder, "I have a few less acres to work and don't mind since I have the time." He and my sister, Anna, have been married twenty years and have one daughter. He certainly is a jokester, but when it comes to getting things done, he is tops!

(29 May 45) Woke up to a beautiful morning. Worked in the big field by myself all day and was able to finish there by 2 pm. Mabel helped me today by discing in the afternoon. Her efforts were focused on preparing the southeast field for planting beans, hopefully by this

coming weekend. I started planting corn in the North field after supper.

While Mabel was working the disc, I used the Fordson to pull the rake out of the machine shed to grease it and get it ready for dragging. I spent about an hour on the rake and she was ready to go. Tomorrow I will unhitch the disc from the Farmall and hook up the rake to start dragging the field across the road.

I relieved Mabel on the disc at around eight-thirty and continued until around ten-thirty. Mabel was such a wonderful help and true companion. When there was work that needed to be done, she was not one to fuss or complain.

As it became clear through the years that God intended for us to have only girls, I realized that I needed Mabel's assistance driving the tractor from time-to-time. I hesitated and gave it considerable thought, but then decided that I would teach Mabel the tricks of the trade. She did quite well and actually enjoyed it. Today Mabel helped me tremendously, discing a 15 acre section like nobody's business. It was quite amusing to see her on the tractor, her slip showing just a trifle.

In the spring when the soil is first worked up and turned over after a long winter is most invigorating. The smell of the earth as I worked it gave off a wonderful and familiar aroma.

Finish Planting Corn

(31 May 45) First thing after breakfast I hooked up the rake to the Farmall and headed across the road. It was easy going with the Farmall and the rake. I finished across the road around 10 am, came back across the road, jumped on the John Deere and took it out with the planter in tow with full intention to finish planting the north forty today.

I was able to get eight rounds of planting in by two, then it started raining so I headed back. It only rained about 30 minutes, so I went back out and finished just before supper, bringing my final total for corn acreage to one hundred ten acres.

As I headed back to the barn, I looked behind me and there was my dear friend Alfie walking right along side me. Linc would always say "Whenever you see Andy, you see that dog. And wherever you see that dog, you see Andy". It was true - we were always together, especially in the field. It always made me feel good to see him there.

"How are you doing boy? Are you getting hungry?" I had a habit of talking to Alfie, and most of the time I think he understood me. He seemed to like it when I talked to him.

"What do you say we head in Alf?" he looked up at me in approval and yipped just a bit in reply.

"Okay Alf. One short round and we'll head back."

JUNE

(1 Jun 45) First thing after chores, I greased the disc and put it away in the machine shed. I took the Farmall up to the piece near the schoolhouse, and finished it by 9:30 am. Back at the farm, I unhitched the corn planter from the John Deere, cleaned it up real good and put it back into the machine shed. I pulled the beans out of the bin in preparation for planting. By then it was time for lunch.

After a quick bite, I started dragging corn in the big field by the house. Alf tagged along and kept me company. Lots of times he would just sit at the end of a row and watch me. I noticed that it was quite a bit hotter today than it was yesterday.

I had been working in the big field for nearly three hours dragging the corn when I decided to head in for a drink of water. I parked the tractor and walked to the house. I returned home and found Mabel very upset. It was around four pm. She was peeling potatoes preparing for supper. Brother Steve and his family were coming over this evening.

"What's wrong Mabel? You look upset," I asked with much concern.

"Anna called," Mabel said, referring to Anna Schank, her sister in Marseilles, "they just received word today that William Fraser, Marjorie's husband, was killed in the war in Europe." She was fighting back tears as she flicked the potato peeler across the potato. Marjorie was Mabel's niece.

"Oh Mabel, I'm so sorry." I didn't quite know what to say. William was so young, and he and Marjorie had a two-year-old son, William Junior. It saddened me to think Marjorie would have to raise that little fellow by herself. It made me think of Albert in the war, and dreaded the thought of hearing the same news of my brother. William was a forward radio operator in an Army field artillery unit.

"Do they know when or where he was killed?" I thought it would be good to break the painful silence by asking a question.

"Somewhere in Germany they said, and he was killed sometime in April. I guess it takes time for the news to get back here. Oh, Marjorie must be devastated, and that poor little boy will never see his father again." Mabel's sorrow was turning into anger. She, like most people, could hardly bear to hear the bad news of our boys dying everyday. With a family member being killed in this war made it much harder to bear.

"Well, he is with the good Lord, now. He died fighting for his country, and we are one of thousands upon thousands of families who have lost loved ones. It doesn't make it any easier I suppose, but he died serving a good cause," I said trying to help Mabel put things into perspective, and I was also trying to convince myself that his death was for our freedom.

"Andy, would you believe they buried William in France? Rather than send him home, they found it best to bury him there, and make arrangements for the Army to bring him home later. This is what the gentlemen who came to their house with the news had said. I just can't fathom that."

"Well, I guess with everything going on in the thick of the war, they had to see that they give him a proper burial there for now. At least they know where he is and it is good to know that he is not lost in some battlefield somewhere. I'm sure they learned from the last war how to take care of such things." I was trying to be as reassuring as possible to help Mabel feel better. I just couldn't imagine how the Army kept it all straight, with soldiers dying all over Europe and in the Pacific.

We talked about the situation a bit longer, and I was relieved to see that Mabel was calming down. I told her again I was sorry and she looked up with a sorrowful smile, then kept right on making the potatoes.

It was just about then that I heard a car pulling into the driveway, and the shuffling of gravel, and figured it was my brother Steve. I walked out the kitchen door and greeted them as they got out of the car. Steve, my sister-in-law Edna, their daughter Mary, and sons Jim, Billy, and Bobby came inside, and after a bit we had supper together, talked and played cards. We spent part of the night talking about the war and the death of William Fraser.

Steve and family left around nine. It looked like rain. Although we could really use a little rain, I hoped it held off another day as tomorrow I wanted to start planting beans. I did my evening chores and went to bed early.

(2 Jun 45) I headed to Ray Bedeker's place to get his planter to plant beans. Ray was in the field kicking up dust, dragging his corn just like I have been doing. He saw me, made another round, stopped by the road and waved me to drive down the road a piece to meet him.

"Hello Ray," I greeted him with a smile and a handshake, "would today be a good time to borrow your planter?"

"Sure Andy," Ray replied. He was such a good soul – always willing to lend a hand or his tools. "You're a couple days ahead of me with the beans. I greased it up just the other day."

"Thanks Ray. I'll make sure I give it a greasing and cleaning when I'm done. I should be just a day or two. I'm hoping one day will do it if all goes well, and get it back to you tomorrow."

"No problem, Andy. I'm starting Monday on the beans. This heat is something else today, I wasn't expecting this," Ray said as he took off his cap and wiped the sweat off his face with his sleeve.

"Okay Ray, I'll let you get back to your work and I will see you tomorrow. Thanks a bunch."

I drove back to Ray's place hitched up the planter to the truck and headed home. I didn't waste any time getting the planter hooked up to the John Deere and headed to the bean field. I worked through lunch planting the beans. Mabel and the little girls brought me lunch around 2:30 pm.

They handed me the cooking pot with four jars inside filled with cold water. I drank two of them right down. I was starting to get a bit of a headache – I felt the water would do me good.

"So what's the lunch special for today Joyce?" I asked the little one who was trying to hand me sandwiches while I drank my water.

"Ham, I think," she replied. I rubbed her little head and thanked her.

"Why don't you head on back," I said to Mabel, "I would like to keep going and finish before supper. I'll hang on to the rest of this water."

She agreed and headed back to the house. I worked another three-and-a-half to four hours and finished. After supper and chores I was pooped out and decided to take a nap to try and get rid of my headache. Earlier in the day, Mabel and I had discussed going into Streator for our usual Saturday night routine. She came into the bedroom, put a cold washcloth on my forehead and asked if I wouldn't mind if she and the kids go into town while I rest.

"That would be fine," I replied, relieved to be able to rest a bit more, "I'll just take a break, then maybe tink around a bit tonight. I want to get the bean planter cleaned and greased for Ray if I can."

I must have really needed the sleep, as I didn't even hear Mabel and kids leave, and slept for over two hours. When I woke up, I felt rested and the headache was gone.

St. Louis Cardinals

(3 Jun 45) Just after supper, my brother George had called to inquire about going to a baseball game at Wrigley Field in Chicago. It only happened a few times a season where we had a chance to see our St. Louis Cardinals play. St. Louis was a lot further than Chicago, and we felt we had to show support for our team to all of the Cubbie fans at Wrigley Field.

"Hello Andy, how you doing?" George's voice was loud and happy.

"Oh, fair to Middlin," I replied.

"How would you like to go up to Chicago Wednesday and see the Cardinals?" George asked me the question expecting only "yes" as the answer. We had talked about it for the past couple of weeks, but knew the game was only three days away. The Cardinals were only in town for one game.

"I think we can do that George. I talked with Mabel and she didn't see any reason why we couldn't get away."

"Hot diggety!" He replied happily, "we are going to have a grand old time brother. I'll drive if that's okay with you."

"You betcha! Do you figure we will have any problem getting tickets?" I wondered since the Cardinals were the World Series winners last year and the Cubs were no slouch.

"We'll be fine. Never have had a problem. If we have to, we will talk to one of the street vendors. Just make sure you bring lots of dough just in case." George belted out a laugh.

"Okay George, see you." George and I have been to many ballgames together, and we tended to take off on the spur of the moment like this. It always seemed to me that you have the best time doing things like this when you don't plan too much.

Many folks asked me why I followed the Cardinals and not the Chicago teams. I always say, "When's the last time the Cubs or White Sox won a World Series?" The Cardinals have won the World Series five times, and twice in the past three years: 1942 and 1944. This year was different as Stan "The Man" Musial was off serving in the U.S. Navy. Stan wasn't the only one serving though. Other Cardinals, like Enos Slaughter, and other great players around the league, like Ted Williams, were serving the call. As those great players took up arms, they urged those players staying behind to keep baseball going. During these times, baseball kept our spirits up and brought people together.

Went to 10:30 am church. Nancy and Esther went with me. Just

100

after lunch, I returned the planter to Ray as promised. Mabel, the little girls, and I went to Howard Olsen's for a potluck dinner. Many of the Olsen family were there – it was almost like a family reunion. We played horseshoes, cards, and had a fine time.

Then we were off to Streator High School in the evening to meet Gladys, Dick, and the Palaschak's to listen to Gladys play in the band. After the program we all went to the Gables.

(4 Jun 45) Spent the entire day dragging corn in the big field, the North field, and the bean field. Cleaned the rake and put it away. Noticed that a soul on one of my shoes had come loose, so I took the time to repair both shoes. Hauled some corn into the horse barn, and put new points in the truck before calling it a day.

Rinker came down the road with his four-horse team after supper to borrow the roller. He and I had to move things around in the machine shed in order to get it out. I hauled it out to the driveway with the Fordson. Paul hitched it up to his team to pull home.

"Paul, you know that I lost one of my horses in February," I said, "would you mind terribly if I could use one of your team for rolling?" I almost hesitated to ask, as Paul was very particular about his animals, as was I.

Paul thought for a bit and then replied, "Well, I suppose since you let me use your roller every year, I can let you use one of my horses for a bit." He continued, "Why don't you let me get done, then I'll return the roller and leave one of them here with you."

"That would be so nice of you Paul, thank you."

"I'll let you use old Bo here. He'll get along just fine with just about any team."

"That would be fine."

He hopped up on the roller and gave the horses the signal to get moving, and off he went.

(6 Jun 45) We woke up to a very cool day. Went to the 8:00 am mass in Ransom in memory of Mother. George, John, and Pete were there, as well as some of my nephews and nieces. I went to Wednesday morning mass from time-to-time. It was a good service, and got me in a good state of mind for the day. My brothers and I chatted for a short spell in the parking lot. They wanted to get home to the work they had scheduled for that day.

Cubs vs. Cardinals – Wrigley Field

(7 Jun 45) George came by at around six-thirty on the day of the game. I was able to get all of my morning chores done, and left a few items for Mabel and the girls to tend to while I was gone. A trip to Chicago was an all-day affair. Mildred, George's wife, made sure she stocked their Pontiac with plenty of snacks, sandwiches, and small ice chest with some cold beer and soda pop. We headed north and picked up US Highway 6 East out of Seneca for almost an hour, where we picked up Route 66 North, which took us all the way into Chicago. By the time we made our way to the ballpark it was around ten-thirty. We met up with some other Cardinal fans and had a beer and shared stories of past baseball games we had attended. George was able to finagle some tickets from a street vendor for five dollars each.

"What did I tell you Andy?" George proclaimed with victory in his voice as he held up two tickets. "On the third base side, twenty-fifth row. What do you think of that?"

"Good job, George," I replied wiping the sweat off of my brow, "getting to be pretty hot boys. Maybe we'll see you inside." We said farewell to our new friends as we headed toward the main gate. Since George was kind enough to buy the tickets, I bought each of us some bright red Cards ball caps, which earned a glare or two from some Cub fans. The Cubs started out strong this year, but had slipped a bit to a record of 19-18 and the Cards were ahead in the standings at 24-18.

We made our way into Wrigley Field fifteen minutes after noon in plenty of time for the one o'clock start. There was nothing like a ballgame in June. Seeing my Cardinals in person was so exciting. Although Stan Musial was missing, the Cardinals still had a strong team with guys like Harry Breechen, a real good pitcher who won sixteen games last year, Whitey Kurowski at third base, and Buster Adams in the outfield. There was also a lot of talk about the new outfielder, Red Schoendienst, who is a blazing hot rookie.

Baseball was a big part of the Durdan family. My Father played ball and he made sure that all of us Durdan boys played as well. Me, George, Peter, John, Steve, Albert, and Edward all played for a team in Grand Ridge. We were getting a bit older, but we had lots of experience and we were all pretty big hitters. I was our first baseman the past few years, as the younger nephews who had more speed were playing the outfield.

The Cubs took an early lead with a couple of home runs in the third inning. The Cardinals went ahead in the sixth with a two run double by the rookie, Red Schoendienst. The Cards held on to the lead the rest of the way and won six to four. We ended up sharing a row with some fun-loving Cub fans. We were shooting jabs at each other throughout the whole game and buying each other beers and hot dogs. By the time it was all over, George and I both realized that we had a few too many and shouldn't drive just yet. We found a diner not far from Wrigley Field and we both had some coffee. We met some more interesting people in the diner and we ended up talking for more than an hour.

George and I started to head home around six o'clock. George handed me the keys as he felt he wasn't in the best shape to drive. He nodded out before we got out of the parking lot. We arrived back at our farm just after nine. With George rested up, he was now okay to drive home. We both agreed that we had a great time and that we need to do it again real soon. The best part of the day was that the Cards were able to get a big win over their archrival Cubs.

Last LST Built at Seneca

(8 Jun 45) Darlene called this morning from Seneca to let us know that the last LST to be built at Seneca Shipyard was completed today.

"We had a big celebration here, but it seems that it won't be too long and many of us will have to leave the shipyard," said Darlene with concern in her voice, "the US Navy contract for building the LSTs expired, causing the company to lay off thousands of workers. I'll most likely be let go by the end of June."

"But what about the war, don't they need these ships anymore?" I asked bewildered by the news.

"I guess they feel that they have enough. Nobody quite understands. But there are many companies here handing out flyers for jobs. Many of the girls are leaving early to take on jobs elsewhere."

"How about you Darlene, what are you going to do?" I asked.

"I think I am going to stay until they let me go. I still have a lot to do, and I'm not ready to go just yet," she said.

Darlene had a good head on her shoulders. That would be the same thing that I would do, I thought. She was a hard worker and wanted to finish the job she started. I used to tell her to put in a hard day's work and then some. The boss will always notice your dedication.

"I think that it is a wise decision. Maybe when you finish up there, you can come back home for a while and catch your breath. You have been working so hard."

"I think I might do that Dad, thanks. Well I better go. Send my love to Mom."

I sent our love back to her and said bye for now.

Decided that today was a day as good as any to paint the crib. I started around ten, had lunch, and painted all the way to dinnertime, finishing the east and west sides of the crib. Although most people I know dread the idea of painting, I actually enjoy it. The fresh colors brighten up the whole farm.

(9 Jun 45) Paul brought the roller back and left Bo with me. I hitched up the three horses, along with Bo, to the roller and took it across the road. The horses got along real well and we rolled the field in about two hours. It was a very pleasant, cool morning. The sky was blue with just a few white clouds. Working with a team always took me back in time. I remembered the first time my Dad let me take out a team by myself. I was about 13 years old, and have always been impressed at the power of these animals and how they worked together to pull in a straight line.

I took the team back across the road to the field by the schoolhouse. By lunch I had finished there, and headed back to the farm to get something to eat and rest. I fed and watered the horses, then started on the big field. At around 5 pm Mabel waved me in. I un-hitched the team and let them graze a bit before I put them in the barn. I cleaned Buster's old stall a bit to get it ready for our guest.

"Andy, I just wanted you to get your chores done so we can go into town. The kids really missed you last week," Mabel said referring to me skipping the trip into town last Saturday due to my bad headache.

"I feel like a million bucks today. It was nice and cool – not like last week," I said to reassure her that I was looking forward to going into town myself.

I did my evening chores, and turned the horses into the barn. Bo didn't fuss a bit at his temporary quarters.

We headed into town and made our usual stops before Mabel and the girls went to the show and I went to Shab's. I played cards and Mabel and the kids met me there afterwards.

"So how was Lassie in this movie?" I asked Esther.

"This movie was called the 'Son of Lassie' and it was really good," Esther replied.

"So Lassie had a son, huh," I replied with interest, "is Lassie Jr. as smart as Lassie?"

"No, he is just a puppy and got into a lot of trouble," she replied.

"Sounds like you enjoyed the show."

She nodded. We got the kids some soda-pop, Mabel and I partnered up for one card game, then we headed home.

In the middle of the night the skies opened up and it poured for about a half-hour. It was music to my ears.

(10 Jun 45) During morning chores I noticed that Sadie was fresh. We have had Garnett and Sadie for years. They have provided us with many gallons of milk and calves. Many of those calves we had butchered for veal. When they bled, we knew that they were said to have come in 'fresh' and then could be mated with a bull. I could either call Ray Bedeker or my brother Pete to provide the bull – as they each had one I could borrow.

Went to 8:30 am church with Nancy and Esther. Left church and drove into Marseilles to pick up Ma Olsen and Darlene. Darlene had spent the night with Ma.

Start Cultivating Corn/Bean Fields

(11 Jun 45) After returning home, I put the cultivator on the John Deere. Now that all of the corn and beans were planted, it was time to turn my efforts towards cultivating. The cultivator, with pointed shovels attached, stirs the soil between the rows and uproots the weeds. Weather permitting, cultivating three times over between now and July was ideal in order to give the corn a chance to flourish. Once the corn got to be knee-high, you were pretty much done cultivating.

It was a good feeling to see the corn sprout up - the shoots had reached about six inches. I would cultivate in the same order in which I planted.

In order to keep focused on my task all day without stopping for lunch, I asked Mabel to send lunch out with the girls. They did like to stroll through the fields, and they were fine by themselves as long as they didn't see a snake. Well, I think they kind of like to come out and see me, and they were very pleased they could help by bringing me some food, as they knew I would be very hungry. It seemed a shame that my busiest time of the year was when the kids had time off from school during the summer. I really liked to see them too.

The weather had been cool and sunny, and the soil had just the right amount of moisture so that the ground worked up just about perfect. Unlike the planter, where I had to continue refilling the corn seed, the only limitation while cultivating was refilling the gas tank. Therefore I could just keep going. I noticed the neighbor's fields had already been cultivated, perhaps for the first time also.

Lunch in the Field

It was around noon when I first saw Nancy, Esther, and Joyce walking across the road, with Nancy carrying a basket covered with a red and white towel, Esther carrying a fruit jar full of water, and Joyce carrying a pot with food inside. The girls knew not to come in the field anywhere close to the tractor. When I reached the end of the row, I shut off the tractor. How serenely quiet it was – this good earth. They came running up.

Lunch in the field, from left to right, Nancy, Joyce, Esther, and Andy (circa 1945)

Nancy reached me first and announced, "We brought your lunch Dad."

"Wow, well thank you girls. I sure am hungry," I continued, "now stay clear of the tractor and the blades of the cultivator. They're very hot, okay."

"Okay Dad," Esther nodded and replied as she handed me the jar of water. These were the same mason jars Mabel used for canning most of the summer months. We had more of these mason jars in the basement than you could count. It seemed like we collect more and more every year. I'm not sure how we got so many, and don't ever remember buying any. In the winter they would be lined up downstairs with tomatoes packed in scarlet juice, dill pickles with seedy flowerets, green string beans, peaches, and corn and even mincemeat with pieces of meat. Mabel spent many summer days canning and preserving food for the winter months.

"Thank you Esther," I thanked her for the water and chugged half of it down. "What do you girls have in that basket, Joyce?"

"Mother sent a couple of sandwiches and a piece of cake," said Joyce as she looked up at me shading the sun from her eyes with one hand. She handed me the two sandwiches wrapped in wax paper.

"One of my favorites, ham sandwich – hopefully with a little horseradish?" I lifted up the piece of bread to see. "Yep! Thank you girls." I could tell by Nancy's smile that she was the one who remembered the horseradish. I was much more interested in the water, and took another chug on the fruit jar. After sitting on the tractor for over two hours, it felt good to stand up for awhile.

I walked over to Joyce, kneeled down towards her and asked, "I think it is someone's birthday today. Do you know who that might be, Joyce?"

With a big smile she replied, "It's my birthday, Dad."

"Oh really," I teased, "and how old are you today?"

"I'm six."

"Well happy birthday to you, sweetheart." I reached down and gave her a big hug. Nancy and Esther wished her a happy birthday as well. Mabel had a plan to surprise Joyce and the girls by taking them into town to the A&W root beer stand to celebrate Joyce's birthday.

I finished the sandwiches, cake, and the jar of water. I rolled a cigarette, lit it, and watched the girls run around and entertain themselves. Joyce kept herself busy shooing flies away from the basket, Esther was picking some dandelions, and Nancy was pointing to a plane, which was a rare occasion. It was most likely headed for Chicago.

"Lunch sure tasted good. Better run along. See you later on." I thanked them and off they were on their way back to the house. They ran to beat the band with the basket, pot, and fruit jar. They certainly had a lot of energy. I could hear Nancy telling the other two girls the next fun thing to do.

"Okay, let's go back and find an animal in the clouds," Nancy exclaimed. The game where they would lay on their back and find animal shapes in the clouds.

Back to the task at hand, I sized up how many rounds I had yet to cultivate, estimated a couple of hours and I should be done with this field. By that time the tractor would need more fuel. I waited for the girls to get back safely to the house before starting the tractor and resuming. The lunch re-energized me and I spent another two and half hours and finished the field across the road.

I had some time before supper and headed into Grand Ridge to Hallet's Nursery to order some fruit trees to plant just south of the house. I ordered two golden delicious, three Burbanks July Elberta Peach, and three Halberta Giant Peach. The total bill came to eighteen dollars and seventy cents. I wrote a check for five dollars as a down payment and arranged for the man to give me a call when the saplings came in.

"About two weeks," he said.

(12 Jun 45) First thing after my morning chores, I loaded up oats and corn into the grain truck in preparation for a trip to Grand Ridge to get chicken feed ground up. Continued plowing the field across the road, finishing around noon. Shortly after lunch I took the oats and corn into town for grinding. Did not want to waste any time today, so I hurried back, unloaded the chicken feed and immediately started plowing the small field by the school.

Sarah Armstrong Cuts Her Toes at Shapland's Creek

(15 Jun 45) With all of the crops finally planted, it was time that we did something fun today. We had been getting lots of rain for the crops, which made me feel very happy. Today there was lots of sunshine, very hot, and the girls had been asking Mabel if they could go to Shapland's creek to go wading and cool off.

"Get ready and let's get going," I said to Nancy and Esther. Mabel gave me a smile because she needed some time to herself. With it being summer, having the girls home all day was tiring.

"Oh, make sure you stop and get Sarah and Patty, they were talking about going wading yesterday." Mabel was always so good about including everyone. The Armstrong girls were like family.

"I'll drop them off at the creek and let them walk home. Maybe you could take Sarah and Patty home when they come back. I need to run into Grand Ridge and get some parts for the hay rack."

"Okay Andy. I think I am going to take a nap while everyone is at the creek," she replied.

It was just after ten when I dropped the girls off at the creek and headed for Grand Ridge. I often worried about the girls there, but the water was so shallow under the bridge, there was nothing to worry about except a few harmless snakes.

The hardware store had the wood, metal rods, and screws I needed to reinforce the hayrack tongue. Over time the wood weakened and needed to be replaced. I got back around 11:30 am and Mabel had just woke up from what she called "a nice little nap". She made me a sandwich for lunch and I headed out to the machine shed to gather my tools for the hayrack job. As I crossed the yard the grasshoppers jumped and scattered out of my path. There seemed to be lots of those little buggers this year. On my way back to the barn Mabel came out of the house a bit startled.

"Minnie just called. It seems Sarah has cut her toe pretty badly on some glass while wading under the bridge." Mabel only completed half of her sentence and she was angling back towards the garage on her way to get the girls.

"Do you need my help? Should I call the Doc?" I offered.

"No, I'll be right back. Minnie said it doesn't look too bad." Mabel had things under control. She backed the car out of the garage and left. It seemed only five minutes had gone by before she was back. All of the girls seemed a little scared, however, Sarah was not in tears as I had expected. Mabel seemed a bit nervous and so was I.

"It was a bottle, Dad. We seen a couple bottles on the side of the creek, but they weren't broken." Nancy was worried we might be mad.

"It's okay honey," I replied to Nancy, "we'll get those bottles cleaned up out of there. These things happen. She's going to be fine. Right Sarah?" Sarah nodded. I took a look at her toe. The cut was pretty deep right across her middle toes. I pictured the hooligans throwing empty bottles out of their car as they drove over the small bridge above the creek and it made me mad. With all of us standing around Sarah, Mabel went inside to call Linc, and to get the iodine and a clean bandage. We consoled Sarah and told her it was going to be fine.

Linc was there in a jiffy, and as was his way, he was laughing, and said to Sarah with a little more compassion, "Maybe we'll take you into Ransom and have Dr. Ryan look at it."

Jokingly I pointed to her ankle and said, "He'll probably only need to cut it off to here." Sarah started crying and I thought, Oh my! "I'm just teasing honey," I softened, "the doctor is going to be very kind and gentle and fix your toe right up."

Linc and Sarah drove off towards Ransom. I drove down to Shapland's and picked up the bottles along the side of the creek, and used a metal garden rake to scoop out the glass that probably cut Sarah. I didn't think I would find anything, but after five minutes or so of dredging, pulled out what looked like glass from two beer bottles. After spending another fifteen minutes or so checking the creek bed up and down, I felt satisfied that it was clear.

Later that afternoon, Linc, Mary, Patty, and Sarah stopped by to show us Sarah's stitches on her toes. She was limping around and said that it did not hurt at all. We all agreed that from this point forward we would wear shoes when wading in Shapland's creek.

(16 Jun 45) It was a beautiful Saturday morning. I had volunteered, along with Gladys, to help clean the church in Ransom. Gladys and I rode over in the family car and talked while we rode along. This time of year it seemed that we were so busy that days and weeks could go by without talking with Gladys as she was so busy. She told me about her and Dick spending time together and how much she admired him.

"Is Dick coming for dinner tonight?" I asked.

"I hope so. He and his Dad have been real busy. I know that he would like to come," she replied.

"Well, if he wants to come late that's okay. Maybe we can play some cards?"

"That would be nice. Oh it is such a beautiful day," she said with a big smile on her face. It was nice to see Gladys so happy.

We spent a good two hours cleaning the church. I did most of the sweeping and helped Father Eagan sort through things in the basement.

"Don't know why we keep things so long, Andy. I just can't seem to get rid of these old boxes full of odds and ends." Father Eagan sounded frustrated as he was looking through old dusty boxes.

"Well, Father, if you have done without it for this long, you probably don't need it anymore," I said trying to relieve any guilt he might have.

"I suppose you're right. Let's take these three and take them out to the trash. Would you mind Andy?"

"Not at all Father. I'll take them out right now." He seemed happy to have made the decision. I carried out the three boxes and set them with the other garbage that had accumulated during the morning.

I dropped Gladys off at home and headed over to Linc's to see if he could stop over and help with the hayrack.

"Sure Andy, let me get a few things done here. Bill's coming over here in a bit to help me with that elevator belt. Maybe we'll stop by for a Meister Brau and then see what we can do about that hayrack." Linc always had a way to make me feel better about things. That hayrack was starting to bug me and I knew that with Linc and Bill's help, it would be fixed today.

I put some beers in a tub of cold water in the pump house so they would be cold by the time the boys got here. Bill, Linc, and I shot the bull, had a couple of beers, and in no time we had the hayrack all fixed up and ready to go.

Cut Hay – First Time

(18 Jun 45) Finished cultivating the big field near the house by 10 am this morning. Spent the rest of the morning fixing a wheel on the wagon. Started cutting hay after lunch. This would be my first cut for the year. It was standing about 20 inches tall. With the sickle bar mower pulled behind the John Deere, I started the piece across the road. I was able to get better than half of the field before a mechanical problem on the mower caused me to stop and head back to the machine shed for tools. An hour later, I got her going again. Just as I finished a round, Mabel waved me down for dinner. Where had the day gone, I thought.

I was able to get a bit more done after dinner, but realized that I would not be able to finish until tomorrow. Overall, I was pleased with my accomplishments for today. Ah, that smell of fresh-cut hay.

(22 Jun 45) Most of the day was spent raking the dried hay. I had finished cutting the piece across the road and the piece by Rinker's and was fortunate enough to have Ray Bedeker and Linc give me a hand raking and loading. Ray and Linc came by around three in the afternoon and helped me hook up the side delivery rake, windrow, load the hay into the hay rack and haul it back to the barn. They also helped me put up loose hay in the loft. Working the hay was at a minimum a two man job, and we were fortunate to have three of us today as it was hotter than blazes – 92 above the last time I checked. We agreed that we would meet at Ray's tomorrow afternoon to cut and rake over at his place.

Ransom Free Show

I took off my cap that I knew was laden with dust, and hit it against my coveralls to shake it free of the dirt, then headed inside to get cleaned up before supper. After supper, the girls helped Mabel get the kitchen cleaned up so we could be on our way to Ransom for the free show. Every Friday night during the months of June, July, and August, Ransom or Grand Ridge hosted free shows – bring your own lawn chairs and blankets. Those wanting to sit in their autos would need to go early to find a suitable parking place where they could view the movie. Ransom was such a small town, everything was on the same street – Main Street. Places of business included a tavern, ice cream shop, bank, grocery store, small hardware store, and the post office. The front of a downtown building is used as the screen and the operator of the projector in the middle of the street. This was really an entertaining way to see everyone and enjoy the show. The same old crowd would be there every week, and everyone you saw during the course of the evening you knew.

A typical movie on a Friday night would be a good old Western with Roy Rogers and Dale Evans, or Gene Autry. Once in awhile they showed a movie with actor Victor Mature, who happens to be Mabel's favorite. She would sit with her friends on lawn chairs, and the girls had it all planned out from the week before which friends they would sit with.

On this particular Friday night, I would have preferred to relax after a long hot day working in the hayfield, but did not want to miss the free show, as it was always a fun evening. Even after the movie was over, families and friends mingled and talked for sometimes an hour or more. As I usually did while the family watched the show, I wandered into the tavern to play some euchre with friends. Bill Koetz was there, and we partnered up for a few games. The girls were counting on their usual ice cream for the ride home.

Night in the Barn

The five-mile trip home from Ransom was quite warm with ice cream cones dripping. I noticed some lightning in the north, and became a little concerned. What if lightening should strike the barn with all of the new mown hay? The hay had a way of staying hot and required days for it to cool down. In addition to the worry of the lightning, the wet hay had a way of creating combustible gases that could ignite with the smallest spark. This created an extreme fire hazard and would burn very easily.

We drove into the yard and straight back to the barn.

"Why aren't you pulling into the garage Andy?" Mabel asked.

"I'm a bit concerned about the fresh hay in the barn and the lightening, it is a bad combination. I think I am going to stay out here for a while and keep watch over things. Go ahead and pull the car into the garage and take the girls inside, it's not good to be out in the lightning."

Sensing the urgency in my voice, Mabel did what I asked of her.

It seemed everyone was tired after such a hot day. I opened up the doors and turned the horses into the barnyard, located the fire extinguishers and found a comfortable place to sit in an area where I could pretty well see all around me, hoping and praying all would be okay.

It took a few hours for the lightning to dissipate, and I let the horses back in the barn, and headed for the house. The house was quiet and everyone was sound asleep. I told Mabel that everything was okay, and rather than crawling into bed, I settled into my comfortable recliner in the living room for the few hours of sleep I could catch before dawn. As I lay down, I pulled one of Mabel's quilts up to my chin and let out a yawn. It was one of those deep, satisfying yawns where I opened my mouth so wide, I almost knocked my jaw out of joint. Then fell fast asleep.

Victory on the Island of Okinawa

(25 Jun 45) At six-thirty, Gabriel Heater reported that US soldiers and marines had claimed victory on the island of Okinawa. Initial report of US casualties were heavy with over 8000 dead and 32,000 wounded. The battle lasted nearly three months. The troops were pushed to exhaustion working cave-by-cave and tunnel-by-tunnel to remove the entrenched Japanese from their holes. The US troops are leary of attacking mainland Japan. Knowing how long it took to conquer this relatively small island of Okinawa, just figure how long it will take to conquer Japan.

This was the first major victory since the Germans surrendered last month. It was wonderful news to hear that our boys took the island. Now we had to think of the scary task of attacking the Japanese on their soil.

(26 Jun 45) Spent the morning cutting hay at Bill Koetz's place. Gerald, Bill's son, a very strong, young-looking boy of about 15 years of age was ready to go to work. Ray Bedeker was there as well helping out. We cut and hauled five loads of hay to the barn, and put up some dry hay to his loft.

Finally finished plowing corn in the North field, then onto the bean field. Finished cultivating the first time for this year. Tomorrow I would start cross-cultivating across the road.

After supper I headed over to Bedeker's to help him put up some hay. We sat outside as the sun went down and had a couple of beers. We saw my brother George driving down the road to beat the band. He must of noticed us out of the corner of his eye. He came to a stop, turned around and came back to join Ray and I for a beer.

"We better watch those Cubs Andy," George said as he leaned back in his chair, "I think they are going to give the Cards a run for their money this season."

"We'll see," I replied, "they'll peter out like most years, you'll see."

We sat and talked about baseball and the war. I just about nodded off.

"Time to go beddy-bie Andy?" George teased.

Yes it was time for bed. I headed home and went straight to bed.

Gage's Ice Cream Social

(30 Jun 45) It was a beautiful Saturday for Gage's annual ice cream social. Gladys and Darlene did not attend as they had other plans today, but Mabel, I, and the little girls were very much looking forward to going, as we do every year. We picked up Nancy and Esther from catechism, then headed to the Gage's farm, which was near Grand Ridge. We knew Lawrence and Mary Gage well, as we see them many times during the year at other occasions. They have two teenage boys at home and they are very nice young gentlemen.

The social started at noon time. We were about the third or fourth car to arrive. My brother Pete, his wife Mary, and two boys pulled in right behind us. We sat around and talked for a short while until everyone had arrived, then Mary announced lunch was ready. The meal was set up in the garage on large tables. It was nice to get inside out of the sun, as it was quite warm. The barbeque was kept hot in an electric fry pan, along with potato salad, garden green beans and cabbage slaw. The Gage's always had root beer on ice, which was Esther's favorite. Mary would open up the ice-cold cans and pour it into paper cups for the girls, with the foam forming at the top of the cup.

After lunch, the oldest teenage boys would gather up the kids for games of tug of war, gunny sack races, and red rover. The kids had remembered the same games from previous years and were eager to play. There were over a dozen kids competing, all of them destined to be the winner. They just played for fun, no prizes, and the adults sure got a lot of laughs watching them.

The main event of the day was the making of ice cream out of the Gage farm dairy milk. All of the kids stood in line to take their turn at the crank on the ice cream churn. When it was done, which took a good while, it was served with cake.

Pete and I teamed up for a game of euchre against Ray Bedeker and his wife. We split four games. Ray and I sat and talked a bit about our threshing plans, which was just about one month away. It got to be about 5:30 pm when we decided to head home. I always enjoy the social – it was an afternoon of fun sure to remember.

PHOTOGRAPHS

Special thanks to Elizabeth Davis and Teresa Italiano Budish for providing these photographs from their memorabilia.

Mabel Olsen and Andy Durdan (January 19, 1921)
Andy was best man for Milt Inks and Mary Durdan at their wedding.

Andy Durdan (circa 1921)

Andy Durdan with Mabel Olsen (circa 1921)

Mabel Olsen (date unknown)

Mabel Olsen and Andy Durdan (circa 1922)
Visiting Starved Rock State Park before their marriage.

Andy and Mabel's Wedding Photo (sitting) (February 25, 1922)
Best Man, Peter Durdan and Maid of Honor, Edith (Bentley) Danielson

Threshing operations at Peter Durdan Senior's farm (date unknown)

Andy Durdan holding first born, Darlene (circa 1923).
Andy at 27 years of age.

Nancy in front (2 years), Gladys (left – 11 years), Darlene (right – 15 years) holding Esther (6 months) (circa 1938)

Gladys pushing mower; Sitting (left to right), Joyce, Esther, Nancy, playing with kittens or rabbits (date unknown)

Gladys relaxing by barbecue (circa 1945)

Playing in Mom's garden (left to right) Nancy, Joyce, Esther. Outhouse at left, barn in rear. (circa 1944)

Lunch in the field, from left to right, Nancy, Joyce, Esther, and Andy (circa 1945)

Gladys adventure outside in winter (December 1945)

Girls playing in front yard with bike and dog (left to right) Joyce, Nancy, Esther (circa 1946)

Girls playing by road with family dog (left to right) Joyce, Esther, Nancy (circa 1946)

Nancy feeding lamb, Joyce (center), and Esther (right) (circa 1948)

Family picture at Illini Park – Olsen Family Reunion.
(left to right) Gladys, Joyce, Andy, Nancy, Mabel, Esther, Darlene
(circa 1948)

Darlene in Mabel's garden (circa 1950)

Darlene cooking at the brick barbeque (left to right) Darlene, Esther, Nancy (date unknown)

Andy working on machinery (date unknown)

Andy after a long hard day in the fields (date unknown)

Andy and Mabel Durdan relaxing (date unknown)

Andy and Mabel Durdan (circa 1957).
Andy 61 years, Mabel 57 years.

JULY

(1 Jul 45) Woke up around six-thirty - a bit early for a Sunday. I was able to get through my chores a bit faster, maybe due to the extra sleep. The little girls and I headed off to Sunday's nine-thirty mass in Ransom. I saw my friend Connors as we walked into church.

"Ready for the game Andy?" Connors asked quietly with a big smile.

"As ready as I'll ever be." Today our baseball team had a game against Ransom at three.

"Are John, Pete, and George coming?" he asked, referring to my brothers.

"John and Pete will be there, but George can't make it. Trouble with his tractor, I think. Maybe I'll go give George a hand, so he can make it."

"We'll need all the help we can get. See you there Andy."

We made our way to our usual spot in the church to partake in the mass.

I never did make it over to George's, as I had my hands full getting the plow ready for the North field tomorrow.

I went alone to the game while Mabel took the kids to Pete's to help the women folk prepare for the potluck supper after the game. It was a hard fought game all the way through to the ninth inning.

We were tied in the top of the ninth, with my brother John on third, my brother-in-law Walter on second, and Pete at the plate. Connors didn't have a hit during the game and suggested that my brother Pete pinch-hit for him. Pete had hurt his hand during warm-ups and initially decided to sit this one out. Pete, our best hitter, accepted the challenge deciding that his hand felt good enough to bat.

Pete hit the first pitch for a clean hit into center field, allowing John and Walter to score. We all screamed and cheered, as did our small cheering section. We continued hitting and scored five more runs. Ransom was deflated and made three quick outs in the bottom of the ninth.

After the game, the Durdan players all went to Pete's to enjoy the potluck supper, brag about our win, and to celebrate our hero, Pete, for hitting in the winning runs.

(2 Jul 45) Starting to cross the North field today but did not quite get

finished, although I had pretty good luck and no problems today. It was pretty cool for July – didn't get much higher than 60 above. As I was making my diary entries for the day, I remembered that tomorrow was Esther's practice for first communion at St. Mary's church. I finished my entries and went to the bedroom to find Mabel sitting up in the bed knitting.

"Esther's got her practice tomorrow," I said to Mabel as I cleaned out my pockets, placing my wallet, keys, and change purse on the dresser.

"Oh, good heavens. Her first communion is this Sunday, isn't it?" Mabel was stumped. "Will you have time to take her tomorrow?"

"Well, sure. I put a good dent in the North field today. I'll take her over."

"Okay. I will finish her belt first thing in the morning." Mabel had finished sewing Esther's white dress quite awhile ago. She had tried it on ten times or so already and thought it was so pretty that she did not mind wearing the hand-me-down veil and white shoes.

(3 Jul 45) Mabel was up before me running the sewing machine making the finishing touches on Esther's communion outfit. By the time I finished my chores Mabel was busy making donuts. I peaked my head into the kitchen to see the donuts bobbing around in the oil. She was using her handy metal donut cutter to shape the donuts. She pulled the hot donuts out of the oil with tongs and rolled them in sugar and cinnamon, then set them on the counter to cool.

"May I?" I pointed to the first donut that had made it through the assembly line.

"Go ahead, it should be cool enough to eat," she replied, keeping a watchful eye on the donuts inside the oil.

"Delicious," I said. Esther walked in with her communion dress on, "look at my sweetie pie in her beautiful dress," I said as I licked the sugar off of my fingers. Esther twirled around to show off her dress.

"Now you're not going to wear that to practice," Mabel said knowing that is what Esther had hoped to do.

"But Mom, I want to wear it," Esther begged.

"That dress is for Sunday, for your real first communion," Mabel continued, "none of the other children will be wearing their dresses or suits for the practice. Now march right back upstairs and change."

"Can I have a donut first?" Esther asked. Her thoughts had clearly shifted from her dress to the delicious treats cooling on the counter.

"Sweetheart, go upstairs and change, then you can have a donut," Mabel's voice was a bit more serious. Esther listened and ran upstairs.

The donuts were absolutely delicious. I grabbed one more and headed outside to get ready for Mr. Gordon, who bought our chickens. Just like the hogs and cows, we had to sell our chickens to market. By July, the baby chicks that we purchased in early spring were full-grown. I will sell the chickens from now through September. We will clean some chickens for our own use. We eat some fresh, and freeze some also. He arrived about 9 am, right on time.

"Good morning Mr. Gordon," I greeted him as he drove into the farmyard.

"Want me to pull up by the chicken coop?" He asked without getting out of his truck. I gestured to him to do just that. His truck was a grain truck loaded up with cages. There were quite a few cages already full of clucking chickens. The back of the truck contained a scale – the chickens were sold by-the-pound.

Together Mr. Gordon and I fetched 30 chickens from the chicken coop. It was fairly easy to catch them using a sturdy long wire with a hook on the end to latch onto their legs. He took his time to carefully weigh the chickens. The total weight came to 109 pounds.

"Well, Andy, the going rate today is 40 cents a pound." Bill then performed multiplication on a notepad and reported the total. "The total will be 43 dollars and 60 cents. Fair enough?"

"Fair enough."

He handed me the check and was on his way. I went downstairs to clean up a bit before taking Esther to the church for rehearsal – which started at 10 am.

Esther had changed her clothes like her mother had asked. She seemed very happy to be going with me to practice. It wasn't very often I was able to spend time alone with just one of the kids.

"Well, whataya say Sweetie Pie, should we get going?" I cupped her face in my hand and we headed out the door.

There were only a few kids receiving the sacrament. Father Eagan took a few minutes to explain the importance of receiving the sacrament of the Eucharist. He explained how they have entered the age of reason and could now participate in the sacramental life of the Catholic Church. Father asked each of us parents if we felt the children were ready for this awesome responsibility. Everyone nodded yes.

The kids practiced their entrance into church as a group and Father walked them through the paces. There were a couple of other neighborhood friends there to shoot the breeze with. We were only there about 45 minutes when Father let everyone go.

After the practice, Esther and I drove to Marseilles. I wanted to check the progress on the porch repairs on my rental property, which was located right on Route 6. It was quite a large house and I have had the same tenants for quite a long time. Ray Wermstrom was about my age, and he and his wife had one daughter. Never could figure why they wanted such a big house for the three of them. I really appreciated the fact he was never late on his rent payments.

Ray wasn't home but his wife answered the door.

"Hello Mrs. Wermstrom," I talked to her through her screen door, "sorry to bother you. I just wanted to check on the porch repairs. Have the workers been by today?"

"Oh, hello Mr. Durdan. No they haven't been by for the past couple of days," she responded politely. "Would you like to come in?" She noticed Esther was in tow. "Well hello there. You are Esther, right?"

"Yes," Esther replied, "I had my first communion practice today."

"Well isn't that nice," she said, "oh please be careful of the boards, there's nails in them."

The porch was mostly torn up and you could see to the dirt below. I must have been visibly upset because Mrs. Wermstrom provided a bit more details on the status of the work, "The men were moving right along. They worked this past Friday and Saturday and removed most of the bad boards. But they haven't been back."

"Well, I will give them a call when I get home," I said, "they probably got hung up doing something else. The squeaky wheel gets the grease I like to say."

"Thanks Mr. Durdan. That would be wonderful. We think they are doing a good job."

"Thanks for offering to have us in, but we should be going," I continued, "we sure feel lucky to have you and your family here in the house, and we are grateful that you keep up the place so nicely. We'll get this porch fixed up lickety-split. Say hello to Ray." I raised my hat and took Esther's hand in mine and we headed back towards home.

It was just about noon and time for lunch, so I asked Esther if she wanted to stop at the A&W Root Beer stand. She thought that was a swell idea. We each ordered a frosty mug of root beer, a hot dog for

Esther, and a hamburger for me. We sat in the car and ate our sandwiches and sipped our root beer in silence.

"Pretty good huh?" I asked after a few minutes of silence. Esther just nodded her head in agreement.

"Whataya say we get an ice cream?" I asked. Esther nodded her head once again. We licked our ice cream cones as we headed for home.

I had plenty of time before dinner to finish cultivating the North field, which would take care of my second cultivation of the season. It was smooth going for well over two hours and I was happy to be done. Decided to take advantage of my good fortunes with time and hauled a load of oats into Grand Ridge for sale.

(5 Jul 45) I was cutting weeds in the front of the house along the road when I saw Mabel walking towards me down the road. She seemed to be clicking along at a good pace, so I didn't feel the need to go after her in the tractor. Something must of happened to the car, I thought.

"What happened, you okay?" I asked as I walked towards her.

"Flat tire, darn it! I was just about home." She was upset but kept her composure.

"How far down?" I asked as she walked by. I think she would have walked right by me, up the driveway and into the house if I hadn't asked.

"Just past the Long's place on the South road." Clearly frustrated with how the day was going, she waved her arm in the general direction of where the car was left and headed for the house.

I finished the weeds along the road, parked the tractor in the driveway, gathered a few tools, made ready one of the bicycles out of the old garage and headed down our road south. I couldn't remember the last time I road a bike. What they say is true – you never forget how to ride. Riding on the gravel was tricky, and I always warned the girls to be careful. We had two good-working bikes and I tried to keep them ready just in case the girls wanted to go on a bike ride, or when the cousins come over to play. There were a couple of bikes in the old garage that I wanted to brush the rust off, paint, and patch up the tires. Mabel had walked quite a ways, no wonder she was upset.

As I turned the corner, there was the car. As I drew closer, I could clearly see that the right-front was flat. Using the jack in the trunk, I was able to change out the bad tire with the spare. I placed the bike in the trunk, with the lid bobbing up and down as I drove, and headed home.

Dinner at the Palaschak's

By supper time Mabel had gotten over the flat tire incident and was getting a basket of cookies and drinks together for our Fourth of July party. We were invited to go to Andy Palaschak's place to shoot off firecrackers, have a few beers, and play cards. Gladys was very happy to have both our family and Dick's family together. There was a lot of excitement knowing that Dick and Gladys were dating and you could tell that their courtship was special. Mabel and I thought the world of Dick. He was tall, handsome, strong, worked hard and had a great sense of humor.

Dick and I had a contest last year to see who could grow the biggest watermelon. We went out to Dick's patch to see how his crop was progressing. Dick kept his eye on me to make sure I didn't cut the stem on one of his prize watermelon.

Last year, it was clear that I would have the biggest watermelon. Dick would walk out to my patch every time he visited to gaze at my big melon. He was sure that I would win and consequently was a little peeved about it. Right before the day of reckoning, which was around July 15th, Dick went out to my patch and disconnected the big melon from the vine and marked it with a black crayon "17 cents per lb", which made it look like it was purchased. That night after dinner we all walked out to look at my prize and I saw the marking. I'll never forget the way Dick laughed when he saw my astonishment. We all laughed and Dick raised my hand in the air to show I was the winner.

So today, I jokingly pulled my pocketknife out and gestured as if I was going to cut the vine on one of his biggest watermelons.

"Now Andy, don't think you're gonna get back at me tonight, because I got my eye on you," Dick belted out followed by a laugh.

"You got some real beauties out here. I think I'll have my work cut out for me this year," I replied.

"Oh, don't be so modest, I've been in your garden to see what you're growing."

"I guess we'll see in a couple weeks."

(6 Jul 45) It was a beautiful morning. I wanted to relax a bit today knowing that it wouldn't be long and I would start harvesting the oats. The harvesting would last from mid-July until the end of August. This effort would include harvesting our oats, and also the fields of all of the men in the threshing gang. Mabel called me in for breakfast, which was

137

a hearty breakfast of eggs easy over, ham, toast, with strawberry jam. Eggs and toast with strawberry jelly just seemed to go together.

"Where are the girls?" I asked Mabel.

"They ate already and are outside playing on the bike," she replied reaching for the toast. She and I sat down to eat. The jelly was especially good. We talked a bit about our trip to Weger's farm near Marseilles where we picked our strawberries. We made our strawberry picking a family outing every spring when the strawberries were at their peak. We would bring a number of our own quart-sized containers, which we filled ourselves, and they charged 11 cents per quart. With all of us picking, it would take no time and we could pick several pecks. The patches of strawberries at Weger's farm totaled approximately eight acres. We always seemed to run into someone we knew and would chat as we picked. The girls always had a good time, and so did Mabel and I.

Once we got the strawberries we had to prepare them for canning. It was quite a job taking the stems off, washing them, making the jam, jarring them while still hot and sealing them in Mason jars. The girls would help with the stemming until their little thumbs got tired. Then they ran outside to play.

We would stick to the job until all the strawberries were jarred. We usually did not can all of the berries, saving quite a few for cereal, ice cream, and to snack on. When Mabel started her canning operations you dare not get in her way or do anything that would slow down the process. She never minded the heat from the stove or the sticky fly tape hanging from the ceiling. The sticky tape was a necessity, and was usually pretty well covered with flies. Sometimes if I was not careful, it would touch the top of my head. Once the jars were sealed, we dated each jar, and carted them to the basement.

So this morning we surely enjoyed the fruits of our labor at breakfast.

Just as I finished breakfast, Nancy bolted in and announced there was a flat tire on the bicycle and asked politely if I could fix it.

"Of course," I replied. The inner tube probably had a hole in it and I would have to patch it.

After I patched up the tube, I headed to Ray Bedeker's place to put up hay. He had quite a bit to do so his son Ron helped. We worked through lunch and finished by three o'clock. I came home, did my chores and we all went into Grand Ridge for supper at the local bar and grill.

Nancy Sewing for the 4-H Fair

(7 Jul 45) I came in for a break around eight am to find Nancy and Mabel quite busy in the dining room hovering over the Singer sewing machine with green material spread out on the table. They had bought the material and pattern quite a while ago. I guess Mabel didn't have time to help her and knew Nancy was quite concerned she would not have her skirt finished in time to model it at the 4-H fair, which was just a week away. So they were busy as bees trying to complete the project.

Esther Hagie is the 4-H group leader for the girls in our area. Each girl selects a project they would work on for the 4-H Fair, held every year at the fairgrounds in Ottawa. The girls select food preparation, flower arranging, sewing, and a variety of other things. Nancy picked out sewing for this year.

It is a national organization which was really great for boys and girls. Bless those group leaders, as they have meetings on a regular basis, and needed to be well versed in a number of things. The sole purpose was to learn fairness to all, helping others, and the community.

The projects for the boys are even more challenging - like raising a good looking and healthy calf, sheep, pig, or rabbit. The boys would have to keep their animals clean and trimmed. Whatever your project, it was entered at the fair. The judges were very critical. The entries received a blue, red or white ribbon.

By lunchtime Nancy had her skirt done and was showing it off as I walked in.

"Well don't you look beautiful? I'd say that's a blue ribbon winner for sure," I said.

"She did really well, and did most of it herself. Once we got the material cut, she took her time stitching and gathering the skirt at the top, and then she hemmed it. Isn't that right Nancy?" Mabel had her hands on her hip, smiling and looking at her daughter with pride. Nancy just smiled and twirled around.

Esther's First Communion

(8 Jul 45) Mabel, the three little girls, and I went to 8 o'clock mass at St Mary's for Esther's First Communion. Dick and Gladys came in a separate car. Linc and Mary Armstrong, and family were there as well. All of the children did splendidly. Esther looked so cute as she got in line to receive the sacrament. She was very serious and Mabel and I were both so proud. We stayed after the mass for group photos in front

of the church.

After church we decided to take a ride north to Triumph, a small town near Mendota, to see the damage done there by the windstorm. We had heard about the terrible storm from some friends at church. Several farms on one road had every building on the place down flat. The storm must have been quite devastating. I felt a little reluctant showing this to Mabel as she worried a lot about these storms. To see such devastation made us appreciate how awful these storms can be. We took our time on our way home looking at the fields. It was a good chance to see how the crops were coming along.

(9 Jul 45) Since we had gotten quite a lot of rain lately, I felt it was a good idea to take a short ride in the old truck to inspect the north field for standing water. Smack dab in the middle of that field was a low-lying area that would not drain properly with too much rain. It was possible to have four or five acres under water. This could be a real problem for the corn, as the water could drown the small shoots quickly. Luckily, it wasn't too bad, and the standing water was limited to a very small area, perhaps one-quarter acre. Nevertheless, I had decided that this year I would make the investment and hire the tilers to come dig the trenches and lay the tile properly so the low area would drain to the creek that ran through the property. It would be worth the time and money.

(10 Jul 45) The cornfields were looking very good, as we had plenty of rain the past week or so. I was sure that we would have a good crop of corn this year if we can keep the corn borers away. The corn borer has become a big problem in Illinois the past few years, and all farmers are worried about the pests. We've been lucky so far, but it is a good idea to inspect the leaves of the corn plants as they grow.

Mabel made plans to go to a real estate sale in Marseilles with Annie. She made arrangements to drop the girls off at the Armstrong's on the way to Marseilles. Many times I was able to watch the girls while Mabel went to town or to Marseilles to see family, but today my entire day would be dedicated to cultivating the corn crops for the third, and hopefully last time this year. Mabel usually had a pretty big workload around the house, but she was very good at planning some time for herself. Of course, Gladys, who always pitched in where needed, shared the workload. Nancy and Esther also helped Mabel with specific chores. When Mabel went away, she always managed to spend a good amount of time, and you never knew what she was going to bring back from these sales.

I cultivated across the road in the morning, broke for lunch, and was able to finish there by three. The weeds were not that big of a problem and the ground was breaking up nicely. I was able to start the small piece near the schoolhouse, but ran out of gas. I had to walk home and get a couple of five-gallon cans with gas and then drove back with the truck. Now I had to get both the tractor and truck back to the property. By the time I was done with all that, it was time to go pick up the girls at the Armstrong's before dinner.

Mabel Found a Light Fixture

It was about five pm when Mabel came home. I had been tinkering around in the garage and listening to Perry Como on the radio when she pulled up. She opened up the trunk and there was a new ceiling light fixture. I was quite taken aback as it was large and would throw out a lot of light.

"Did you get this at the sale?" I asked, knowing full well she did.

"Yes, could you install it? It's for the dining room," she said, getting right to the point. She called the girls over to the car. "I brought you some Cracker Jack." They loved to eat the caramel corn out of the box. After a couple of kernels they would dig around for the prize – there was one in every box.

Mabel bringing home the light fixture reminded me of the time she bought a toilet at a sale and asked me if I could install it. Imagine doing away with the outhouse, which was in the back yard near the garden, and actually using a flushing toilet in the bathroom. We didn't have any pipes to drain the toilet to the outside, or a drainage tank in the ground near the house. Mabel didn't really think about those things. I think she just thought that we could bolt it to the floor and it would work just fine. I was really taken aback then. I was pretty good at keeping farm machinery all tuned up and running, but plumbing and installing a toilet was a horse of a different color. That time I had asked my brother George to help me, as he was pretty good at plumbing and things of that sort. We got the job done, and now we couldn't imagine going back to the outhouse.

So to make Mabel happy I didn't give her a hard time and said "I'm certain we can get the light installed. All I need is a little time to figure it out."

As usual, after Mabel's day out, she really had to hustle to get supper on by six, so we could go to Streator to take our eggs to the Kollar's market and spend some time in town.

(12 Jul 45) Finally finished cultivating the corn and bean fields for the final time. Spent a good amount of time cleaning and greasing the cultivator to get it ready to put away. I set the wheels in on the John Deere in preparation for cutting oats.

Tiling the North Field

(14 Jul 45) After morning chores, I made the call to schedule the tilers to have them come out to the farm and give an estimate for the job. I called an outfit called Taylor and Sons out of Marseilles that had done similar work for Bill Koetz, did an outstanding job, and were fairly reasonable in price.

"Taylor here." It was a deep voice on the other end of the phone line that I assumed was Taylor and not one of the sons.

"Yes, Mr. Taylor. This is Andy Durdan from Grand Ridge. I'm Bill Koetz's neighbor out here and you did some tiling for him awhile back, I believe it was a year ago or so. Do you recall?"

"Sure, sure I remember. So are you one of Peter Durdan's sons?" He asked.

"The oldest, and the best looking," I responded with a chuckle, and he chuckled as well. I continued, "I've done smaller jobs to get water away from the fields, but this job is a pretty big deal, with a low spot about four or five acres wide."

"I think we can help you, Andy. The way we normally do things is we come out check it over and write up an estimate. Can't really say how much it's going to cost over the phone without looking it over."

"Okay Mr. Taylor. Any day next week is good for me. Now I don't want the work done until the fall, after the harvest and before the frost. Hope that's okay by you?" I didn't want him to think that I wanted it done anytime soon, that I just wanted to get it planned.

"How does Monday afternoon, say around two sound?" He said.

I told him that would be fine and I started to give him directions, but he remembered where Bill Koetz lived and told me no need.

"We'll see you on Monday," Mr. Taylor said happily, "and thanks for your business, Andy."

"You betcha. Bye now." I wished all things went that smoothly. I was proud of myself for calling, as this is a job that has been weighing on my mind for some time. There's no sense in worrying about spending the money, as it had to be done. Besides last year's crop was very good and I was able to put away a few extra dollars for something like this.

Just as I hung up the phone, Mabel made the announcement.

"Okay everyone, let's get ready, we are leaving for the 4-H Fair in 10 minutes."

Nancy Wins Blue Ribbon

It was time for Nancy to enter her new outfit into the competition at the 4-H Fair in Ottawa. It seemed everyone went at least once during the three-day event. The fairgrounds were buzzing with activity. We walked around for about an hour - looking at the animals, vegetables, flowers, baked goods, jams, tool demonstrations, tractors, and all kinds of fun stuff. Esther and Joyce had cotton candy and lemonade. Nancy was nervous and passed on the snack, and was extra careful not to get her outfit dirty.

Nancy did a fine job modeling her outfit in front of quite a few people. We were very proud of her. She was awarded a blue ribbon, and was happy it was all over.

Walking by the tractors, Mabel and I looked at each other and smiled remembering last year's little incident. It was last year's fair that Esther had decided to take one of the tractors, that was on demonstration, for a little ride. She had climbed up on one of the tractors, pushed a few levers and the tractor started rolling oh so slowly down the hill. She realized what she had done, jumped off, and ran away. Mabel and I were standing close by when an alert gentleman yelled, "Hey, that tractor is moving." He jumped on the tractor and brought it to a complete stop. We did not scold Esther and ignored the fact that we knew it was she that started the tractor rolling down the hill. She probably wondered if we knew it was her that caused the commotion. It's funny now – but it wasn't funny then. Thank God nobody was hurt.

(15 Jul 45) First thing after chores, I hooked up the binder to the John Deere, pulled it across the road, and started cutting the oats. I had to make some minor adjustments which slowed me up just a bit. The binder wasn't kicking the bundles out like it should. I was able to make three rounds before lunch. Things were going pretty good, so I continued there a while longer.

Ray Bedeker came over and helped me shock the bundles. We were both huffing and puffing pretty good after stacking for about an hour. We took a break and drank some water that we had brought in a thermos.

"And we're just starting, Andy," Ray said as he sat on the ground with his arms over his knees, "did you ever wonder how our Dads could do this into their 60's?"

"I guess they learned to pace themselves," was my reply. Nothing was more taxing on a farmer's body than oats and threshing. It is a lot of work. Just then, Ray's son Ron rode over on his bike. We told him we appreciated his help.

Together we were able to cut and shock the field across the road and cut some by the schoolhouse before calling it a day. Tomorrow would go easier as Bill Koetz would be joining us here in the morning. Then we will be off to Bill's in the afternoon to cut and shock his oats.

(16 Jul 45) I had to leave Bill's place at about quarter till two in order to meet the tiling man. Alfie was making high-pitched sounds and darting around a bit.

"What's wrong Alf?" I asked him. He stopped and stared at me for a second or two, and then continued making his sounds.

"Is there a storm coming boy?" Most dogs I ever owned seemed to know when a storm was brewing and Alf was no exception. Dogs could sense a storm long before people could.

He looked at me again as if to say "Can't you tell?"

Mr. Taylor drove up about ten minutes before two. He drove a fairly new truck with "Taylor and Sons Tiling Services" and phone number painted on the side. He had pipes strapped to a rack and a number of shovels and other tools cluttered in the back. He said hello and gave me a brief introduction of what services he provided. The tiling that I have done in the past was fairly simple, and from what Mr. Taylor was saying, there were a few things that I was doing wrong.

He explained that tiling involves burying a system of clay tile below the surface of a field that allows water to be collected and drained off the field underground rather than run off the surface. He went into detail about how the water that collected on the surface increased the level of salt in the soil. I didn't get many of the details, but I could tell that he was much more than a ditch-digger and he knew what he was talking about. We went in his truck to the area in the field where we had the problem and he sketched out a diagram on his clipboard. He spent a good while looking over the land and near the road, I imagine, to see where the water would drain.

We headed back to the house, went into the kitchen and sat down at the kitchen table for a glass of lemonade and Mr. Taylor wrote up an estimate.

Mr. Taylor broke the silence when he completed scratching out the estimate. "Andy, I'm going to give you an estimate for $325. However, I wrote in there that if we run into rock or have unforeseen trouble, the cost will increase and from that point it would be time and material. Of course we will inform you of any problems, and we won't do anything without your okay."

I looked it over and it seemed okay to me. Mabel looked over my shoulder and we made eye contact and she seemed pleased with the estimate. I signed the paper and he gave me the carbon copy. We agreed to a date of 15 October and he went on his way.

After seeing Mr. Taylor off, I noticed the sky getting darker. Looks like my little weather forecaster was right again. I picked up a few tools that I had sitting out on a cart in the barnyard and headed to the old garage to store them away out of the rain. There was Alf under the workbench.

"You were right again old boy. Let's get inside before it starts coming down," I said as I slapped my thigh. Alf followed me in through the pantry door. We just got inside when the rain drops started falling.

(17 Jul 45) "My hollyhocks are blooming Andy, look it there," Mabel exclaimed full of joy as she looked out the back entrance this morning.

"Yes, I noticed them yesterday starting to open up," I replied looking over her shoulder at the beautiful lavender and pink flowers.

"The girls will be so happy when they see them," she spoke of Nancy, Esther, and Joyce getting ready to make their floating dolls. Mabel loved her hollyhocks and planted them near the horse tank at the back of the barnyard. The flowers made such a beautiful backdrop. She also had planted a few in different places around the yard. They never failed to return each year. When they bloomed, it was a sign we were well into summer – the best time of the year – all the crops are in and thriving.

The girls would make dolls out of the hollyhocks and float them in the horse tank. One flower in full bloom would become the skirt, and a bud not quite in full bloom would be the top of the doll. They just hooked them together and spent hours floating them around on the water. What a way to keep cool. If the dolls drifted too far away they would have to get a stick and pull them in.

While looking at the horse tank and thinking of the floating hollyhocks, I realized that I should put out a salt block for the cattle. During the summer, I keep a salt block for the cattle mounted on a wooden structure. This helps the cattle deal with the heat. The cows would lick it from inside their fenced-in area. We would eat salt pills on really hot days in the fields. My Dad would warn us that if we are sweating a lot in the fields, we should take salt tablets. I would notice that if I didn't take the salt tablets I would get really tired or get a headache. When the girls were playing they would get the urge to lick the salt block. Yee gads! I thought it was the strangest thing I ever saw. It certainly wouldn't hurt them I don't think, but Mabel tried to discourage it. There had to have been flies, ants, and whatnot crawling on it.

Darlene Moves Home – Leaves Seneca Shipyard

(18 Jul 45) Darlene moved back home today after living in Seneca for quite awhile now. She had called home two nights ago to tell us the news. We had known for some time that the Prairie shipyard had completed building ships for the war effort over a month ago.

"Your room is ready," we told her. Mabel and I were tickled to have her home again. George and I headed up towards Seneca in the grain truck to help clear out her apartment and haul all of her stuff home. She had some furniture, clothes, record player, records, books, many boxes, and other odds and ends. By the time we got everything packed up it was 10:30 pm. We were all pretty pooped after we unloaded everything in the house.

"I didn't realize how many things I have acquired," Darlene said looking with astonishment at all of her belongings stacked up in the living room and in her room upstairs.

"We'll get you all settled in," I said smiling and gave her a hug, "welcome home."

Albert Durdan Home from the Army

(19 Jul 45) Decided after dinner that it would be a good time to dig up some of the new potatoes in the garden. We planted potatoes in March, and by mid-summer the new potatoes are ready for picking. They take anywhere from 3 to 4 months to mature in the ground. I use a pitchfork to bring them to the surface, being careful not to damage any. I picked about two bushels and left the rest for later. I will be able to dig

146

potatoes off and on for the next month or so. In the fall, we can harvest the late potatoes for storage in the basement through the winter.

I gathered about ten potatoes in the front of my shirt and headed inside to find Gladys in the kitchen cleaning up after dinner.

"What do you say we have some fresh potato chips tonight?" I said to Gladys.

"I just cleaned up Dad!" Gladys replied.

Gladys knew how much I enjoyed her potato chips. It was one of my favorite treats, and Gladys made them extra special.

"Couldn't you do it for dear old Dad?" I begged.

"Okay, let me just do a few things upstairs and I will start peeling in a bit. Maybe I can get Nancy to help."

Just after Gladys walked upstairs the phone rang, and it was for us.

"Hello".

"Andy? Guess who this is?" A familiar voice came across the line. It sounded like Albert.

"Al?" My brother in the Army.

"Yep, how'd you guess."

"Where are you? Are you overseas?" I was very confused because I had not talked to Albert in a good while.

"I'm at Dad's. I got home about an hour ago. Dad picked me up in Streator at the train station." Silence. "Are you there Andy?"

"Yeah, yeah, I'm here. I just can't believe it. Well that's wonderful," I was so happy, almost in tears and I continued, "so are you all in one piece?"

"Sound as a pound, as they say. It's been a long time since I've been home," Albert said and continued, "it sure feels good to be here. We have lots of catching up to do. Everything looks wonderful. The corn looks great, and Dad looks good too." Albert was just bursting with joy over the phone. I couldn't imagine what it must feel like to come back after being gone nearly three and a half years.

"Why don't I get everybody together and head over there," I suggested.

"Good. We'll be here. Say hello to Mabel and the rest of the family. The last time I saw all of you is when your youngest was barely talking."

"Joyce is six now and growing like a weed. Wait until you see how tall Nancy has gotten. And Esther has been going to the country school a while now." Al was laughing into the phone as I was talking.

"Well I'll be. Well, get on over here so I can get a look at you. See you soon," Al said as he signed off.

"Okay, see you soon," I replied and hung up.

Mabel came up from the basement unaware of who I had just gotten off the phone with.

"Well, that was Albert calling from Dad's. He's home from the Army," I said.

Mabel was as astonished as I was initially

"You mean home for good?" Mabel asked – she seemed flabbergasted.

"Well, I don't know if he is home for good, but he's at Dad's right now - that was him on the phone," I said gathering my thoughts and continued, "I never thought to ask him if he is home for good. I only assumed that he has been discharged. I'll be sure to ask him. Let's get everybody together and get over to Dad's."

Gladys walked into the room and stopped in her tracks as she saw the joy in her Mother's face.

"Cancel the potatoes," I said as I reached out to hug Mabel, "better yet, let's sack them up and take them over to your Grandpa's to see your Uncle Albert. He's home from the Army!"

After a bit of silence, Gladys said, "He's home from overseas, for good?"

"We believe so," I replied. Like Mother, like Daughter I thought.

So, we eventually got everyone loaded up in the car, along with the sack of potatoes to fry at Dad's. I wondered how long it had been since Albert had homemade potato chips. My mind was racing all the way to Dad's place.

We pulled up and jumped out of the car. Albert came out in his uniform. He looked taller and thinner than I had remembered him. We first gave each other a firm handshake, then a hug. I was fighting back tears, and so was he. Albert then hugged Mabel, then Gladys, and looked down at the little girls.

"Hi Nancy. Hi Esther – do you remember me?" Albert said to Esther as he lightly grabbed her earlobe.

"Hi, Uncle Albert," Nancy said, "I remember you. We listen to the radio all the time and we pray that you are okay." Esther looked up at her Uncle. I'm pretty sure Esther remembered him – but she didn't say anything. But Joyce certainly did not recognize her Uncle, as she was just a little tyke.

"And there is the little one," Albert said as he looked at Joyce who was hiding behind Nancy, being bashful. "Well, let's go inside," Albert continued, "Dad, Irene and the neighbors are here and are looking over some mementos I brought home."

We all went inside and talked for hours. Gladys made numerous bowls of fresh potato chips. Albert told us of his service, and we told him of how things had changed back home. One by one all of the brothers and sisters and their families arrived. We were happy to confirm that Albert was officially discharged from the Army and home to stay.

School Board Meeting

(20 Jul 45) After lunch, I went back to the field for a very short time, as I had a school meeting at three pm at the Union School, which was two miles north of us, at the intersection of our road and the Grand Ridge road. For some time now, I have been maintaining the property around the country school, and also making small repairs to the school from time-to-time. The superintendent of the school district had commented on how much he appreciated my help in maintaining the school and had asked if I would like to serve on the board of directors. When he called me at the end of last week and asked me to attend the board meeting, I had a gut feeling that he was going to officially offer me a position on the board. The district included several small schools in the township. Each school had a member serving on the Board of Directors, and I would be the person officially representing our little country school. Our little school had only seven students attending, and the Union school had around fourteen students. There was talk of someday combining the two schools into one, considering they were so close together.

I arrived at Union School and waited in the parking lot only a few minutes when the superintendent, Fred Johnson, pulled up and greeted me.

"Hi Andy. Thanks for coming out," he said. Fred was a big man, very happy and friendly.

"My pleasure, Mr. Johnson," I didn't want to assume we were on a first name basis.

"Oh, please call me Fred. I want to ask you to be a member of our board, and help us make decisions for the district, and more importantly, for our little country school that you take such good care of." Fred didn't want to beat around the bush.

"I'd be delighted, Fred. I'm not sure what I would have to do other than what I'm already doing. I have a pretty good handle on the standard chores, such as mowing, keeping the coal stocked up, and general upkeep as needed."

"You have done a great job, Andy, and I appreciate it. Well, the whole board appreciates it, and we hope that you can join the board and help us in a bigger way." He was very enthusiastic, was a real good leader, and I couldn't think of any reason why I wouldn't want to help the school district more than I am at the present time.

"Well, you know I have two daughters attending the country school. I want to make sure that things are kept up so the teachers don't have to worry about anything but teaching the kids."

"Well, I'm sure that the teachers would be happy to hear you say that, and that is exactly why we want you on the board. Okay then, Andy, why don't we go inside and get started." Fred shook my hand again and gave me another smile.

The meeting inside was very business-like. The board members talked about the last meeting, and new business. A majority of the time was spent on deciding which teachers should be retained, hired, or let go. All the members seemed very happy with the teachers in the district. Everyone on the board spoke very positive about the teacher at our country school, Miss Kates. The board voted unanimously that she should be retained. Nancy and Esther loved Miss Kates, and she truly enjoyed teaching at our little school. She only lived two miles away and she felt it was convenient for her. There was discussion of one teacher who was leaving the district and would have to be replaced. I didn't say a whole lot at my first meeting as a board member, but voted on a number of issues. I'm sure that I would have more to say during future meetings. The superintendent handed out a checklist on how to prepare for the start of the upcoming school year.

After the meeting the board members sat and talked over coffee. I knew everyone there pretty well, so I felt very comfortable. I felt both excited and nervous about being on the board, especially since I only managed to make it through the seventh grade. I wanted my kids to finish their schooling and get a good education. On the way home I started thinking "What have I gotten myself into?" But then I realized that I have been doing the work for a few years, and the only thing that has changed is I am being recognized as an official board member. Sitting at the meeting, and now having an official checklist, made it seem that much more important. I figured that it would not take up a whole lot of my time, as most of the teachers were organized by assigning the students small tasks to help keep up with the building, such as sweeping the floors, dusting erasures, and cleaning the chalk board. Sometimes the teacher would stoke up the furnace in the wintertime, and some of the time she would ask one of the bigger boys to do it. The teacher would go directly to the superintendent for books and school supplies. They did a whole lot more than they were expected to do.

The first item on my checklist would be to meet Miss Kates at the schoolhouse and discuss what had to be done to the building for the upcoming year. Sometimes the windows would have to be mended, and the floor would have to be cleaned. I decided to stop by the school on the way home to look it over prior to my meeting with Miss Kates. I pulled my little notepad out of my pocket and jotted down a few items that needed repair.

The school is a pretty good-sized building with a front door and a fire exit door at the back. There are three very tall windows on each side. As you came in the front door there is a cloakroom. Like most of the older country schools in the county, there is no indoor plumbing – still use an outhouse. Along one wall there is a big white table with edges, and it is filled with sand - for the little kids. A little bird told me that the girls sometimes go down to the school when the school is not in session, push up a window from the outside, and somehow manage to get inside to play in the sand. All along the front wall there are chalk boards and above that there are pictures of George Washington and Abraham Lincoln. The teacher's desk is also at the front of the room with a big school bell sitting in one corner. There are three rows of desks of various sizes in the center of the room. It always smells of chalk dust, new crayons and white library paste. At any given time, there are probably ten to twelve kids attending.

Mabel was at one time a teacher after graduating from Northern Illinois State Teacher's College in DeKalb. She earned her certificate after successfully completing the teacher's program in 1919. She was hired by the LaSalle County School District 188 shortly after receiving her certificate, and taught at Diehl School of Farm Ridge Township a short time before we got married in 1922. I am sure that Mabel will help by giving me some direction on how and why things should be done at the schoolhouse. Her training has also been invaluable to our children over the years.

When Nancy and Esther first started they were the only girls, and of course they got teased terribly. I am sure the teacher watched over them pretty close. Sometimes the girls would come home with all their little complaints like "the boys are teasing us", or "Billy pushed me on the swing really high, the bell rang, and I couldn't stop the swing because my feet couldn't touch the ground." One thing that I did not like was the boys throw the hedge balls at the girls.

Hedge Balls

The hedgerows produce hedge balls in later summer – early fall. The hedge balls are round, green, with a bumpy, pitted surface. They range in size from that of a hardball or as large as a softball; depending on how much rain we got over the summer. The more rain, the larger the hedge balls would become. Regardless of size, they are very hard and drop to the ground like fruit after they mature. People use them in their basements to keep spiders and bugs out, the spiders do not like the aroma the hedge balls give off. The more common use found for hedge balls: the mischievous country boys pick them up on the way home from school and pack snow around them. The hedge balls are transformed into a very hard snowball, and those monster boys would throw them at the girls. Sometimes, when the girls got home from school, they would be crying, running to me and wanting me to do something about it. I would not retaliate in order to keep peace in the neighborhood, but I made a mental note to talk to the boy's fathers the next time I saw them.

(21 Jul 45) By the third week in July, we had used the binder to cut and shock about 75% of my oats crop. Not only did we get our oats done, but we also completed Bill Koetz's oat crop as well as the crop for Hanusik, Long, Connors, and Ray Bedeker. This was our threshing gang. Linc was not part of our gang, but part of another group that lived north and east of us.

Bill, Ray, and I were each harvesting a portion of our oats crop using the windrower and combine. I completed windrowing a section across the road and a larger field next to Rinker's place. This is a new method of harvesting where the windrower lays the oats in a long row ready for the combine to come along and separate the straw from the oats. This saves us the hassle of shocking the oats.

In the evening, I tinked around with the combine to get it ready to go once the cut oats dry in the field. I took a ride to Missel's to get some repair parts for the combine.

(27 Jul 45) Ran the combine all morning picking up the oats in the

field across the road, and started in the field by Rinker's place. Finished hauling three loads when the cut out bearing somehow got damaged. Ran to Missell's to pick up the part. Spent a better part of the afternoon getting the combine fixed and running again.

Got back out to the field near Rinker's, got done with one load and ran out of gas. I guess it just wasn't my day. Decided to take a little break to give me time to cool down as I was getting frustrated.

Able to gas up the tractor and get going again after supper. It was smooth sailing the rest of the evening. I was able to complete three more loads before nightfall.

(28 Jul 45) Tonight we held an 18th birthday party for Gladys. Mabel invited everybody over for lunch. She made a big pot of barbecue for sandwiches. Everyone brought a dish to share. My brother John and Anna, brother Steve and Edna, and brother George and Mildred and all of the cousins were all there to celebrate. All the kids played outside in the yard. It was very hot today – into the 90's. Gladys made sure that Dick and his parents were there for the celebration. Gladys looked so beautiful and happy to be celebrating her birthday with so many family members. It turned into an all-day event, with many of us ending up playing euchre past midnight. We didn't get to bed until past one am.

AUGUST

The first few days of August had been particularly hot - not a trace of a breeze to cool the body down. August is typically one of the busiest months of the year. Our threshing gang will spend many days together over the next three to four weeks. The heat is somewhat expected this time of year. The humidity would tend to bring up heavy rains, which we were glad to see to provide some needed relief. Everyone stayed inside most of the time during the day to keep cool - unless there was work that had to be done. Even the animals felt the heat. They would find shade and would remain stark still. They ate less, drank more water, and their saliva would drool from their mouth.

(1 Aug 45) I started the day repairing and replacing shingles that had come loose on the north side of the old garage. Now that the summer rains were in full swing, I figured it would be best to get them replaced now. After strapping on my tool belt, I inserted my tack hammer and filled the pouch with nails. I got the big ladder out and pulled some spare shingles out of a box where I stored them in the garage. I was happy to see that it was pretty shady on that side of the garage.

I was only working 10 or 15 minutes when I noticed the sky was starting to get very dark in the west. The breeze I felt kept getting stronger, with occasional strong gusts, and I thought it would be best to get off the ladder. I could see some leaves flying through the air and other debris picking up and blowing around. The barn side door was opening and banging shut and Alfie starting barking and howling. As I lowered the ladder to the ground, the tree branches and power lines were swaying and whipping around. That was all the evidence I needed to know that this was not a normal occurrence.

Not long after my realization that a pretty bad storm was coming Mabel stepped out the back door and yelled above the wind.

"Andy, you better come in, there is a storm headed our way."

I ran towards her and she held the door for me to come inside. Everyone was pretty scared. The wind must be around 40 mph, with gusts up to 50, I thought.

"Everything will be fine, it will blow over in no time," I said trying to stay calm as not to startle everyone and continued, " I'm going outside just long enough to see if I can get the cows into the barn. Just remain calm, okay."

The cows and horses did strange things in bad weather and I did not want them outside if I could help it. The horses were already inside.

It had started to rain and the wind was vicious carrying the rain sideways. It was a short way to the barn and the cows were all huddled by the back sliding doors. After opening the sliding door they wasted no time getting inside.

I then searched for something to provide cover on my way back to the house. Tucked under a support beam I found a good-sized piece of plastic that was used to cover my woodpile in the winter and put it over my head and held it tight. The wind was relentless and the rain was pelting the plastic as I made my way back to the house. Mabel seemed a little upset as I entered the house. She looked out one window, and then the next.

"Do you think there is a tornado coming?" Mabel said worriedly.

"We better get ready to go down in the cellar if it gets any worse," I replied joining Mabel gazing out of the windows for signs of a twister.

Just about then the hail started coming down. Many times in the past, this meant a tornado was close by.

"Where are the girls?" I asked.

"They are behind the couch hiding."

"Well, let's get everybody down in the cellar until it blows over."

The girls heard us talking about going downstairs. They ran towards the basement steps first, ahead of Mabel. I looked over towards the back door entry and Alfie looked at me as if to say "Me too, Andy?"

"Come on Alf, let's go boy - down the cellar," I beckoned my friend. He bolted for the cellar and I followed him down.

The birds were awfully quiet. Mabel started straightening things up, which probably helped to calm her nerves.

"Look at these cobwebs, jeepers crow," she said.

"Leave it to you to clean during a tornado," I said jokingly.

After what seemed like a very long time, it started to let up a little. I found some old magazines in a box and thumbed through them. Nancy found a deck of cards and her and Esther played rummy. After the wind died down we all went back upstairs, and Alf and I went outside to survey the damage. We did need the rain, I thought, but certainly not all this wind. There were many branches down in the orchard and some by the old garage. The cleanup would take awhile. Thank God that none of the branches hit any buildings, and the power lines were still up. I could only hope that the crops were not wind blown too badly.

Start Threshing

(3 Aug 45) The day had come to start threshing the oats that we had harvested during the month of July. Started out for Connors' place at around 7:30 am. We had planned to meet there by 8:00 am. Bill's threshing machine had been delivered there the day before and set near the barn ready to go. I had stopped to see Bill yesterday to make sure that everything would be all set for us to start today.

Bill and Long got there before me, and Elmer Kates, Hanusik, and Ray Bedeker showed up shortly after I did. We sat around drinking coffee and shooting the breeze for a little while before getting started. Bill got us motivated to start working by cranking up the threshing machine. There were a number of shocks in the hayrack ready to be fed into the threshing machine.

By noon, we had filled the length of the loft of Connors' barn with straw. While Bill kept busy feeding coal to the thresher, Long, Ray and his son Ron, and myself were feeding the shock bundles into the hopper. Connors, Hanusik, and Elmer fetched the shocks from the field and brought them to the barn in the hayrack. We worked right through lunch. Carrie Koetz brought out an assortment of drinks, a picnic basket full of chicken salad sandwiches, potato salad and served the whole crew and handed them out to each of us.

With the temperature in the 90s, we were all tuckered out by around 4 pm. Carrie had a tub of cold beers waiting for us under a shade tree.

"Well, you must have taken good care of that thresher, Bill," Long pointed out, "because she was running like a sewing machine today."

"Let's just hope it stays that way," Bill replied, "we don't want to put a jinx on her."

I headed home around 5 pm for supper and to clean up in time for the Grand Ridge Free Show. Saw Connors and Ray there and shot the breeze with them after the show.

(4 Aug 45) We spent all morning at Connors' place and finished with his oats crop by lunchtime. I helped Bill prepare the thresher to be hauled over to Long's place. A few of the guys headed over to Long's in advance to start hauling the shocks to the barn. We got the thresher to Long's by 2:30 pm and started operations shortly thereafter. Virgil, Long's son, strolled out of the house to help – he didn't appear to anxious to work with us, but he did. I don't think he is too keen on

farming. I went to the truck and pulled a John Deere hat out from behind the seat and handed it to Virgil to cover up from the hot sun. It was smooth going and we were able to get five loads done before quitting time.

Mabel met me at the door to inform me of our evening plans.

"Andy, please clean up and get ready," she said with a slight panic in her voice. I could tell that she had big plans and we were behind schedule already for the evening, "We are going into Grand Ridge for dinner, then we are going to drop the kids off at Anna's to spend the night," she took a short breath and continued, "Gladys is going to meet us in Grand Ridge. Ma is going to stay with the kids, and Gladys, Anna, and I are going to Chicago."

I figured that this plan was already in motion, so I simply nodded my head and cleaned up, changed clothes, and we were on the road. It was a fun evening, everyone in a good mood. After Anna, Mabel and Gladys left, I spent some time talking to Ma before I left for home.

(5 Aug 45) Woke up to a quiet house – just me and Alf. It was drizzling most of the morning. Didn't go to church today, mostly due to laziness. Went into Ransom in the afternoon to see a ballgame. Ransom needed a player, so I got to play a game. They put me in right field. I caught a few and couldn't quite catch up to a few balls that came out my way. I was used to playing first base on our team.

Started pouring down rain around chore time. Headed to Marseilles around 8 pm to pick up Mabel, Gladys, and the girls. Everyone was pretty much tuckered out on the ride home. Everyone except Gladys fell asleep.

(6 Aug 45) Received a call from Ray Bedeker first thing and he informed me that the threshing gang would not meet today due to the hard rain.

"I think it's best to give the grain a day to dry, okay Andy?" Ray suggested.

"I was waiting for your call, Ray. See you Tuesday," I said agreeing to his plan. You would be asking for trouble trying to thresh when the grain is wet. I was happy in a way, because the refrigerator was acting up, and in need of repair.

"It's not cooling again, Andy," Mabel had said during breakfast in frustration. I removed the part that I suspected was giving me the problem and took it into town for a replacement. I spent most of the morning on the repair, but felt confident that I had found the problem.

"Give it some time to cool down," I said to Mabel, "about two or three hours and you should feel a difference."

"I think it's working," Mabel said while sticking her hand inside the ice box. She was giving me assurance that my work was not in vain.

Atomic Bomb Dropped on Hiroshima

With great alarm, Gabriel Heater reported that President Truman released a statement today an atomic bomb, possessing more power than twenty thousand tons of TNT, had been dropped on Japan. This one bomb had a destructive force equal to that of 2000 US Air Force bomber planes filled to the gills. The president stated that we have entered the age of atomic energy, and that 16 hours earlier an American plane had dropped the bomb on the Japanese city of Hiroshima, an important army center. It was the president's hope that the Japanese would unconditionally surrender. If they did not, we would continue to drop these horrible bombs on Japan until we thoroughly eliminated the Japanese ability to continue the war. These bombs would hopefully bring an end to the war and eliminate the need to send our troops to Japan and perhaps lose hundreds of thousands of men. Apparently this huge bomb has been under development for years under complete secrecy.

"What do you make of that?" I asked Mabel.

"About what?" she replied.

"Did you hear what Gabriel Heater just reported about the new bomb? He said that it had the power of 2000 bomber planes. Can you imagine that?"

"I'm not sure what to think about it. I'm getting so worried about this war. I can't tell you how happy I am that Albert is home."

"Well it sounds like we're really letting them have it."

Darlene Moves to Joliet for New Job

(8 Aug 45) Darlene hadn't been home three weeks when she had taken a job in Joliet. One of her close friends, Mary, from the shipyard had taken a job with a construction company. Mary had gotten the job by responding to flyers handed out at the Seneca Shipyard when news had spread of the Navy contracts ending there. Since the girls had gained such good experience at the shipyard, construction firms were seeking out these skilled workers for construction jobs. Mary was able to get her

an interview. Apparently the boss was very impressed with Darlene as she was hired on the spot.

As the job was only temporary, perhaps two or three months, Darlene decided to take only what she needed with her to Joliet. Mary agreed to come and pick her up and they could go together. It wasn't a whole lot further than Seneca. She would be able to come home on the weekends, and Mabel and Gladys promised to visit her often.

(9 Aug 45) We started threshing at Koetz's place today. Bill's son, Gerald, was there to help. We finished Long's yesterday. All-in-all things were going very well for the threshing gang. We were getting a lot of rain, but that didn't bother us too much as the rainy days gave us time to rest up.

Atomic Bomb Dropped on Nagasaki

The evening radio report included news of another atomic bomb dropped on Japan. This time the bomb was dropped on the city of Nagasaki. The promise by President Truman that the US would continue to drop these bombs until Japan surrenders is being kept. There is no telling how many Japanese lives were lost from this atomic bomb and the atomic bomb dropped on Hiroshima just three days ago. This bomb was again dropped by a B-29 Bomber.

"Well, looks like we hit them with one of the super bombs again," I said to Mabel, who was listening from the kitchen.

"How they ever make those bombs is beyond me," was her reply, "it is simply astounding, isn't it?"

"I wonder how many more we have of those bombs? I don't think the Japanese want to find out. Maybe we won't have to fight on the Japanese mainland after all."

(11 Aug 45) Woke up this morning to still more rain. It rained all day yesterday, and it looked like today was going to be more of the same. After lunch I was able to cut a few weeds around the place, before it started raining again. I tinkered in the old garage for a while.

Afternoon with Milt and Mary Inks

Around two-thirty I heard a car pull up in the driveway and was pleased to see it was Milt and Mary.

"Hi Andy, thought you'd be around and not in the fields with all of this rain, so decided to stop for a short visit," called Milt from the open car window.

"Well, it sure is nice to see you both," I said to them as they were getting out of their big shiny Oldsmobile. Milt married my sister Mary, the eldest girl in the Peter Durdan family. They live in Lansing, Michigan, where Milt works for the GMC Oldsmobile automobile company. We knew they were in the area as they always come the same time every year.

"She's a real beauty Milt," I said admiringly.

"This one's a 1940 Olds 78 Model. It's got a Hydramatic Drive transmission." Milt paused waiting to see if I knew what he meant, but I didn't. He continued, "It's automatic. No need to shift gears." He pointed to the lever on the steering column. "That lever puts her in gear and away you go."

"Well, sure I've heard of the new transmissions," I replied scratching my head, "how do you like it?"

"I really like it, and I don't think I want to go back to a standard. When this war is over, I'm going get a new one. They haven't made any cars since 1942, did you know that Andy?" Milt replied as he rubbed the fender of his car.

"Yes, you had mentioned that before. I guess it is all for the war now."

"Yep," said Milt, "you wouldn't believe the things the automakers are building for the war effort. It's out of this world. We have built tanks, military trucks, aircraft engines, you name it and we're building it. Hopefully this war will be over soon."

We all went inside where Mabel had been doing some sewing. Esther and Joyce took a break from playing with their paper dolls, came downstairs and said hello. They gave their Aunt and Uncle a hug, and then kind of shied away. They knew Uncle Milt was overly generous with his hugs and kisses, and they did not grasp that idea too well.

Mary stated they had arrived a couple of days ago and were staying at my Dad's place. Milt and I proceeded to walk around the farm a bit, while Mabel and Mary talked and started preparing a little snack. Mabel always worried about food preparation when they came, so she kept a five pound canned ham in the refrigerator specifically for this occasion.

We had a nice visit and soon they were off, confident we would see them again before they left for home, most likely at Dad's or at one of my brothers for a get-together.

My Sisters

It's ironic my other sisters live in the area, and I feel that I talk more to Mary than any of them, and she lives so far away. I see them often enough, usually at family gatherings, but very seldom do I ever have the opportunity to talk to one of them at length. Usually at gatherings the men sit and talk in the basement or the garage, while the women prepare food or have tea in the sitting room and chat amongst themselves.

Clara married Dennis Kehoe in 1930, and lives on the other side of Blackstone, about 15 miles as the crow files. She and Anna look more alike out of all the sisters. Anna is more serious minded, but her husband, Walt, is a fun-loving guy that laughs enough to make up for Anna's shortcomings. She is so supportive, and helps Walt a lot with the farm chores. Anna and Walt were married in 1925.

Margaret is always kidding around - she has a really good sense of humor. She likes to tease her husband, Chuck. The last time we went to their house, Chuck was saying that he was hungry. I asked Margaret what she was planning for supper. She responded jokingly "I occasionally feed my husband chicken bones." Margaret and Chuck were married in 1934.

Irene is the youngest in the family. She and Michael Vercimak were married just last year. Michael is serving in the US Army in the European theatre. He entered the military March 28, 1941. While they were engaged, Michael came home on furlough and asked Irene if she would marry him while he was home – and she said yes. They surely didn't have much time to plan the wedding. They were married at St. Stephens Church on Tuesday, January 18th 1944 and Michael returned on the following Saturday. Our Darlene served as Maid of Honor and my brother Edward as Best Man. Michael was very proud to be serving his country and wore his Army uniform at the wedding. Everybody pitched in to help with food and preparations. You would think someone else could have milked the cows for her the morning of the wedding, but she insisted on doing her chores even on that special day.

Trading Eggs at Kollar's Grocery Store

It was not long after Milt and Mary left that we made preparations to go to Streator to trade our eggs. Mabel and the kids wanted to go to the show. Before we left we had Nancy and Esther gather up all of the eggs that we had collected the past week so we could take them to the market for trade. The eggs had to be gathered every day. This daily responsibility belonged to Nancy and Esther. They each would retrieve a wire basket from the basement and head to the chicken coup to gather the eggs, and then take them downstairs to be stored where it is cool. They did not like this job because they hated the feeling of lice crawling up their arms. The chickens would shed lice in their nests.

Each egg was put under a strong light, or "candled" as it is called, to determine if the eggs are stale or infertile. I first taught Nancy how to do this and she in turn taught Esther. Once the eggs are candled, they are packed in a crate. The crate held five-dozen eggs packed in layers, with a dozen per layer separated by a piece of cardboard. The cardboard has egg-shaped grooves to protect the eggs during storage and transport. The girls came out of the basement each carrying two crates by the handle at the top. They were both proud of their task and made sure they handled the precious cargo with extreme care.

We headed straight to Kollar's Grocery Store on Main Street in Streator. Two Kollar brothers, Albert and Edward, ran the store. These two gentlemen were Sully's Uncles and were so easy to do business with. The two families ran the store together, and I was very impressed at how well it was managed.

I drove the family car behind the store to a parking space where we could easily unload our eggs, climb the cement steps, and enter the back of the store where there was a big room where refrigerators and freezers were kept. There were also many boxes of fresh fruits and vegetables, some of which were probably from a local farmer. The front section of the store where the customers could enter from Main Street and select their merchandise was separated from the back of the store by large swinging double doors. The store always had a fresh meat smell to it. In the summer months they would have produce in front of the store on the sidewalk in bushel baskets. Customers would buy bushels of peaches, apples and pears to can, as well as sweet corn, cucumbers, and other vegetables. Often times if we had a large crop of apples, pears, or peaches we would bring them in for trade with the Kollars. As it was getting close to six o'clock closing time, Albert and Edward were in the process of putting everything back inside the store and starting to close up shop.

Mabel was moving extra fast in order to get all of her shopping in before closing. We didn't buy perishable items, as when Mabel was done selecting what we needed, we headed towards the movie theatre, and wouldn't be going home for a while.

Along the south wall of the store were the meat coolers with a walk-in area behind. The glass was always very clean and you could see all of the fresh meat. The Kollar's made sausage and lunchmeats in the store. Their specialty is headcheese made out of pork. They have a meat slicer and huge butcher block and sharp knives to cut up special orders. Sawdust is spread on the floor to absorb the blood and moisture from the meats and to prevent the Butchers from slipping. Along the north wall there are shelves with canned goods, cereals, breads and other staples.

Albert approached to do the business at hand. Both he and Edward always wore long white aprons, and not very clean.

"Just eggs tonight Andy?" Albert asked.

"That's right Al, four crates. The girls set them in the back," I gestured towards the large swinging doors. He started preparing our invoice. "I think this war will be over soon, with the big bombs being dropped on the Japs and all."

"I sure hope so," Al replied while using his adding machine, "I think we have had just about enough of this war. I think you're right Andy, those were amazing bombs they dropped. We need to show them Japs that we mean business, don't we?" He gestured by making a fist while he added up our cost for the grocery items. He then deducted what was owed for our eggs.

"We certainly do mean business," I agreed, "those bombs will show them."

The girls were amazed by the adding machine, and would mimic the Kollars when they played store in the corncrib. They would set up a grocery store complete with counter, adding machine, empty cereal boxes and cans. They would take turns being the owner of the grocery store and the customer.

Mabel brought the last few items to the counter and when all of the adding and subtracting was done, we owed Al six dollars and fifteen cents. We paid him in cash and I headed out the back of the store with our goods to store in the trunk, while Mabel and the girls headed out the front door to get in a little shopping before the movie started.

Saturday Evening in Streator

I met up with Mabel and the girls at the five and dime store. They each got fifty cents to buy what candy they wanted for the movie. It was always funny to see what they would pick out with their small fortune. Sometimes they would have their own money tied in the corner of a handkerchief. Of course they would trade with each other as we walked down the sidewalk. The movie theatre was close by, and I left them off there after paying for their tickets and headed for Shab's Tavern. Sometimes I went to the movies with them, but tonight I was more in the mood for cards, and the movie playing was a comedy I didn't think I would care for.

By ten in the evening we were all pretty tuckered out but had a very nice evening in town. I played cards with George and Rudy and a few others I play with often. Mabel and the girls enjoyed their movie and we headed home. Not five minutes into the drive and the girls were asleep and Mabel was nodding off also. The moon was shining bright through the breaking clouds. Looks like the rain was going to stop and hopefully we would have a good day tomorrow.

(13 Aug 45) It was nice and dry this morning with the sun shining. The threshing gang met at Bill's place at 10 am. We got a good start and worked hard all day, finishing Bill's place by 7:30 pm.

"Whataya say we wait until the morning to move everything over to your place, Andy?" Bill suggested.

"Okay Bill, we're all pretty tuckered out," I replied, "I'll be here at eight."

Bill nodded in agreement.

Mabel informed me when I got home that the family car would not start.

"Did it turn over at all, Mabel?" I asked.

"Not really, no," she replied, "all I hear is 'click, click' when I turn the key." She used her hand, turning it to show me the motion she used to attempt to start the car.

"Sounds like the starter again," I said angrily, "that's the third starter this year if that's the case."

"Andy, I don't need the car tomorrow for anything. Mary offered to drive me if I needed to get anywhere."

"Okay, that would help. We're starting threshing here first thing tomorrow. I'll try to get into town tomorrow afternoon."

I went out to the garage and tried to start the car. I knew from past experience that it was no doubt the starter. It took me no more than 10 minutes to take it out and set it in the truck to take into town tomorrow.

Victory Over Japan Pronounced

(14 Aug 45) The six-thirty radio report was extra special tonight. President Truman pronounced victory over Japan today as Japan has

accepted unconditional surrender. Truman said that he was making arrangements for the formal signing of the peace treaty at the earliest possible moment, and the surrender would be made to General Douglas MacArthur, Supreme Allied Commander. President Truman also stated that the draft would be reduced from 80,000 men a month to 50,000, and that he hoped to release five million to five and a half million men in the next year and a half. The president's final announcement was to decree holidays for Wednesday and Thursday, 15 and 16 August.

Mabel and I could hardly contain our enjoyment as the report came to a close. We could not believe our ears. We waited so long for the war to end that we didn't quite know how to react when the word finally came. Mabel called the girls downstairs and explained to them that the Japanese had surrendered and the war was over. Mabel and the kids were dancing around the kitchen in a circle.

I joined them in their celebration, holding hands and dancing around. I started to hear the sound of guns firing in the distance. It was our neighbors firing shotguns and rifles into the air. I ran outside and heard the shots coming from all directions. I figured what the heck, I might as well join them. I ran to our closet and pulled my 12 gauge out and searched for the shells a few minutes before I could find a box. I went outside and fired off half of a box.

The next three hours were total delirium. We received phone calls from Darlene in Joliet, Milt and Mary, Linc Armstrong, and other friends and family members. Albert called and asked us to come to Dad's for a party. We accepted his offer and Mabel, I and the three little girls headed over there. We left a note for Gladys, who was in Streator with Dick, to come over to Dad's when she got home.

At Dad's we drank champagne and danced to records on the victrola. The gunfire and firecrackers could be heard in the distance. It was a very joyous evening, many of us letting off a lot of steam, totally relieved that this horrible war was over.

Gladys and Dick arrived at 9:30 pm to tell us of the celebrations going on downtown Streator.

"The streets are filled with people. They are having parades and honking their car horns. People are dancing in the streets," Gladys was so excited, as was Dick.

"Andy, you wouldn't believe it if you saw it," Dick added to Gladys' explanation of the events, "they have all of the fire engines out of the stations, blowing their horns. The bars are bringing the whiskey out into street and giving it away. It's a real sight to see."

"We couldn't get out of town," Gladys shouted over the music, "we saw your note and headed straight over."

We celebrated well past midnight. The party slowly died down and we sat around talking about what is next for our country. The kids were fast asleep in the living room. I scooped Joyce up and woke up Nancy and Esther and we headed home. As Mabel and I laid down to sleep, she laid her head on my shoulder and I put my arm around her as she fell asleep. It just then dawned on me how much effort Mabel put into supporting the war effort. From the Home Bureau, Royal Neighbors, Victory Gardens, and rationing, Mabel sacrificed a lot for our family and countrymen. Tomorrow will be a brand new start.

(15 Aug 45) Spent most of the day cleaning out the ditches along our road. Over time they would tend to get filled up with too many grass clippings, weeds and loose gravel, even sometimes garbage and papers. So every once in a while I dig them out using the Fordson.

Shoe Repair

After putting the Fordson away and cleaning up a bit, Mabel reminded me that Nancy and Esther would be going back to school soon and it was time to look at their shoes for repairing. If they were beyond repair, then we would have to put some new shoes on order. New shoes always brought about a little enthusiasm for returning to the classroom. Sears and Roebuck did not have much of a selection of children's shoes, but at 98 cents a pair they lasted a pretty long time. They would last longer if you made a few repairs here and there – which was pretty easy if you had the right tools.

I purchased my shoe repair tool kit from Sears a few years back. It came complete with bootjack, shoe pegs, nails, souls, and rubber heel and toe protectors for under three dollars. I was pretty well set up to repair shoes of just about any size. Nancy was the first one to come out to the garage with her shoes for inspection.

"Dad, can I get a new pair of shoes for school? I asked Mom and she said to ask you," Nancy said as she handed me her shoes.

"Let's take a look," I replied. I could tell she was hoping I would say that the shoes were no longer fit to wear. But I could see that her shoes were in pretty good shape. I put them on the bootjack to have a closer look.

I dreaded giving her the bad news. "These look pretty good yet. I'll tack some new souls on the bottom, and if you give them a little shoe polish, they'll look good as new."

"Okay," she said with drooped shoulders and pouting just a bit.

It only took me about five minutes to cut the leather souls to fit, tacked them on, and handed them back to Nancy.

"There. That should do it. Now go ask Mother for the shoe polish."

Nancy headed for the house with the shoes in tow and said, "Thanks, Dad," and smiled. I was able to fix Esther's and Joycie's shoes as well. However, I could not save Mabel's shoes.

"How in heaven's name did you walk in these shoes?" I asked her.

"Oh, they seemed fine to me." Mabel was not one to complain.

We put in an order to get Mother a new pair of shoes.

We went over to my Dad's in the evening to say goodbye to Milt and Mary, as they were heading back to Michigan in the morning. Steve was there, and I had been asking him to give me a hair cut. We went over to his place where he gave me a trim.

(17 Aug 45) The threshing gang had taken a couple days off due to more rain and a needed break. All the guys except for Elmer Kates, who had a family commitment, met at our farm to start there. Bill had staged the machine here a couple of days ago, so we were pretty much ready to go by 9 am. I manned the thresher today, making sure it kept running and properly shot the stock out into the barn, and the oats into the bin. Gerald worked right along side of me, but left by noon to go to Missel's to pick up parts Bill had on order for his weed cutter.

It was pretty good going most of the day. We had a bit of a problem with my hayrack. Repairs I had done to the hayrack in June slightly came undone. Ray and Bill were able to get her fixed in about an hour and we were back in business. We did not finish at our place today, but the men thought that three more hours in the morning should do the trick. Once we are done here, we will head to Ray Bedeker's place.

Olsen Family Reunion - Marseilles

(19 Aug 45) Went to church this morning in Streator alone for the nine o'clock mass. I didn't chat with anyone too long after church as I wanted to get home due to the fact today was the day for the Olsen Family Reunion in Marseilles.

I wasn't home very long and we were on our way to Marseilles, which was about a 15 to 20 minute ride to the north. Mabel brought fried chicken that she spent most of the morning cooking. She seemed happy to sit for the first time today during our short drive there. She poured her and I a cup of coffee from the thermos that she brought along, as she said that she hadn't had her first cup yet being that she was so busy. While en route, just two miles north of Grand Ridge road, I noticed some cornfields with ears a might bigger than mine. I had heard they had a good rain lately that we did not get.

"Looks like they've been getting a bit more rain here, wouldn't you say Andy?" Mabel said.

"Yeah, we'll catch up," I said, as I thought to myself that Mabel sometimes knew what I was thinking.

"Our corn looks wonderful. We will catch up in no time," she responded.

I gave Mabel a big smile and a nod. She had a way of making me feel better about things. We seldom had real dry spells, however when there was no rain, and too dry for the crops to survive, the priest on Sunday would ask the whole congregation to join in prayer for rain.

This was our chance to see Mabel's side of the family – Aunts, Uncles, Grandparents, and cousins. Illini Park was on the banks of the Illinois River. One of Mabel's nephews from Marseilles usually went out early to secure the shelter. The girls were not to go down by the river, but they surely had a good time playing with cousins their age. We took a walk down by the river, you could see the town of Marseilles just across from where we stood.

We talked about the US Navy submarines that were built at a shipyard in Wisconsin and floated down the Illinois River. Many folks met here at this very park in 1943 to watch the first submarine being sent down the river to be used in the war. The submarines sailed the same path as the LST ships from Seneca – down the Illinois to the Mississippi and onto the Gulf of Mexico. We never got to see the submarine – but I guess it was an incredible sight.

I always looked forward to playing horseshoes with Nick Schank, who I usually partnered with. We would have small wagers to make it interesting. The older kids played baseball and the women gathered together to catch up on all of the news.

Ma was 83 years old, and looked forward to the picnic. She made sure she was on time, and she was usually the first one in line for dinner. She wore her white hair short with a lot of hairpins to hold it in place, a cotton dress, cotton stockings, and little black shoes. She recognized most of the family members present; except for some of the little ones.

She would ask who the children belonged to and would give them a kiss and a hug.

Around four in the afternoon, Nick, having opened the black insulated container, was suddenly surrounded by children laughing and singing.

"I scream, you scream, we all scream for ice cream."

Inside the container, packed with dry ice, were ice cream slices. Each slice was individually wrapped and Nick made sure each child got at least one. This was traditional at the Olsen Family Reunions, and it was the highlight of the day. The kids had to eat the ice cream fast, as it was eighty degrees, a little cooler in the shade.

Not long after the ice cream, we started packing up the car to head home. We said our goodbyes to those we might not see again for another year.

That evening after we put the kids to bed, Mabel and I sat and talked about all of the goings on with the family. Mabel always seemed to have news to pass along after big events like the family reunion. After attending one of her club meetings, after a dance at the Moose, or just talking on the phone, she would proceed to tell me the latest news. I guess you might call it gossip.

"Well, I guess that Beth's planning a wedding in the fall sometime," said Mabel.

"That soon huh, what's the rush?" I replied having an idea what she meant.

"I understand she's in a family way." Which meant she was with child.

"Well, you know Mabel, the first one can come anytime, after that it takes 9 months," I joked. Mabel laughed, jumped out of her chair, waved her hands at me, and went into the kitchen to clean up a few things before heading to bed.

It was nice having a day to relax. We had been pretty busy threshing the past few weeks. We only have the Hanusik's place to complete and we will be done for the year.

After making my diary entry for the day, I joined Mabel in bed and I fell asleep the moment my head hit the pillow.

(23 Aug 45) Finished up threshing for everyone in our gang today. We finished up Ray's in one day, took a few days off, then went to Hanusik's place, the last. We had a little party over there this evening to

169

celebrate. It was a very successful harvest and we were all very relieved to be done. Tomorrow we will meet at Bill's to spend a good part of the day cleaning and greasing the thresher. We would surely discover some parts that need replacing, which we would all pitch in to purchase. All of us would now concentrate on hauling our oats into town for sale and turn our attention to the corn. Now is the time to cut the thistles, which I had been doing in my spare time over the past week already.

(25 Aug 45) When I came in from chores Mabel was gathering her overnight bag and sacks full of food including chocolate chip cookies and canned goods to take to Joliet to spend the night with Darlene.

"Andy don't forget to pick up some ground beef and steaks at the locker when you go into town," Mabel said looking over her list of things to remember. "Oh, and please ask Nancy to pull the clothes off of the line outside."

"Yes Mother," I replied, "you go ahead and get going – we have things under control here."

She was a bit flustered getting everything together, but we finally got all of her stuff gathered and loaded into the car. I gave her a peck on the cheek and she was on her way.

The little girls and I headed into Streator for the afternoon show. Afterwards, we stopped at Kollar's to trade some eggs, and then headed to the locker to get the meat that Mabel had requested. For supper, I made the girls hamburgers and Gladys made some potato chips.

(26 Aug 45) Gladys, the three little girls, and I went to 9:30 am. church in Ransom. After church we met the Durdan clan in Streator for a baseball game. We won 9-3 thanks to a six run inning capped off by a bases-clearing triple by yours truly. After the game we went to Pete's for dinner. Mabel showed up at Pete's around 7 pm. She had gotten home from Joliet earlier than planned.

"How did you know we were here?" I asked Mabel.

"Mary mentioned the other day that you guys had a ballgame today," she replied.

"How is Darlene?"

"Oh she is doing just fine. She sends her love and says she will be home next weekend for the Mendota fair."

(30 Aug 45) End of August already and it is Nancy's birthday. She

turned nine today. Mabel spent the better part of the last two weeks making her a special dress. She was being careful not to let Nancy see what she was making her.

This morning when Nancy came downstairs for breakfast Mabel had it laying out on the dining room table.

"Is that for me?" Nancy asked with excitement.

"Happy birthday, Nancy," said Mabel, "why don't you go in our room and try it on."

Nancy changed from her play clothes into her dress in lickety split. She came back into the dining room and did a couple twirls.

"I would say it fits pretty nicely," Mabel said, "what do you think, Dad?" she asked me.

"Well, I think it's perfect," I said with approval, "now don't you look beautiful in that dress."

She gave us both a big smile, we wished her a happy birthday, and each gave her a hug.

"I have to make one little correction on the hem," Mabel said studying how the dress fit Nancy, "I need to bring it up just a tad."

Nancy changed again into her play clothes and Mabel immediately set up her sewing machine on the dining room table and fixed the hem.

SEPTEMBER

With the oats harvest and threshing behind us, I would focus on making a final cut on the hay, then plow it under to prepare for corn to be planted in it's place next year. September was a relatively easy month compared to July and August. By the end of the month we would have cooler weather. As part of the plowing, I would put down tons of phosphate as fertilizer.

Mabel was busy this time of year getting the kids ready to go back to school. Nancy at nine was starting the fourth grade, Esther at 7 was starting third grade, and Joyce was now six and will be starting first grade. Mabel spent a good amount of time making new clothes for the kids and going to town for pencils, paper, erasers, paste, and whatnot for school supplies.

This year would be quite an adjustment as all of the girls would be out of the house during the day. With this being Joycie's first year, it would be somewhat difficult for Mabel. School would start just after the Labor Day holiday.

Visit to the Kollar Farm, Kangley

(1 Sep 45) After a late lunch, Mabel and I went to visit the Andrew Koller family. We had visited them a few times before. We ran into them at the Kollar's Grocery store the previous Saturday, and they had invited us out to their farm in Kangley. We were so fond of the Kollars, as they always came to our house on Christmas to bring a box of chocolates covered cherries for the girls, a real treat for them and they were thrilled. The Kollars were good people, and we were so pleased that Darlene and Sully would be getting married after his overseas duty.

No matter what time of the day you went to their farmhouse, Molly was always sitting on a stool near the stove cooking. With six boys, she spent most of her time preparing vittles. It was a momentous time for them because they had three sons in the military: Louis, Elmer, and Sully. Ray was planning to go into the Navy as soon as he was old enough, which would make it four boys serving.

Everything in her kitchen, where we sat and talked, seemed to be right at your fingertips. There was always coffee mugs on the table along with sugar, a cup full of spoons, and lunch plates. Making soup was something that went on all of the time, winter or summer, especially during the summer with all of the garden fresh vegetables available. Buff, thier oldest son was always there with grease all over his clothes and hands. He was just naturally talented repairing machinery, and he made a good living at it. He could take a motor apart no matter how many pieces, and put it back together. Buff absolutely loves to talk, just about anything that came to mind. His wife, Juanita, helped Molly a lot around the farmhouse. Andy Kollar sat and talked with us and Molly just kept right on cooking. Along with the farming, the Kollar boys had many outside jobs, including the rendering works.

We stayed about two hours and headed back to our farm to prepare for evening company. Linc, Mary, and their kids were coming over for a few games of cards and socializing.

Darlene and Gladys had arrived from Joliet by mid-afternoon. Gladys has driven to Joliet to spend some time the night before last to bring Darlene home. They both helped Mabel make supper for our guests.

(2 Sep 45) Darlene, Gladys, Nancy, Esther, and I went to 9:30 am church. We went home after church just long enough to pick up Mabel and Joyce, pack up our picnic basket and head to the Mendota Fair. We try to go every year. It is always so much fun for all of us. I enjoy watching the horse and buggy races. The kids played the carnival games and toured the barns to see the animals. The local farm merchants showed off their new tractors and equipment. The merchants hand out little souvenirs and trinkets that the girls like to collect throughout the day. We all get our fill of corn dogs, candy apples, and lemonade. By 4:00 pm, we were all pretty tired and ready to go home. It was nice to have the whole family together today.

When we got home, I gave Dad a call. I was always concerned about Dad after Mom died, and made it a point to call him quite often just to make sure he wasn't trying to do too much, and to see if he needed help. I also kept in mind that Ed, Albert, and Irene were there to keep an eye on him.

"Hi Dad," I said over the line, "are you all set for the Sandwich Fair tomorrow?"

"I suppose so," he replied, "wasn't sure if I'd be able to get away, but tomorrow seems okay to go."

Dad, slow to show any excitement, was probably as excited about going as I was. He and I went to the Sandwich Fair every year together

173

over Labor Day. Sandwich is a small farming town in DeKalb County.

"I'll pick you up in the morning."

"Okay, see you tomorrow, Andy."

Sandwich Fair with Dad

(3 Sep 45) Arrived at Dad's at around 7:45 am. Albert and Ed were just finishing up with breakfast prepared by Irene. They were heading off to the field to cut some clover seed.

"Where's Dad?" I asked Irene.

"Oh, he's getting ready," she replied, "you know how important this day is to him, he's getting his nice suit on."

Dad and I always dressed up for the fair. It has gotten less formal over the years, but Dad still dressed up real nice, as did I.

Dad came into the kitchen looking spiffy with a nice hat to go along with his suit, vest and tie.

"Well, don't you look dapper," I complimented him.

"You look nice too, son," he said, nodding in approval.

"Did you eat, Dad?" I asked.

"Sure did, I say we get going," he replied.

"Irene, you're welcome to come along," Dad asked sincerely, "it's going to be a beautiful day."

"That's fine Dad," she replied with assurance, "I have plenty here to do. Besides, who is going to feed Ed and Albert?" She giggled.

"Well, okay," Dad said to Irene, "we probably won't be home for dinner. Please ask Ed to clean and grease the plow, I meant to do that yesterday, but didn't get to it."

"Okay, Dad, I'll tell them. You and Andy have a good time and drive careful."

Sandwich was over an hour away north of us. We took the country roads up through Marseilles and jumped on Route 71 into Norway. From there we took the road north through Sheridan and into Sandwich.

There are so many interesting displays of new machinery and equipment that we wanted to look over. There were always new inventions and enhancements that Dad didn't really care for. They say you can't teach an old dog new tricks. The tractor dealers had the new John Deere and International tractors on display. Neither Dad nor I purchased new equipment due to the high cost. We relied on farm sales for most of our equipment, but it was nice to look at what was coming down the pike.

We saw many people we knew, but did not spend a lot of time

talking to them, as everyone was scurrying about trying to take in everything in just a few hours. We tried to select the best food stand for a quick bite. It was near to 7:00 pm before we headed home. It was another successful trip to the Sandwich Fair. I glanced over at Dad as we were driving home. He had a pleasant smile on his face. He caught me admiring him, and he smiled even wider. It was a special moment between us that words could not describe.

Dad always had a way of waiting for just the right time to tell a story or to pass along some good news.

"Rafel phoned yesterday," he said very calmly, "his discharge date from the Army is September 25th."

I was so relieved and happy as we had not heard from Ray in a great while. We just looked at each other - I was trying to concentrate on my driving and control my feelings.

Then Dad let out with, "Hurray! Soon they'll all be home. Your mother would be so happy. She is probably smiling down from Heaven."

(4 Sep 45) Saw the girls off to school this morning, including Joyce, who started her first day today. They all walked up the road together to the country school on our corner. Mabel stood in the yard, in her apron, watching the three of them leave. I walked over to see if she was okay.

"Well, there they go Mabel," I said. I saw a few tears forming in her eyes and put my arm around her. "Now, now Mabel. They'll be back in a few hours for lunch," I tried my best to make her feel better.

"They are growing up so fast," she replied wiping her tears away, "it's going to be quiet this morning."

It was definitely a quiet morning. Mabel seemed to be okay – she spent some time in her flower garden pulling weeds.

Spent the past two days raking clover seed from the clover crops. We did this to extract the seeds from the existing crops in order to plant it in new fields next year. I could gather about 20 to 25 bushels of clover seed during the harvest.

This afternoon I went to Dad's to help cut hay. We spent a good four hours there and cut a whole field.

"Dad, why don't we call it a day, and Pete and I will be back tomorrow or the next day and finish here," I suggested.

"I'll get the rake going tomorrow Andy," he said, "I know you got things you need to be doing. Besides Ed will give me a hand tomorrow

175

afternoon."

"Okay then. I'll give you a call."

Cut Hay – Final Cut

(5 Sep 45) Spent first part of the morning pulling the sickle bar mower out of the machine shed, which I had put away after cutting hay in June. I hitched the mower up to the John Deere and hauled it across the road to start cutting. I was able to get the entire piece across the road cut by supper time. After supper, I unhitched the mower and hitched up the side delivery rake to prepare for raking across the road tomorrow.

I called Dad to see how he was getting along. Ed and Pete had spent part of the morning and early afternoon cutting hay so they were getting along good. I was happy that Dad was getting his hay done.

Darlene's friend Mary Solon, who came for dinner, took Darlene back to Joliet around 8:00 pm. Mabel always packed Darlene up with leftover food. Although Darlene has been out on her own for some time, it still is a bit sad to see her go.

(8 Sep 45) Raked clover seed in the hay field near Rinker's. Finished up there in time to get ready for the family to go into town. We made our usual stop at Kollar's grocery to drop eggs off and stopped at the locker to pick up some meat. We went to the theatre to watch "The Bells of St. Mary's". It was an excellent show starring Bing Crosby. It was the best movie we had seen in a long time. We bought some ice cream for the ride home. The kids were asleep when we pulled into the driveway.

(12 Sep 45) Spent the better part of the past couple of days finishing up with cutting and raking the hay. Linc and Ed came over mid morning to help with the hayrack and loader to get the hay back to the barn.

"How about a beer, Andy?" Linc asked after the first couple of loads.

Without hesitation I walked over to the pump house to pull a couple of cold beers out of a tub of cold water.

"Here you go," I said.

"Got a bottle opener, Andy?" Ed asked.

"Oh, shoot, let me go get one." I had a couple of bottle openers in the old garage.

We were just about done with our beer and my Dad pulled in.

"Looks like you boys are working real hard," he said laughing.

"Well hold on now, we've been working our tail off," Linc said half-jokingly.

"How is it looking, Andy?" Dad asked, "what can I do?"

"You can be the bartender, we'll be back in just a bit," said Linc. He is always so quick witted.

Ed, Linc, and I headed back out to the field to get another load. The weather was just right for working hay. It was a little on the cool side and a slight breeze. After unloading, Dad set us up with another round, then another. We started to get a little too relaxed.

"Okay, boys, let's get back at it," Dad said, prodding us to our feet and back into the field.

We hauled two more loads before stopping again for a cold refreshment. By supper time we were able to finish the hay and finish the tub of beer. Needless to say, we were all feeling pretty good by quitting time.

With the hay cut, I would focus on plowing the fields to prepare them for next year's corn.

Swarm of Bees

(14 Sep 45) After morning chores, I spent about one hour replacing the brake cable on the truck. Decided that I would test it by driving to Grand Ridge to have the water pump fixed. This is the pump I used to fill the cistern that is attached to the windmill. I dropped the pump off at the machine shop in town, and decided that it was a good time to stop and pick up a load of coal for the schoolhouse. On the way back, as I was coming up the hill past Shapland's creek I saw a big black swaying cloud heading south. I knew instantly what they were - a swarm of bees. I would see them occasionally during the summer months. This swarm was a big one and I became really scared thinking that the kids or Mabel might be outside. The memory of the bee stings I endured this past spring quickly came to mind. I had been stung many times while pulling the posthole digger out from next to the old garage. I pressed the accelerator pedal down to get home as quickly as I could.

Sure enough, Nancy and Esther were out playing in the front yard. I turned quickly into the driveway.

"Nancy, Esther, go inside. I see some bees coming up the road," I said as I walked briskly towards them. They didn't move as quickly as I wanted them to, so I gave them a little nudge on their backs towards the front door.

"Go on in and stay there until I tell you. You don't want to be out here if those bees come this way."

"Are you coming in Dad?" Esther asked before shutting the door. She had a concerned look on her face.

"I'll be right in," I said giving her a smile.

I looked around to see if the bees had made their way up the road. I felt it would be best to go inside for awhile until I was sure the bees were gone. I'm not sure what type of bees they were – bumble bees or honey bees? They seemed to travel close to the road. I asked everyone to stay indoors at least until dinner time just to be safe.

Music in our Family

We always had a piano in the living room. Mabel did play quite well, as she took lessons when she was younger. The piano is a "Spinet" and we have one of those piano benches that she sits on when playing - the kind that the top lifts up and holds all of her sheet music. I really loved to hear her play. Some of the old favorites are: "Tennessee Waltz", "Always", "Goodnight Irene", and "When Johnny Comes Marching Home Again." She also has sheet music of patriotic songs, like the "Star Spangled Banner." She plays at special occasions like Christmas Eve or birthday parties, and often plays when she is all alone in the house, and I can hear her from outside. Often times I've come in the house from outside just to listen to her play. What a pleasant sound to come home to. None of the girls picked it up so far, as they rarely sat down at the piano for any length of time.

Gladys has taken drum lessons and plays in a band. Gladys also plays the accordion quite well, and takes tap dancing lessons.

I play the violin a little and would get it out once in a while just to keep it in tune. From time-to-time I would try to play along with Mabel, but that mixed both of us up. I guess you might say I just learned the violin by picking away at it as the years went by. It was hard for me to hit the right strings, as my hands were kind of big for the violin.

Mabel and I love listening to big band music. Our favorite was the Glenn Miller Orchestra. Unfortunately, Glenn Miller was killed while in the service just last year. He played for the Army Air Force band and was killed while on a trip to Paris France to entertain our soldiers. Captain Miller's plane was lost on that trip and they never really knew what happened nor did they find any remains. We had been listening to Glenn Miller long before he joined the service. His band had an outstanding, different kind of sound as he had many trombones, coronets, and other great sounding brass instruments. The big band music is so easy to dance to. We also enjoyed listening to Jim Dorsey, Artie Shaw and Benny Goodman. We can tune in their music right on our radio, and we often dance right there in the living room.

The school district hired a music teacher – Mr. Kirby Todd, so now the children have a pleasant break from reading, writing, and arithmetic. Mr. Todd teaches chorus and some instruments. Nancy and Esther learned how to read the basic notes from printed sheets and play simple tunes. He has taught in several schools, seems very knowledgeable, and the kids really like him. For a good while, all we heard around the house were the girls practicing their red tonettes. They paid particular attention to their hair and what clothes they were going to wear the day Mr. Todd was coming to the school. He also helps with the annual Christmas programs at the school.

(17 Sep 45) Albert came over for breakfast this morning. He and I had planned to go to Grand Ridge to purchase and haul 10 ton of phosphate back to the farm. As I plow the field, I will incorporate the fertilizer as I go along.

"Good morning Albert," I got up to meet my brother at the door, "I appreciate your help today."

"Oh, my pleasure Andy," Albert said graciously, "I'm just glad to be home to help you."

"Well, it sure is a blessing to have you back with us."

"Albert, can I get you some eggs?" Mabel asked with a smile.

"Never turned down your food Mabel," was his reply, "yes please."

"What is Dad up to today?" I asked him.

"Oh, he's tinkering around with his truck. I think it needs some major work. He is being stubborn and thinks he can fix it himself."

"Could it be bad gas?" I suggested. "You know I had a heck of a time with my truck a couple weeks back. Turned out to be bad gas. I had to drain the tank."

"I'll mention it to him."

Albert and I ate our breakfast and then took the grain truck and headed into Grand Ridge. Alfie came along with us – he didn't want to be left behind.

"How old is this dog Andy?" Albert asked.

"Not sure, he's gotta be eight or nine I guess."

"He's a good old boy," Albert said while scratching Alfie's neck.

We purchased the first load in Grand Ridge and headed back for home. We could haul a little over one ton per trip. I could have it delivered, but it is quite costly. If we haul one ton at a time, we can distribute it around the farm easier.

Once back to the farm, we pulled the panels off the back of the grain truck and shoveled the phosphate onto the field. This was pretty tiring work, but we could rest on the way back to Grand Ridge for the next load.

In eight hours, we were able to haul all of the phosphate needed. Mabel made us dinner, and Albert and I relaxed for a bit listening to the radio report.

Spread Phosphate as Fertilizer

(18 Sep 45) Went to Pete's this morning to get the phosphate spreader. I hooked the spreader up to the F30 and headed to the field across the road to start there. I pulled up to the pile of phosphate Albert and I had dropped off yesterday and shoveled the fertilizer into the spreader. Was able to get two ton spread today. After supper I worked on the plow a bit.

(21 Sep 45) Woke up at four in the morning to use the bathroom to find that there was no electricity. I flipped the switch in the bathroom a few times and checked other rooms to see if it might be a fuse. Glanced outside to notice that the farmyard light was out also. Seemed like the whole house was out. Looked out the front porch window to find everything pitch black – not even a yard light anywhere. It reminded me of one of our blackout drills. Even though the war was over it still gave me the chills.

The Civil Defense Service conducted blackouts to extinguish all lights in the event of an air raid by enemy forces. The warning sign to turn off lights was either by a loud boom from town or whistle blasts from factories. Later they used air raid sirens, which were easier to distinguish. The sirens really gave me the creeps. All cars had to pull off the road. We weren't even supposed to light a cigarette outside. There were big fines for those who decided not to follow these rules.

Confident that the problem was at the power station and not an attack from the Japanese, I went back to bed.

Disposing of Garbage

(22 Sep 45) After supper I decided to take the trash down to Kangley. Quite often I made a trip over to the Kollar mines to discard the trash. Most of the household trash was fed to the hogs or chickens,

but cans, bottles, paper trash, and whatnot I store in an old wagon until it is full and ready for dumping.

I invited Alf to come along for the ride and he gladly accepted the offer. I hitched the wagon to the truck and headed toward Kangley. The trash was dumped near the mine slag piles. Buff Kollar was out there with his earthmover covering over trash with dirt. Buff pointed to where he wanted me to dump the garbage. I unloaded the trash where he asked and Alf and I were on our way. I paid the Kollars by check to dispose of the garbage.

(25 Sep 45) Butchered a calf today for veal and took it to the Meadow King store on Lundy Street in Streator. Occasionally Mrs. Uhren would call and request it. This was one of two twin calves that Rita had birthed this year. Rita was one our best producers. Each milk cow produced at least one calf per year, sometimes two. Very seldom do we have twins, like Rita had. I decided to call Lloyd Provance before I left for Streator, and asked him to come by this week and pick up the second calf and one cow to take to the Chicago stockyards and sell.

"Won't be able to come until Friday or maybe next Monday if that's okay Andy?" Lloyd replied.

"That would be fine Lloyd. Please give me a call when you know you'll be coming."

"All right then." Lloyd hung up the phone without saying goodbye. I was used to that. It was not that Lloyd was being rude – everyone was different.

(28 Sep 45) Received a call from Lloyd Provance last evening and he informed me that he would be by tomorrow around eleven to pick up Rita's calf and one cow. He arrived a bit late on account of some trouble loading some cows at Hallet's place.

I assured Lloyd that it was no problem. As usual Lloyd made the job look easy and had the calf and the cow onboard his rig in 15 minutes and was on his way.

After eating a quick lunch, I got in the truck and headed into Grand Ridge for a load of coal. The weather was starting to dip into the thirties, and I figured we would get our first frost very soon. The Farmer's Almanac predicted our first frost by the second week in October.

(30 Sep 45) Mabel called me inside for an early lunch as she wanted

to go to see Edith Bentley in the hospital by noon. Edith had her gallbladder removed and I guess she would be in the hospital quite a few days. Edith was in our wedding and was a very nice person.

Mabel set down a big bowl of chicken noodle soup with crackers.

"How did she know she needed her gallbladder out?" I asked as I held the soup spoon in front of my lips blowing it cool.

"Oh, she had been having terrible pains," Mabel replied, "it took the doctor quite a while to figure it out."

"Makes you wonder why you have a gallbladder to begin with if you can have it removed. I hope she is all right now."

"Well, I'll see how she is doing and let you know." Mabel paused and told me that there is plenty of soup on the stove if I wanted more and said she would be on her way.

I walked outside with Mabel to see her off and decided to get the mail out front. I was surprised and very annoyed when I saw deep ruts in our front yard close to the roadway. You could see where a car or truck came onto the grass and the ruts were extended about 20 yards. Just missed the mailbox! It must have been a heavy pickup, I thought, that could cause the turf to be torn up like that. Damn that reckless driver! Probably had a few too many. Of all the work I have to do, and now this.

I glanced down the road apiece and I saw a sack laying on the ground. I walked to it, picked it up, and found two empty beer bottles. Hooligans! I wished I had the license number – I would report it for sure.

I trucked the beer bottles up to the house along with the mail. I figured I would finish my soup, and then fill those ruts with dirt. I was madder than a hornet by that time, and wasn't hungry anymore. I headed outside to get some dirt to haul it to the front to patch up the grass so I didn't have to think about it anymore.

OCTOBER

When Gladys cooked she preferred to prepare the full menu all by herself. It was usually the supper meal that she prepared as she was generally occupied during the day. When Mabel was not home or extremely busy, Gladys would start cooking without being asked, and she is very good at it.

Oddly enough, Gladys' favorite place to talk to her mother was while she was in the kitchen. If something was on her mind, Gladys would bear her soul. This is how we learned about her feelings for Dick, or trouble she was having at school, or anything that was bothering her at the time. As I was making my diary entries, I overheard Gladys start a conversation with Mom to get something off her chest.

"Mother, Dick and I were sitting on the couch the night before last, and Nancy, Esther, and Joyce were peeking down at us through the upstairs register in Darlene's room, and we didn't have any privacy at all. It's so embarrassing. They should have been asleep in their own rooms. But no, we could hear them tiptoeing around upstairs giggling and whispering. You probably didn't hear them in your room, but we sure did. I wonder if you could talk to them and tell them to stop doing that?"

I was fighting back my laughter as I eavesdropped on their conversation.

"Well," said Mother, "we can close Darlene's register since there isn't anyone sleeping in that room now. The kids won't like it, but that will solve the problem." Mabel then added with a snicker. "Next thing they'll be creeping down the stairs and peeking around the corner."

"They were doing that too. They are being little pests. All I want is a little privacy."

"Okay, Gladys. I'll have a talk with them. It really is harmless," Mabel consoled Gladys. "Let's get this dinner on the table shall we?"

It was pretty obvious to me that the girls were watching Gladys and Dick kissing on the couch. Mabel and I knew that they spent an awful lot of time sitting on that couch without making a sound and lots of times chatting away.

(2 Oct 45) With the fall coming soon it was time to take all of the window screens down and put up the storm windows. I made it a point to get this done before the corn harvest. I stored the screen and storm

183

windows in the old garage. The first step was to haul all of the windows out of the garage into the yard for cleaning. We had about a dozen windows on the first floor and eight on the second floor. We also had the screen doors leading into the pantry, kitchen, and two in the front porch. I could not replace all of the windows in one day.

I started with the kitchen windows, and after putting them up I noticed the newly painted shutters made the windows look a little drabby. After some hesitation, I decided to pull them back down and paint them. I sifted through the windows to determine how many needed painting and how many could wait another year. With more than half of them needing painting, I set them back in the old garage for later. I now had to identify where the good windows belonged. All of the windows were marked on the edge where they went, so it should not be difficult.

I must have painted the upstairs windows recently, because all of those windows were in the "good" pile. I got out the long ladder and one-by-one replaced all the screens on the second floor.

Mabel headed to town to stock up on canning supplies for next year. She spent a good amount of time downstairs cleaning up. With the kids at school she had more time to get things organized.

Cubs Play in World Series

(3 Oct 45) Gabriel Heater reported that the Cubs had won Game 1 of the 1945 World Series. The Cubs had beat out my Cardinals in the National League Pennant race, ending the season three games in front. Unfortunately for the Cubs, they had to face the Detroit Tigers, the team that had beat them in the last World Series the Cubs had played in 1935. The Cubs clobbered the Tigers, in their stadium, 9-0 today behind the pitching of Hank Borowy and a home run from their star first baseman Phil Cavarretta.

Michael Vercimak Coming Home from the Military

(4 Oct 45) Headed to Ransom early this morning to purchase a light pole. I had decided that I need to add an extra outside light near the machine shed. There were too many times when I wished I had a light out there.

As I parked the truck outside the hardware store, I saw Edward coming down the road in Dad's truck to beat the band. He was waving one arm out the window.

"What is it Ed?" I asked, it was obvious he was excited about something.

"Michael is coming home, Andy," Ed said with a big smile.

"Vercimak, from the military?" I was referring to Irene's husband. They were married almost two years ago when he was home on leave. Irene had been waiting so long for him to come home.

"That's right," Ed confirmed, "he is due to be home October 31st. Irene is so happy. You have to bring the family over to Dad's tonight and celebrate."

"You betcha, Ed, we'll be there." I remembered how excited it was when Albert came home from the war this past July, and Ray will be home real soon. I couldn't imagine how wonderful it must feel for Irene. They have been writing back and forth all this time.

I spent most of the morning putting in my new light pole. Couldn't quite finish as I did not have enough electrical hardware. Decided to start prepping the machine shed roof for painting.

After dinner, Mabel, I and the kids went to Dad's to celebrate the news of Michael coming home. Irene was so happy, bouncing around the house. We pulled out the pictures from their wedding. Irene pulled out the calendar and counted the days until her husband would return. Thank God that he was okay and made it through the war.

(5 Oct 45) Spent this morning making a list of farm machinery maintenance items that I needed to attend to before the corn harvest gets underway. I spent a good two hours looking over all of my equipment and listing with paper and pencil what needed to be done. Most of the time all the equipment needed was lubrication, oil changes, and general cleaning. There were some things that I put off until now because I was just too busy to fix earlier on. The binder was not working as good as it should be. Some of the mechanical parts were old, like the chains, and some of the parts in the bundler. I made a note to spend some money and time getting her back in shape. Some machinery, like the cultivator, had been in service for quite a few years and did not need any maintenance at all. I did not want to push my luck too much. There is standard upkeep to do on the engines like sparkplugs, wires, belts, magnetos, and whatnot. Some parts were simply broken and needed welding. For that I would remove the part and take it into town to be welded at a professional machine shop.

With my list in hand, I headed to Missel's to buy the parts I would need for a few of my higher priority items. I didn't mind driving to town, as it gave me a chance to get in the truck, rest my legs and look around at how some of the other neighbors were progressing. Truth be known, certain times of the year, like early October, when there was not a whole lot to do, I enjoyed sitting in our old red leather recliner and dozing off for a short time.

(8 Oct 45) Went over George's today to listen to the Cubs on the radio. Today was Game 6 of the World Series at Wrigley Field. Cubs were down in the series 3-2. It was really a good game, going into extra innings tied 7-7. The Cubs put Borowy in to relieve in the ninth and the Cubs finally won it in the bottom of the twelfth. Borowy got his second win of the series. The deciding Game 7 will be played in two days in Chicago.

Cubs Lose World Series to Tigers in Game 7

(10 Oct 45) Didn't listen to the World Series today, but George came over after supper to tell me that the Tigers beat the Cubs 9-3.

"The Cubs just can't get past those Tigers, huh Andy," George said smugly, happy that the Cards archrivals had another failed attempt against the Tigers. "You know they pitched that Borowy again."

"You don't say," I replied, "well he was the best pitcher they had."

"Well, they must of thought he was going to finish them off like he did in Game 6, but the Tigers got all over him in the first."

"Well, maybe next year."

"Next year is going to be exciting, Andy. All the players are returning from the war – Joe Dimaggio and Ted Williams."

"That will be nice to have those guys back in the lineup."

(12 Oct 45) Received a phone call from Taylor & Sons Tiling Services to remind us that they would be out Tuesday or Wednesday of next week to start tiling. It took me a little off guard that he was coming so soon.

"Well, that's great," I said, "I'm glad you called first because I had totally forgotten."

"Well, Mr. Durdan," this must have been Taylor's son as it was a younger voice, "we have here that we would start 15 October. We are running a couple days behind on a current job, so we will be a couple days late if that's okay."

"Oh, that would be fine." I needed a few days to get ready for them anyway. "We'll see you then. Oh, and thanks for calling. Bye now."

Darlene Finishes Job in Joliet – Moves Back Home

(16 Oct 45) Received a letter from Darlene today to tell us the details on her construction job in Joliet - that the work is now complete and she will be let go on the 22nd of October. Darlene knew all along that the job would be temporary. Mabel and I thought that she worked a bit too hard for a woman. All those hours working outside in all weather conditions was very hard on her. Now that the war was at its end, the men were coming back home and assuming their former positions.

Mabel folded laundry on the kitchen table and stated, "Well, I am glad she is coming home. She needs a break. She also needs to start thinking about Sully coming home and planning their wedding."

"She has certainly earned some time off," I said, "she's a hard worker. Just like you Mabel." I gave her a big smile, and she gave me a peck on the cheek.

(17 Oct 45) Taylor & Sons were on the job by 8:30 am. They had five people in all working on the tiling job. I watched them for a bit and was very impressed with their work. Mr. Taylor had told me he expected that it would take them all of today and half-day tomorrow, unless they ran into trouble. Rather than bother them by watching over their shoulders, I decided to hook up the plow to the F30 and plow the hayfield under next to Paul's place.

Husk a Jag of Corn for Pigs

(18 Oct 45) As the corn picking season approached, I would go out and hand pick some corn to see how the corn was progressing and also to husk a jag for the pigs. A jag is nothing more than a small load. I'd go out into the field with a sack over my shoulder and pick the ears right off the stalk and put them into my bag. I would make as many trips as needed to get a good-sized load.

After returning from the field, I husked a few to see how the corn looked. I threw about one-third of the load into the pig pen. The hogs would devour the whole ear, husk and all. I stored the rest of the load in the crib. I would do this five or six times during the fall. If you picked too much this time of year, the corn would get moldy, as it was not dry enough to store for very long.

Before heading in for supper I drove out to check on the tiling job. Mr. Taylor had stopped by the house about 3 pm to let us know he was done. I paid him the agreed upon amount and he said that if there was anything wrong with the tiling job, he would come out, no problem. I walked around the field and had a hard time noticing if they were even there. I guess the only true way to tell if it worked is to see how it held up after a heavy rain. Overall, I was happy with the work they had done. I know that I would have spent much more time and energy to do the same job. It was nice to have it all done, now I can put it out of my mind.

Combine Beans

(19 Oct 45) Cleaned oats out of the bean bin this morning to prepare for the new crop. Shoveled the remaining oats into the old brooder house for the chicks. Pulled the combine out of the machine shed. Tink around with the combine a bit and felt she was pretty much ready to go since I had done good maintenance when I put it away last time. Hooked the plow to the John Deere and worked the piece by Rinkers.

(20 Oct 45) Looked like rain this morning , but by 9:30 am it cleared up real nice. Got the combine ready, and was in the bean field by 10:30 am. Spent all day on the beans and finished by dark. The bean field was small and did not take much time at all to harvest.

(21 Oct 45) Linc brought his truck by this morning and we hauled my beans into Ransom for sale. I left enough in the bin for the livestock. Got back late morning. Mabel fixed Linc and I some lunch. Afterwards, I spent a better part of the day plowing and did not get done till dark. The soil worked up real good and it was easy going.

(22 Oct 45) Darlene called while we were having breakfast to tell us that her last day is today and that she would be heading home after work.

"Would you mind if I bring Mary and some friends home to spend the evening?" Darlene asked.

"Oh, that would be fine. We have plenty of room and we would love to see your friends," Mabel replied.

Mabel and I never minded having Darlene and her friends over. It was nice to have young people around. The kids also loved it when they came.

After breakfast I headed to the North field to husk some corn by hand. The corn was still not quite ready for harvest. I picked one load by hand for the livestock.

After lunch I culled the chickens. This was a process where we eliminate those hens that are not healthy or are not producing eggs. Right now the hens are laying many eggs and it is easy to see who is not producing. I cleared eight or ten out, slayed them and gave them to Mabel for cleaning. Most of them were okay to eat, some were clearly scrawny and probably diseased. Getting rid of the bad hens gave the good egg layers more space, and in the long run produced more eggs.

The rest of the afternoon was spent updating the machinery. First on the list was fixing the tongue on the side delivery rake.

Kerosene Lamp on Fence Post

After dinner I cleaned the horse stalls and stacked some lumber along the west wall. There was some wood that could be used by the roofers that are working on the barn next week. Worked in the barn well past dark - this is the time of year the sun sets before 6 pm. When I stepped outside I noticed there was a pretty dense fog in the air. By 8 pm it was so foggy that I couldn't see more than one-quarter mile down the road in either direction. I immediately thought of Darlene and her girlfriends trying to find their way on the country roads, with only the head lights.

She would be traveling on the Grand Ridge road coming from the east and what if she couldn't see which corner to turn? So I decided to drive out to the corner where she was to turn south toward our farm, lit a kerosene lamp, and hung it on a fence post. I just hoped she would see it. Of course, I had no idea what time she would be arriving

I sat in a chair in the front porch looking for signs of Darlene coming down the road. It wasn't until around 9:30 pm that I saw a pair of headlights in the distance. I was hoping it was them – I don't think anybody else would be on the roads on a night like tonight.

As the headlights got closer and closer, I could make out that it was Darlene and her friends.

"Dad, did you put that light on the pole on the corner?" Darlene asked walking towards the front porch, "we would never had known where to turn."

"You betcha I did," I said, "glad you saw it - so relieved you made it in this fog."

After welcoming the ladies inside I took a ride out to retrieve my kerosene lamp from the Grand Ridge road corner.

(28 Oct 45) Sunday morning was extra special with Darlene home from Joliet. The kitchen was full of activity. Mabel and Gladys were

busy making breakfast and Darlene was playing with the girls in the living room.

"Aren't the Palaschak's coming over tonight, Gladys?" I asked, vaguely remembering Gladys mentioning a visit today. We have had Dick and his parent's over on Sundays a few times over the past few months.

"I'm pretty sure they are," was her response. "Should we have them for dinner?"

"Mother?" I asked Mabel. I did not want to agree without knowing what Mabel had in mind.

"Oh, that would be fine. I have plenty of chicken in the freezer." Mabel agreed with no fuss. We all looked forward to Mabel's fried chicken and potato salad on Sundays.

Darlene and Gladys left in the family car to attend the 8:30 am mass at St. Mary's. I tinkered around in the garage a bit and decided to go to 10:30 am church in Ransom. I wanted to grind up some cow feed and pull the corn picker out of the machine shed, look it over, and give it a good greasing.

There were items that I had purchased for the picker that needed attention. I went ahead replacing those parts and when I was finished, felt that the picker was ready for harvest.

Halloween

(31 Oct 45) Today was Halloween; a day where the kids looked forward to a party at school. We sent the kids off to school with some candy to share with the classmates. The girls wore jeans rolled up to the knee with long socks, and oversized old flannel shirts with the sleeves rolled up, and a piece of twine for a belt. Each of the girls wore a facemask with a rubber band wrapped around the back of their head. Mabel always enjoyed dressing them.

"And who is this little girl with the mask on?" I said to Joyce as she walked around the house. "Do you know where my little Joycie is?"

"It's me, look," Joyce lifted up her mask and giggled.

"I thought it was you," I played with Joyce a bit and said to Mabel, "well, I better get ready for the carpenters."

"Oh, that's right. You're starting the barn today."

The carpenters, who were recommended by my Dad, came by around ten am and worked a better part of the day. The entire barn roof had to be replaced. It was leaking pretty bad for quite some time.

They were working at a pretty serious pace, tearing the old roof off and throwing the pieces in big piles around the barn. After inspecting a good part of the old wood, I was happy to have it replaced. Most of it was tattered and brittle. The carpenters had promised to replace the entire roof in three days time. I had to leave the horses and cows in the pasture all day as they would not like the noise and I feared they might get hit in the head. The carpenters said that they would make provisions to allow the animals to be stored overnight during their construction.

I made two trips to the lumber yard in Ransom to give the boys plenty to work with once they started putting up the new pieces. By four pm, they pretty near had one whole side of the roof pulled down, and one of the guys was putting up the new pieces.

At seven, it was time to take the girls to a few neighbors' houses to show off their costumes. The neighbors would give them candy to eat while making the rounds or store in their little brown sacks. We stopped by the Armstrong's, the Koetz's, and brother Steve's and brother George's place before heading to Myrtle and George Hallett's place for the main Halloween attraction. Each year we would go to the Hallett's for a fun party. This year was no different than any other year. Myrtle was such a character, even though she was Mabel's age, she dressed up in a homemade costume and would do so much clowning around, you just had to watch her and laugh. Her daughter Marilyn dressed up as well, in a cheerleading outfit complete with hat and pompoms. The kids were laughing and enjoying the fun the second we got there. Myrtle served the kids soda, told them it was magic potion, and told them spooky stories. The adults would sit around the living room as Myrtle told her stories and kept real quiet. We would try to keep a straight face, and then everyone would belt out laughing.

George Hallett and I sat together watching the kids play and drank a few beers. I told George about the new barn roof, and he told me of the different chores he was tending to around his place. We headed home around ten. The girls all fell asleep on the way home with their bags of candy in their laps. I'm sure that one of them will be up tonight with a bellyache.

NOVEMBER

Picking corn made November a very busy month. By now the corn should be dry and ready for harvest. The first day of November was cold at 29 above. If the weather stays this cold it could make for a long November. I had to ensure that the John Deere, two-row corn picker, and wagon were ready for the task ahead. The corn picker has a special place in my heart because I bought it the day Esther was born, November 17, 1937.

I had a difficult time finding necessary replacement parts for the John Deere hookup the past couple of days. After unsuccessfully trying Missel's and a couple other tractor supply outfits, I finally found what I needed in Grand Ridge. The wagon had to be slightly modified for picking corn, and it had to be greased and ready to go.

I could pick corn by myself, but it went a bit smoother if you had two men using a two-row corn picker pulled behind the tractor. Behind the corn picker I pulled an 80-bushel wagon. The corn picker plucks the ear off the corn stalk, husks it, and shoots it into the wagon. In a good year, I could fill the wagon in one round, which is one time around the field. I would start on the outer part of the field, say by the road, and go all the way around the field, then work my way in. When the wagon is full, un-hitch it and truck it to the corn crib, load it onto the elevator, and into the crib. Returning with the empty wagon, I am now ready to make another round. If you had two men, one man would drive the grain truck to and from the field. The other drove the tractor and filled a second wagon. We soon adapted to this routine, and we certainly did not waste any time.

The picking would be completed hopefully by Thanksgiving, or as late as the middle of December. There are usually many cold days near the end of the harvest. But once the harvest is done, we could look forward to relaxing over the holidays. So the cycle of planting and harvesting goes on year after year.

Start Picking Corn

(3 Nov 45) Officially started picking corn today, although the first two loads were husked by hand. We picked corn south of the house. My friend Bill Schroeder came over to help me out to make sure that the corn looked good and we were all set to go. Despite the weather being very

cold and windy, I was excited to get started.

(4 Nov 45) Went to 10:30 am church this morning with Esther and Nancy. Headed straight home to pick up Joyce and Mabel, then went to Marseilles to celebrate Ma's 83rd birthday. Darlene and Gladys met us there. Food was served potluck style, and the place was decorated up real nice. All of the Olsen families were represented, each bringing their favorite dish to share. Ma was in good spirits and truly enjoyed herself. Didn't come home from Marseilles until after dark. Not long after we were home, the Armstrong's came over and Mabel and I played cards with Mary and Linc, while the kids played in the living room.

(5 Nov 45) Had a few more maintenance items to tend to before hooking up the tractor, corn picker, and wagon together. Just after 2 pm I hauled the rig across the road to starting picking there. It was slow going the first round, but I nearly filled the wagon, which is a good indicator the crop would be a good, bountiful harvest. I walked back across the road to get the grain truck to haul the newly picked corn back to the crib for unloading. I unhitched the wagon from the picker and hitched it up to the truck and drove it back across the road.

I started the elevator across the road to feed the corn up into the crib. It ran for about two minutes and the motor died. I realized that I had not spent any time getting the elevator ready to go. I spent the better part of an hour getting her going and got the load up into the crib.

Every time I look at that grain elevator that feeds the corn into the crib, I think of how close Darlene came to losing her leg. Darlene was about 14 or 15 years old and she was helping me unload corn from the wagon onto the elevator – this was on our rented farm. She got a little too close to the chain and gears and it caught her pant leg and was slowly pulling her in. Thank God she yelled right away and I was close enough to immediately stop the motor. I had to quickly tear away her pant leg and took a firm grip on the chain to reverse it enough to get her leg free. After the incident she cried so hard and her whole body seemed to quiver, as I quickly took her to Ransom to the doctor's office. She needed many stitches and her leg was left permanently scarred. Ever since that accident, I am very careful not to let the kids get too close to machinery. I can get plenty of help from my brothers and friends, Linc and Bill, if need be.

I was able to get two more rounds completed in the field across the road and into the crib. By then it was dark. I left the tractor and picker in the field overnight.

Geese Flying South

(6 Nov 45) As I walked outside this morning I could hear the sound of geese flying south. I searched the sky for them. What a beautiful sight to see – all of the geese flying in their V shape. There must have been around 40 of them. Seemed like just a few of them making that honking noise that bounced down to earth. I looked for another group, but there was no more. There were times I could see two or three groups. In no time they were out of sight and on their way to their next stop. In the distance I watched them gracefully make their decent - flying what seemed like lower and lower out of sight. The leader of the pack needs to find a good place to land near a body of water and where they can feed on grains and bugs.

By noon time it was 60 above which was very warm for this time of year. I thought of the geese maybe thinking they were farther south than they thought. I picked all morning by myself and continued into the afternoon. By the end of the day I completed eight loads. The wind really picked up as the afternoon went on. On the way back to the house I waved to Darlene and Gladys in the family car heading north on our road. I wondered for a bit where they might be going, but I remember that they were going to Ottawa to spend time with Darlene's friend.

(7 Nov 45) Cleaned the cow and horse barn today. Also picked some carrots, beets, and turnips that needed to be dug before the ground froze. Due to some unexpected rain in the middle of the night, I decided to hold off picking corn today. I heard the mailman make his stop in front of the house and continued on his route. The mail was a little early today - it being only 10:30 am. Mabel brought the mail in, and there was an invitation to a 25th anniversary party for the Rinker's to be held in Grand Ridge a few weeks from now. This is not the same Rinker family on our square mile, as they were brother and sister. They had a large family living in this area.

"Andy, I think we should go," Mabel stated happily.

"Maybe you can make that new dress that you have been talking about," I replied. I knew what was first and foremost on Mabel's mind. She had been talking about a new pattern she had found.

"Oh yes. I think I should go to Montgomery Wards first thing tomorrow and get some material. I really could use that new dress for the upcoming shivaree."

Mabel went directly to a chest of drawers in the dining room and pulled out her pattern. She did love to sew and she was very good at it. She sewed most of her dresses, plus clothes for the kids. It seems her old Singer sewing machine just keeps on percolating - as long as we keep it oiled and cleaned. Whenever she has a problem following directions in the pattern, she picks up the whole thing and takes it to her niece, Katherine, in Marseilles. Together they could always figure it out.

Darlene Starts Working at Owens Glass

(9 Nov 45) Saw Darlene off to her new job this morning at Owens Glass factory in Ottawa. It took Darlene less than three weeks to find this job after being let go from her job in Joliet.

Darlene had the window rolled down and I leaned in to ask, "So are you sure you're ready to go back to work?"

"You betcha," Darlene replied with a big smile.

"Well at least this job is close enough for you to come home every night."

"Yeah, I think I can get use to that. I have a feeling I'm going to like this job."

"I'm sure you will do just fine. Well, you have a good first day." I patted the hood of the car a couple times to shove her off. She bought a good used car in town with the money she had saved. I promised that I would give it a good tune-up soon.

Andy Falls Down Basement Stairs

Started picking corn across the road by 9 am. It was pretty sticky going, but got better as the morning sun dried the soil up a bit. I was going along just fine until the last round and the sky opened up and rain came down hard. It wasn't too long and I was stuck and decided to leave the picker in the field and walk home in the rain.

Mabel had left me a note that my dinner was on the counter. It was still raining when I finished with my evening chores. I stepped in the kitchen door and decided it was best to head downstairs and get my wet, muddy clothes off. With wet shoes, I slipped on the first step and landed hard on my behind and slid and bumped all the way to the bottom of the steps. I felt the pain in my back instantly. I felt my rump and legs to make sure I didn't break anything. I laid there for a bit to gather my thoughts. What if I had hit my head, I thought. No one was home. How long would I have laid there before Mabel found me? I put all of those thoughts out of my head because I was obviously okay, with the exception of the pain in my back. I have had problems over the past few years throwing my back out now and then. In previous cases, our family doctor was able to tape my back up and prescribed rest, and it was eventually healed. What a time for this to happen, I thought, during picking season.

After sitting and thinking for 10 minutes or so, I managed to stand up and stretch a bit. That brought a sharp pain that shot up my spine. I found it was best to stay hunched over. It was about that time that I heard the gravel in the driveway. Thank God, Mabel was home. I heard her heals on the floor above me.

Sensing something was wrong she called out, "Andy, are you down there?"

"Yes, dear, I could use your help."

She came down the stairs seeing me hunched over. "For heaven's sake Andrew, what happened?"

"You're dear old husband fell down the stairs."

She performed her quick inspection and felt it was best to get the wet clothes off and see if we could get up the stairs. We took one stair at a time and made it through the kitchen, dining room, and finally into the bedroom to lie down. After taking a couple of aspirin I finally found a position that was the most comfortable and fell asleep.

(10 Nov 45) Mabel called the family doctor first thing in the morning and he agreed to meet us at his medical office despite it being Saturday. He taped my back up and pleaded that I stay off my feet for the weekend. The tape gave my back the stability I needed to stand up straighter without the pain. By the time I got home I started feeling much better. I was half out the kitchen door to get back to work when Mabel stopped me.

"Now Andy, you know what the doctor said," she scolded, "you are doing too much."

"It feels pretty good, Mabel," I replied, "I promise not to work too hard."

"Well, for heaven's sake, be careful."

After ensuring Mabel that I would take it easy, I headed into Grand Ridge to buy some wood to patch the hole in our roof. When I returned, I headed out to the field across the road to get the tractor and picker out of the mud. Was able to get the rig moving and decided to pick for a while. The back was holding up fine and I was able to pick two small loads before the sun went down.

"Dad, if your back hurts, don't feel like you have to take us into town," Gladys stated sincerely knowing that I had fallen down the stairs.

"I will be fine," I assured her that I was up to the task, "besides, I feel like dancing."

We packed up her drums and gear, picked up one of her friends, and headed to Ottawa for the dance. I listened to the band play, but did not dance. The band played till just after midnight. We got home around 1:00 am.

Hunting Season

(11 Nov 45) Fall plowing was going very well as the weather held fairly pleasant and there was just enough moisture in the ground. There were plenty of pheasants and rabbits seeking the corn stalks for shelter. When they heard the tractor or the ground tremor a bit, they would run to beat hell. The pheasants were beautiful. Hunting season was just a few weeks away.

We had met some couples at the Moose Lodge in Marseilles a few years back. The men in this group sure liked their hunting and had asked me if they could come out and hunt on our property. I consented and they were sure appreciative. I would just have to stay out of the fields the short time they were there, as I didn't want to be the recipient of a stray bullet. I was not a hunter myself, but those guys sure loved the sport.

Depending on their catch, they always left us a generous share – a couple of rabbits or a pheasant. Perhaps more if they had real good luck. Our family did not care for cooked pheasant. To us it seemed very dry and Mabel did not like to prepare it. We preferred rabbit as long as it was not too shot up. I skinned them and cut them up and Mabel sure knew how to cook them.

"But Mom, I can't eat that. I always think of the little rabbits running around," Nancy would say. She would just make herself a bologna sandwich instead.

We had tame rabbits in a pen that was mounted on stilts by the new garage. The girls would take the rabbits out and play with them. It was their job to feed and take care of them. I certainly could see how Nancy did not want to eat rabbit.

It really seemed to me that those who liked to hunt were from the city. Those who had the resources right at their fingertips, like us country folk, did not care for the sport.

(14 Nov 45) With nearly two weeks into the corn harvest, I had finished the field across the road and the small piece by the schoolhouse, and started in the big field. Ray Wilson came over today and was a tremendous help. Ray, discharged from the Army, was happy to be back home from the war. Despite the field being very muddy, Ray and I were able to pick eight good-sized loads.

Back at the house Mabel was gearing up for the Home Bureau meeting at the Koetz' place.

"So what are you gals up to tonight?" I asked Mabel.

"Well, tonight we are putting together welcome home packages for our soldiers," Mabel was busy getting her notes together for the meeting, "we need to get ready for the train that is coming in Friday."

Our boys were coming home in droves from the war. The Streator train station was extremely busy these days. So many troops are passing through on their way home, and many of our local boys will be home to stay.

"Tonight is extra-special," Mabel continued, "we are teaming up with the Royal Neighbors group. That is the group that sponsored the war bond drive, remember?"

"Sure, I remember. That is very nice of you women to support our community the way you do."

"Well, we all pitch in."

Vick's Vapor Rub

(15 Nov 45) Woke to 25 above temperatures and a pretty hard frost on the ground. It was still pretty good conditions for picking. I was finishing my diary entries for the day when Mabel walked by on her way upstairs.

"It seems Joyce has a bit of a cold tonight. I think I better get the Vicks Vapor Rub out." Mabel spoke of her proven method to cure the common cold. I followed Mabel up the stairs to check on Joyce. Mabel rubbed Joyce's chest with Vicks, then wrapped a warm sock around her neck. She would warm the sock in the oven. Mabel would perform this regimen every night until her cold subsided.

"How long do I have to do this?" cried Joyce.

Joking I said, "It will take seven days to cure a cold with this treatment, but it would take a whole week without it."

We did not need much in our medicine cabinet: Vicks, Milk of

Magnesia, Mercurochrome, iodine, some bandages, and tape.

Bird in the Kitchen

(17 Nov 45) Esther turns eight today. Mabel made her and the girls pancakes this morning for breakfast. Mabel startled us all by announcing that we had a little visitor in our house.

"Andy! There's a bird in here." She was looking up above our heads in the light fixture. I glanced up and saw the little bird perched there. "I think it's a sparrow, Andy." Mabel definitely knew her birds. Just then, the bird took to flight and was circling the kitchen in a frenzy. The girls were screaming and Mabel laughing.

"Open the kitchen window Mabel," I said hoping that the bird would fly out. She did so, but the bird did not recognize the exit that we had prepared for it. Nancy was chasing it around and Esther and Joyce were laughing and screaming under the kitchen table. The poor bird was running into the cupboards and walls and I feared it may hurt itself.

"Get me a towel," I said hoping that I could catch it and take it outside and release it. I never imagined how hard it would be to catch such a little bird. I wasn't quite tall enough to catch the bird in the open towel. Around and around I went. The bird managed to find his way into the living room. There he had even more places to fly and hide. I found myself getting extremely tired and could not stop laughing. It was the kind of laughing that makes your stomach hurt. Mabel ran to the porch door and I chased the little bird into the porch.

"Now shut the door Mabel and we can leave him in the porch for now," I suggested.

Mabel opened up the door to the outside and left it open. We figured in time the bird would fly out. I sat in the chair in the living room utterly exhausted. We sat and watched the bird for a while. He seemed as tired as we were.

Mabel and I went into Streator to have the doctor look my back over. He re-taped it after I told him that I still felt a bit of pain. I didn't want to tell him that I hardly slowed down since I injured it. The tape was keeping me stronger so I could keep working in the fields.

When we got home Nancy reported that the bird had finally left.

"We tried to feed it water and bread, but he did not eat or drink anything," said Nancy, "he seemed pretty scared."

"We saw him there one minute," Esther added, "then we came out a little bit later and he was gone."

Mabel and I were relieved that our little friend was okay.

"Well, now he can get back to his family," I said.

I went to the North field to husk some corn by hand to see if it was ready for picking, and it was. I had a majority of the big field and the North field left to pick.

Went to George's place after dinner to prepare to engage sheller tomorrow. Pete and Dad were there. We shot the breeze and had a couple of beers. We agreed to meet first thing in the morning.

(21 Nov 45) The rain the past two nights put a damper on my picking operations and caused George to postpone his shelling engagement until today. We got it all done, but I was unable to pick today since I got home after dark. Decided to grease the picker and pull wagons out into the field to get ready for tomorrow. Noticed the mercury dipping fast tonight so I put the heater in the horse tank and put alcohol in the tractor.

(24 Nov 45) Had pretty good luck the past couple of days, but the temperatures had been below freezing the past three days. Headed to the big field to find the picker, tractor, and wagon froze to the ground. I had worried about this. Spent a good amount of time trying to get the tractor going, then finally got her to turn over. Nothing would budge. Walked back to the barn to get picks and pry bars. After putting another layer of clothes on to stay warm, I put the tools in the truck and headed back to the field.

After a better part of two hours picking and prying, I freed the tractor, picker, and wagon. Started getting things rolling, but didn't go 50 rods before the axle in the picker broke clean in two. Headed back to the house and got on the phone with Walter in Grand Ridge.

"Hi Walter, this is Andy Durdan."

"Andy," he responded, "how are things out your way?"

"Oh, going slow today. Broke the axle on my McCormick picker. It's a two-row."

"You and about 15 other people in the past two days calling about broken axles and such. I'm sorry to say that I don't have any right now. Won't have any for a week or two."

"You don't say."

"You might try Ottawa or Serena."

"Thanks Walter, let me give it a shot." I rang off with Walter and tried Ottawa with no luck, but was able to find one in Serena. The gentlemen assured me that he would hold it for me. I left at about 3:30 pm and told Mabel not to expect me for dinner.

"Are we still going into town tonight?" Mabel asked with concern.

"Sure we will," I responded, "I should be back by 6:00 pm. I'll stop off at A&W for supper."

Got to the tractor dealer just before they closed. The clerk had a hard time finding the part. I explained that I called ahead. It took about 20 minutes for him to realize that it was set aside up front.

Despite getting back home a bit later than expected, we were all headed to Streator in the family car by 7:00 pm for our Saturday night show.

(25 Nov 45) I went out to the picker first thing after chores and replaced the broken axle. After a couple trips between the field and the machine shed for the right tools and hardware, I was able to fix the picker and give it a test run. Got all done with the repair in time to pick 4 small loads before lunch.

Moved the equipment from the field to the barn before sundown to prevent the wheels from freezing to the ground again overnight. Cleaned the mud off the F30 before evening chores.

(26 Nov 45) It was 26 above during morning chores. Decided to wait awhile before I headed to the field. By noon, the temperature went up to 44, so I finally got started for the day. Picked 5 loads and was able to finish the big field by the end of the day. I was glad to have taken the careful approach – not to fight the elements. Patience with the weather was paying off.

(30 Nov 45) My hopes of getting the corn picking done by the end of November had been lost due to my back slowing me up a bit, and the cold and muddy conditions. But I did realize that I wasn't having any more or less trouble than the neighbors. After all I had only the North field to finish and with a little luck the weather would hold up in order to finish in the next week to 10 days.

DECEMBER

(1 Dec 45) Up until the night of November 30th, we did not have an accumulation of snow for the winter. Waking up to December we found that we had our first snowfall. The snow started coming down as we were going to bed at around eleven last evening. By the morning, it was quite possible we could have an accumulation of six inches. I could always get a good idea of how much snow had fallen by looking out the kitchen window at the old garage roof where the light would shine on it just right.

I was up around seven and put on coffee, as usual. Everyone else was still asleep. Gladys had played drums for a dance in Ottawa last evening. Luckily, she made it home safely before the snow was too bad.

After my morning chores I got the Fordson tractor out and attached the front-end scoop, and started clearing the snow away on the drive and in front of the garages. The first snow of the season was always exciting. I guess it gave me something new to do – plow the snow and get the farm up and running. Alfie was having himself a ball rolling in the snow and running around. The girls would be just as excited to play fox and goose and make snow angels. I'm sure that the girls will not be attending their Saturday morning Catechism and would have all day to play. I smiled to myself thinking that I had all of my girls snowbound at home.

I came back inside to have my first cup of coffee. I decided to write a few checks, one to the phone company, and one to the power company. I fiddled at my desk cleaning up a bit. I thought to myself that I must remember to ask Gladys to pick up a new blotter and a bottle of ink at the office supply.

Mabel was the first one up this morning.

"Got some snow, huh Andy? It looks so beautiful," she said as she wrapped her robe tight gazing out the window.

"About six inches I figure. Good clean snow – no slush," I replied. I never liked the slushy snow that is hard to plow and freezes up to make ice.

"I'll put on some oatmeal for breakfast." Mabel liked to make a good-sized pot of oatmeal on cold mornings along with a few slices of toast.

I was pretty sure the mailman would get through, since his vehicle was equipped with chains, so I went outside and put the checks in the mail to be picked up.

I took a shovel and cleaned the sidewalks at the back entrance, side door entrance, and the front porch entrance. By the time I went back inside, Gladys and Darlene were sitting at the kitchen table talking.

"Hi Dad. I see you got the plowing done already," Darlene said cheerily. She looked beautiful as always.

"You betcha – first thing this morning."

"Are you still going to be able to pull the old furnace out of the schoolhouse?" Gladys asked.

"Oh, I think so." I replied. "I don't see why not. Elmer should be down around ten." Elmer Kates had agreed to help me pull out the old furnace at the country schoolhouse. We had been talking about changing that old furnace for months. Fred Johnson had agreed to buy one, but time got away from us. Luckily the furnace worked pretty good until just before Thanksgiving. We'd have the new furnace put in by professionals. But Elmer and I would take the old one out to save some money for the school.

"Always something to do, huh Dad?" Darlene said while blowing on her coffee.

Along about 9 am, Mabel served the oatmeal with buttered toast. We had a nice time talking and relaxing. Just then Elmer knocked and came through the kitchen door, all smiles.

"Little snow never stopped us, right Andy?" Elmer belted out. He said hello to everyone. "It sure is nice to see everyone. How are you Darlene? Gosh, I haven't seen you in a while."

"Good to see you too, Elmer. How about some of Mom's oatmeal?" Darlene, always courteous to guests, offered some nourishment.

Elmer ate some oats and we headed to the schoolhouse with all of the necessary tools. It took us a better part of two hours to remove the old furnace. We stored it in the old garage until the furnace installers picked it up on Monday to either be repaired and reused or disposed of. We arranged for the new furnace to be installed Monday morning, first thing. For that reason, the kids did not have school Monday.

Gladys – Swimsuit in Winter

Gladys and Darlene must have been in an adventurous mood. Just after Elmer had left, I went inside and saw Gladys coming down from upstairs with her bathing suit on, a scarf, gloves, her hair styled up in a pompadour, and some toeless shoes. I could hardly believe my eyes. Darlene and Gladys went outside, with Darlene in her winter coat and the Brownie camera in tow. They went in front of the house and took some pictures of Gladys dressed in her extreme attire, her feet implanted into the snow. Mabel was glancing out the porch window, and the little girls quickly put on their snow gear and raced outside. Mabel and I were shocked to say the least, but couldn't help but laugh at their antics.

Mabel looked at me and said, "Have they taken leave of their senses?"

They were not outside very long, just long enough to cut up a bit, and take the photos. Just as they started making their way back inside, the mailman rolled up. He didn't quite know what to make of what he was seeing. He just about knocked over the mailbox as he was looking our way. He pulled my envelopes out of the mailbox and threw some mail back in, and slowly rolled away looking back as Gladys and Darlene ran inside the front porch door.

"Oh my goodness gracious, get inside you crazy girls," Mabel said sharply while rustling Gladys and Darlene back inside, holding back her laughter.

Sometimes I worry about those girls and what enters their minds to do something like that. Perhaps tonight we will be getting the Vicks Vapor Rub out to doctor up a few sore throats. I laughed it off and thought that maybe we all had a case of cabin fever.

Fox and Goose

(2 Dec 45) After church we stopped by the Armstrong's to pick up the children to come to our house to play in the new-fallen snow. The

kids were so excited about the snow. Nancy and Esther were talking about playing Fox and Goose with the Armstrongs all last evening and this morning.

When we stopped by the Armstrong's house to see if it was okay for the kids to play together, Mary and Linc were keen about the idea.

"Much obliged, Andy," Mary said with a smile and continued, "oh these kids just love to go to your house and play. Linc and I need to run a few errands. Perhaps we will stop by for a visit and pick up the kids a little bit later on?"

"Okay, then," I replied, "see you in a bit."

At home, the kids barreled out of the car and wasted no time creating their Fox and Goose play area. Mabel made sure they were bundled up good with hat, scarf, and gloves. I watched them from the kitchen table as they played in the yard.

First, they made a large circle using their feet to cut paths in the snow. The circle was about 40 feet in diameter. They cut paths in the center of the circle - just like pie slices. The outer circle and the trails in the middle of the circle (pie slices), were areas where the kids could travel. The center of the circle was the safe area. The person who was "it" was the Fox. Neither the Fox nor the "Goose" could run outside the trails cut in the snow, or they would be tagged "it" and become the Fox. The Fox chased the Geese down these trails trying to tag someone before they got to the center, and if so, the person tagged became the Fox.

I must have watched the kids run around and around that circle for 30 minutes or more. The Armstrong boys, Jack and Bob, were faster than the girls and I noticed they would let the girls make it to the center safely on more than one occasion. Little Patty Armstrong was having so much fun. Joyce got disinterested with the game and was making snow angels.

Eventually the circle was trampled over and the original clean paths indistinguishable. One-by-one they got tired and retreated to the warm house for hot cocoa. Mabel attended to each of them to make sure they took off any wet clothes and placed them near the register to dry. Linc and Mary arrived and had a cup of hot cocoa with Mabel and I. The first snowfall was always the most fun.

Finished Picking Corn

(9 Dec 45) It was 20 above and very windy. Nobody went to church today. I went out to pick, bound and determined to finish the corn today, for I only had six acres remaining. It was pretty smooth going all

morning. I was so excited at the possibility of finishing I didn't stop for lunch. By 2:00 pm I made my final round. I jumped off of the F30 and took a look around and felt like a million bucks.

I headed back towards home, face into the wind. Nothing could take away the smile on my face knowing that the corn harvest was done. Tomorrow I will open the gate leading to the North field and the cattle can feed on the ears of corn that somehow fell to the ground. When they get their fill, they will wander back into the barnyard.

Start Christmas Preparations

(11 Dec 45) I woke up this morning feeling light as a feather. With the corn harvest completed and the hard work of picking all of that corn behind me, I could now focus on the greatest time of the year – Christmas. This year seemed extra special. With Albert, Ray, and Michael home from the war, and Sully Kollar coming home for Christmas with his discharge right around the corner, it was going to be a Christmas to remember.

Before breakfast, I took Gladys to the Maple Grove School corner. Tink around until early lunch then went to a sale with my brother John to a farm east of Ransom. We didn't buy anything, just enjoyed relaxing a bit and talking with the regular auction shoppers. After dropping John off at his place and visiting with Anna, I decided to make my way back to the school to pick Gladys up.

"What do you say we head over to Hallet's Nursery and pick up a Christmas tree?" I asked Gladys as she jumped into the car. "Your Uncle John mentioned they just got some fresh trees in."

"Why sure, but we better make sure that we get home in time for Mother to go to club tonight," said Gladys. Mabel had a meeting with the Royal Neighbors club. They met during the holidays to make Christmas gifts for the needy. Tonight was the night to start the drive.

"Oh sure, we'll be home in plenty of time."

Gladys and I picked out a real pretty blue spruce from the nursery's fresh shipment and headed home.

The kids were home and were so excited to see the tree. Mabel had dinner ready and was a little antsy to get going.

"Let me get the car gassed up before you head into Marseilles, Mabel," I said as I headed back out the kitchen door, pulled the car up to the gas tanks, and filled her up. The sun was just about down and the wind was starting to whip and it was chilly. At least I'm not out in the field again picking corn, I thought.

When I was on my way back inside, Mabel was on her way out.

"Thanks Andy. I should be home no later than eleven," she said as she breathed in the cold air, "whoo, it's nippy."

"Drive safely." This is not a night you want a breakdown. I was a little worried about the battery failing her. I would make a point to get that changed out real soon. "Stay on the main roads if you can - to get help if you need it."

I got the tree all set up in the stand and leveled it out.

"Can we decorate it tonight?" Esther asked as she was eager to get started.

"Not tonight Esther. We need to wait for Mom. We can do it tomorrow as soon as you get home from school. That will give me time to get all of the lights and bulbs and whatnot out of the attic." I was sorry to break the bad news, but they would have something to look forward to tomorrow. I figured I would wait until the morning to get everything out.

I laid down about 10:30 pm a little worried about Mabel, but she drove in just past 11:00 pm. Knowing she was home safely, I quickly fell asleep after vowing to get that new battery tomorrow first thing.

(12 Dec 45) Had breakfast a bit early this morning and dropped Gladys off at the school corner and headed straight into Streator to get a battery. "Are you sure you don't want me to take you to work?" I had asked Gladys, since she worked in town. She declined because she had not forewarned her friend that she would not be at the corner for her ride into town. Gladys was always thoughtful of others.

I paid the gentlemen at Montgomery Wards for the battery and headed home. Finished my morning chores and changed the battery in the car. Decided to change the oil and anti-freeze while I was at it.

Just before lunch I went up into the attic and found the Christmas boxes and hauled them down into the living room to get ready for decorating tonight. I untangled the strings of lights, and inspected for faulty bulbs. Only found a couple bad ones, but luckily had enough spares to light all of the strings.

After lunch I greased the corn picker real good and put it back in the machine shed. I thought to truly finish the corn harvest I had to fix the broken elevator under the crib. After only a five-minute inspection it seemed that the motor bearings were burnt out. I guess it lasted just long enough to get the crops in. I got the necessary tools and pulled the motor out. I had done it so many times before, I had it out in 15 minutes. I would go to Missel's to drop off the motor to get repaired in the morning.

After dinner Mabel, the three little ones, and Gladys decorated the tree. Mabel turned on Perry Como on the Philco. We had just finished putting up the lights when Darlene came home.

"How was your day?" Mabel asked Darlene.

"Very busy as usual," Darlene replied as she threw her coat on the sofa. She shrugged off the day, gave us a big smile and offered to help, "What can I do?"

"Well, we could use your height to put some ornaments near the top," I said handing Darlene an ornament with her name on it. Mabel had made each of our girls an ornament, five different colors, with their names on the side with shiny glitter. After the lights and ornaments, came the strands of paper rope and silver icicles. It was my job every year to put the angel on top and then connect the power cord into the socket to light the tree.

"Let me go see how it looks," Mabel said and gestured to Nancy to grab her coat and follow her outside. Mabel always needed to see how the tree looked from the driveway. She came back inside and made a few adjustments to the tree. She must have also noticed cobwebs in the windows when she viewed the house from outside because soon as she was done fixing the tree, she ran to the kitchen and found the duster. She immediately dusted and cleaned the front windows from one corner to the other.

"Oh, I need to set up the manger," Mabel said as she shuffled around looking for the manger in the boxes on the floor. "Andy, did you pull the box with the manger out of the attic?"

"I thought I did – let me have a look-see," I responded by scanning the floor. "Well, I guess not. Let me go and have another look."

Mabel loved her manger with Mary, Joseph and baby Jesus. She always set it up in the living room. The manger was pretty good-sized and was made out of cardboard – and it was quite old.

I came back in just a few minutes with the manger boxes. Mabel was happy. She and Nancy set it up in the same place as the previous years.

"Mabel, I found something else in the attic that we need to put up," I said hiding the mistletoe behind my back.

She smiled as I pulled the mistletoe from behind my back, raised it above her head and gave her a kiss on the cheek and said "Merry Christmas". I then hung the mistletoe in the middle of the room like we did every year.

Christmas had officially begun at the Durdan household.

Cracking Walnuts for Christmas

(15 Dec 45) As I walked down the stairs into the basement, I heard Mabel giving instructions to Nancy and Esther on the best way to crack walnuts.

"Now if you can't crack it with pliers, hold the pliers in place and swiftly come down right about here with the hammer." Mabel gave it a tap and the walnut cracked open. "You see, now you go ahead and try it." She gave the pliers and hammer to Nancy.

Mabel always had Christmas planned out very well and she carried out her plan equal to the precision of a military operation. She wanted to start preparations for baking her cookies long before the 25th. You could tell Nancy and Esther were thoroughly excited to help. Joyce was getting involved also.

"Can I crack one Esther?" Joyce asked.

"When we get a small one, we'll let you try it, okay?" Esther replied. "Why don't you hold the bowl and we'll give you the nuts from inside." The walnuts would be used in the cookies. Joyce gladly accepted her role in the effort.

Just as Joyce held the bowl out, Nancy dropped the nuts from the first few walnuts. I snuck in behind Joyce and grabbed them right out of the bowl and popped them into my mouth.

"Hey Dad, those are for the Christmas cookies," Nancy complained and said to Joyce. "You need to guard those walnuts Joyce. Mom says we need all of them."

"I'm sorry, but they looked so good. I won't eat any more – promise," I said as Nancy smiled knowing I was just teasing them.

The walnut cracking job would take a while as we only had one nutcracker, and there was quite a sack-full to get through. Mabel and I would check on them periodically to see if they needed any help. Every once in awhile you would hear them spatting with each other.

Miss Kates, their school teacher, had quite a curriculum for the kids during Christmas. Nancy came home so excited yesterday telling Mom that the kids had starting making Christmas cards and presents for the parents. Miss Kates must have an awful lot of patience with all of the kids needing help with their projects at the same time. They also had to prepare for a Christmas party that was put on for the parents – this party was next week.

Christmas Party at Country School

(17 Dec 45) Quite a lot of snow had fallen last night to add to the already treacherous conditions. The mercury read ten above and it was windy. Got Nancy, Esther, and Joyce all bundled up and ready for school. Today was the Christmas party for the parents. They had prepared for the better part of two weeks for this event and we weren't going to let a little snow get in our way.

"Make sure you have everything girls," Mabel said as she tied Joyce's scarf around her neck and chin.

"Off we go," I said and headed out to the car, which I had stationed on the driveway, warmed up and ready to go.

At around one pm, Mabel and I headed up the road to the school for the party. There were quite a few cars there, but I imagine some parents would not make it on account of the weather. The party was a good time to chat with the neighbors. Everyone was starting to catch the holiday spirit. Miss Kates was buzzing around getting everyone in place for the holiday chorus. Mr. Todd, the School District's Music Director, was there on this special occasion. The kids sang Christmas carols – Silent Night, Hark the Herald Angels Sing, and We Wish You a Merry Christmas. They also played a few numbers on their tonettes. Every once in a while one of the kids would miss a note on their tonette that would let out a shrieking sound. The parents chuckled. You could tell that the kids practiced quite a long time for this event. After the program, the kids presented their parents' with the gifts handcrafted in the schoolhouse. Then we enjoyed a variety of cookies that several Mothers had volunteered to bring to the party.

Miss Kates approached me as we were having cookies.

"Andy, can you do me a favor please?" she asked.

"Of course. Great program, Miss Kates, the kids did a great job."

"Thank you. The kids worked really hard." She smiled and continued. "My car will not start. I had a feeling it was going to give me trouble today. It was very hard to start this morning and I tried it around lunchtime and it wouldn't even turn over."

"Froze up, I suppose?" I asked.

"I'm afraid so. Could you possibly drive me back to my Dad's? He said that if I had trouble, he would come out and give me a hand."

"Why of course I can. You just let us know when you are ready," I replied, "would you like me to give you a tow back there? It wouldn't be a bother – I can drop Mabel and the kids off at home and get the truck."

"No" Miss Kates replied, "giving me a ride would be just fine."

So we dropped Miss Kates at Elmer's and headed home. The kids were happy to have their teacher riding in the back seat with them.

(18 Dec 45) My Dad had a party at his place every year at Christmas time. Mabel, all five of our girls, and I headed over around 7 pm. Most of the brothers and sisters, and their family members were present. The house was plum full of Durdans. The men mostly congregated in the kitchen drinking egg nog. The little kids were running about with new toys. My Dad always had gifts to give to all of the grandchildren. Usually he bought gifts at the five and dime – little dolls, cars, trucks, and planes.

We all gathered in the living room for the gift exchange around 8 pm. Everyone, adults and kids alike, opened up presents. Nancy, Esther, and Joyce each got a kewpie doll from their Aunt Margaret. Mabel was pleased to get a hat and homemade skirt. Uncle Pete bought me a new baseball glove – he told me that he had had enough of me making errors and that now I could no longer blame it on my old glove. We all had a good laugh at that one. Gladys received a photo album and Darlene a nice purse.

By 9:30 pm Mabel developed quite a headache and Esther and Joyce started to get very tired, so we decided to head on home.

(19 Dec 45) After taking Gladys to the corner to catch her ride to Streator, I came home to do my morning chores and eat breakfast. Darlene had spent the past two nights waiting and hoping Sully would arrive soon on Christmas leave. She knew that he was coming home for the holidays but was not sure of the exact date. Sully's parents had received a telegram that stated he would be home yesterday. But with all of the snow that had fallen the past week, the trains were not able to make their destinations on schedule. The highlight of the telegram was that Sully was expecting to be discharged sometime in January. There will probably be a wedding in our family sometime next year.

Darlene's car was acting up quite a lot lately, so I went into Grand Ridge yesterday and purchased some new plugs and wires. I had her battery on charge most of yesterday. I figured while I was as it, I would clean the plugs in the truck. The past couple of days have been a real challenge keeping autos running and snow cleared away. In addition to Darlene's car conking out once at the Kollar's place, and once in Streator, I had to help brother Pete with his auto and Miss Kates' car stalled at the schoolhouse.

By lunchtime, I had Darlene's car up and running.

"Thanks Dad," said Darlene as she jumped in the car.

"Heading to Kangley?" I asked referring to the Kollar place, "I have a feeling Sully will be home today."

"Oh, me too. I'm on pins and needles." Hopefully Sully will only have to go back one more time before getting discharged.

"You drive safe," I warned Darlene, "the roads aren't too bad right now, but once that sun goes down, watch out. Just spend the night there if it gets too bad, okay."

She nodded, smiled and drove off. The car sounded pretty good and I felt confident that the plugs and wires did the trick.

Sully Home for Christmas

(23 Dec 45) Darlene spent the night at the Kollar's waiting for Sully to arrive. He had called three days ago to tell Darlene that he would hopefully be home by the 22nd, but as of 10 pm last evening, he had not arrived. The phone rang at breakfast. Mabel answered the phone.

"He made it in, that's wonderful," Mabel replied to who I assumed was Darlene. "Oh, that would be good," Mabel finished her conversation and hung up the phone.

"What time did he get in?" I asked her.

"Two o'oclock this morning," she replied, "he was stuck in Chicago for the past two nights. He came in on a bus."

"A bus? I thought he would come in on the train."

"Darlene said it was a real mess with thousands of soldiers and sailors trying to get home. She said it doesn't matter as long as he is home."

"So are they coming over?"

"Well, Sully is sleeping right now. I guess he was pretty tired," she continued, "they'll be here about two pm."

Mabel spent the next four hours cleaning the house and getting ready for Sully's arrival. It had been quite a while since we last saw him. I was looking forward to hearing of his experiences. I can't imagine how excited he must be to be home and so close to being discharged.

It started to snow just before lunch, and by the time Sully and Darlene arrived, the roads were covered with two inches of snow. We all ran outside to meet them. Sully looked great with a big smile and Darlene looked radiant. In fact, I don't believe I have ever seen her so happy.

Sully gave the little girls a big hug and said, "Let's go inside girls, I bought each of you a present." The girls looked up at Sully with starry eyes. They had been talking about him all morning.

Inside, Mabel made coffee and served walnut cookies. The kids opened their presents from Sully – they each received a beautiful Christmas ornament. They were excited to hear that they were purchased in Chicago. We relaxed and talked for two hours or more before Sully and Darlene got up to leave. They had promised to head back to Sully's parent's place to see the rest of his family for dinner.

The snow stopped falling by supper time, but was beginning to drift. I cleared the driveway with the Fordson, then did my evening chores. A truck pulled into the driveway that I did not recognize. I walked over and met the truck in front of the new garage and Sully and Darlene jumped out.

"Thanks for the ride sir, I appreciate it," Sully said to the man inside, shut the door, and waved him off.

"Andy, we tried to get back to Dad's, but I ran the car into the ditch," said Sully.

"Oh boy, you both look alright," I replied, "are you okay?"

"Oh we're fine, just a little cold," he said, then asked Darlene to go inside and get warm.

"The car is fine," he assured me, "it's on Richard's Road not far from Route 23."

"Do you think we need the tractor? Or maybe the truck will do."

He thought for a second, "I think the truck will do it. It's not too far in the ditch."

We spent a few minutes pulling the necessary tools, ropes, and chains together to do the job. I went downstairs and got Sully some boots, gloves, and a hat.

"Here you go Sully, put these on. They should fit," I said referring to the boots, "and why don't you put this hat on, your ears look like they are freezing."

"I don't know Andy," Sully said with a big smile, "I can't feel them anymore."

The roads were very treacherous, but we made it to Richard's Road without too much trouble.

213

We went about three miles west on Richard's Road when I saw what I thought was Darlene's car on the side of the road.

"That's not it Andy," Sully said, "we are on the opposite side of the road."

We pulled up closer and saw a couple inside. The passenger car window rolled down half way and the woman waved to us. Sully jumped out and went over to help her get out of the car. I figured they must not have been there long if Sully and Darlene just came through here while getting a ride from the friendly stranger.

Sully helped the woman inside the cab of the truck. I got a better look at her face and realized that she was quite young, probably Gladys' age or a bit younger.

"Why don't you sit here and get warmed up," I said, "are you both okay."

"We're okay, just cold," she replied with shivering lips and chattering teeth.

Sully and I helped the man out of the car. The car was at quite an angle with the driver's door pushed up against the snow bank. We rigged up the combination of rope and chains between the frame of his car and the back end of the truck. The car came out pretty smoothly with Sully steering from the inside.

The young couple were visibly shaken and scared to drive. They stated that they only lived a short piece up the road, so I pulled the car along with the rope and chain rig and Sully steered the car. The couple stayed inside the cab of the truck with me where it was nice and warm.

We pulled the car into what turned out to be the young woman's parent's farm. A man came outside and appeared not too happy to see what I assumed to be the family car being towed by a rope and chain. He thanked us for our help and we were on our way.

We drove past the spot where the couple went into the ditch and just beyond that point we ran into a pretty good-sized snow drift. This was no doubt what caused the couple to go into the ditch. Another mile down the road, and we saw Darlene's car. It wasn't as far in the ditch as the couple's car, but stuck good nonetheless.

Like old pros, Sully and I eased Darlene's car out of the ditch and kept right on going all the way back to the house. We told Mabel, Darlene, and Gladys of our adventurous night, and Sully made a quick phone call to his parents telling them they wouldn't be there due to the snow and bad roads. He and I both felt good about helping the young couple get home. We talked for a bit, then turned in around midnight.

Oyster Stew on Christmas Eve

(24 Dec 45) Sully was sleeping soundly on the couch this morning when I came out of the bedroom. What a night we all had last night fighting the elements. Started the coffee and headed downstairs to stoke the coals and get the furnace going. Went outside and surveyed the roads a bit. Looked like the roads were drifted and blocked both north and south. The tire tracks from last night were all drifted over. I hustled back inside not sure how to attack this morning's chores. Decided to get the Fordson going and plow the drive first, then tend to the animals.

Back inside, Mabel had quietly started putting breakfast together.

"It's blocked both north and south this morning. Don't think we'll be going anywhere anytime soon," I said, settling in for coffee and cereal.

"Good thing you got my oysters Saturday, and didn't wait until today," Mabel replied. She never missed a Christmas Eve without serving oyster stew, and this year would be no exception. Each year I would go to town and purchase her a quart of oysters.

"Does Sully like oysters?" I inquired.

"Sure he does. I asked him last night and he said that his mother makes oyster stew from time-to-time," she continued with a whisper, "but not as good as mine I'm sure." Mabel snickered as she handed me a plate of toast and jelly.

We heard Sully stirring in the living room.

"Andy, go see if he wants some breakfast," Mabel prodded me to be a good host.

I stood up and met Sully half-way. He was tall, about my height, and slender. He had dark hair and had grown a mustache since the last time we saw him.

"Come join us for breakfast Sully. We have fresh coffee, cereal, and toast," I said.

"Wow, that sounds good. I'm pretty hungry after all that work last night getting that car out of the ditch. Cheese and crackers that was a bugger," Sully replied with a laugh He is a good-hearted soul. Never took things too seriously. After all he's been through on that ship, I imagine this was nothing to get upset about.

We had a nice breakfast. I got busy with feeding the animals, and took a little extra time cleaning out the barn. I didn't mind spending more time in the barn considering it was much warmer than being outside. Sully gave me a hand with shoveling snow around the entrances and around the new garage to clear the way if we were able to get out today.

We relaxed inside talking with Darlene, Gladys, and Sully through lunch. Darlene and Gladys helped Mabel make chicken casserole and salad. Sully wanted to see the 1939 Farmall F-30 I bought this past May.

"Too early for a beer?" I asked Sully.

"Are you kidding me," he replied, "remember you're talking to a Navy man, Mr. Durdan." He laughed and followed me to the basement where I stored my Meister Brau. We walked out to the barn and looked at the tractor.

"She's a real beauty Andy," Sully commented, "get a load of these big steel wheels."

"Yeah, she's really made my job easier. This was the last model year for the F-30. She has real good ground clearance and it is very easy to cultivate with. It really is a smooth running tractor."

"Where did you find it?"

"At a farm sale in Marseilles. Got a good deal."

We looked around a bit more and then headed back to the house.

Mabel's oyster stew was delicious. The only ones who didn't like the stew was Nancy, Esther, and Joyce.

"You'll like it one day, when you are older like us," I teased Nancy and Esther.

"I don't even like to look at them ugly oysters," Esther said as she made a funny face.

In addition to the oysters, I also purchased a quart of pickled pigs feet, which was my special Christmas Eve treat. One sight of those pigs feet and the girls ran for the hills.

(25 Dec 45) As tradition prevails, we opened gifts on Christmas Eve. The little girls opened an array of gifts from us, along with some home-knitted hats, as Mabel was so practical. They opened fun things from Gladys and Darlene. The older girls gave me a nice new billfold, and Mom a bracelet. This morning the kids raced downstairs to see if Santa had been here and to see what he had put in their stockings the night before – oranges, Hershey bars, hard candy, and suckers.

(28 Dec 45) We had more snow on Christmas day and flurries now and again throughout the week. Spent most of my time the past few days

just doing my normal chores, tinkering around the machine shed and old garage, clearing the driveway and sidewalks of snow, and on occasion, pulling someone out of a ditch or helping someone get a car going. Sully and Darlene were spending precious time together before Sully had to return to the Navy. They were starting to make plans for their wedding when Sully was discharged.

We normally kept the Christmas decorations through the new year, so the mood was still festive for the holidays. We were all getting a bit of cabin fever.

(31 Dec 45) We all went to Dad's for the New Year's Eve celebration this year. I believe everyone was there - all of my brothers and sisters, except for Mary and Milt. The house was full. Everyone seemed happy and content. This year certainly ended on a much higher note than it started. Albert and Ray were home, Sully was home and near coming home for good after his discharge, and Irene's husband Michael was home from the Army. I thought of William Fraser who did not return, and all of those who gave their lives for our country so that we could live here in America in peace and freedom. We will start 1946 with a renewed sense of hope, starting our year without war. Gradually, our lives would return to normal.

At midnight, we raised our glasses to a new year. It wasn't until after 1 am that the party died down. We found the three girls sleeping on their Grandpa's bed snuggled up to the coats that were piled up there. Mabel picked up Joycie, and I woke up Nancy and Esther. We all got home and nestled into bed.

"Andy, could you please stoke the coals, it's quite chilly in here," Mabel asked.

"You betcha," I replied.

Epilogue

Durdan Family Picture (1960)
From left to right (back row): Joyce (21), Gladys (33), Darlene (37),
Nancy (24), Esther (23); Mabel (59) and Andrew (64) in front.

Andrew Durdan (1896 – 1964)

Andrew Durdan died on April 1st, 1964. Isn't it ironic that he died on a day that he enjoyed so much, April Fool's Day. As Andy's health deteriorated, he moved from the farm into the home of Leland and Nancy (Durdan) Shields in Streator Illinois until he died. Andy is buried in Riverview Cemetery, Streator Illinois.

Mabel Durdan (1901 – 1962)

Mabel Durdan raised five beautiful daughters, each finding and marrying five true gentlemen. Mabel died in 1962 and is buried next to Andy in Riverview Cemetery.

Darlene (Durdan) Kollar (1923 – 1962)
Darlene married Albert Kollar in 1946 after his discharge from the United States Navy. They moved to Chicago after their wedding. Albert Kollar started his own air conditioning business in Chicago and he and Darlene had four children: Kenneth, Mark, Kathleen, and Albert. Darlene died in 1962 at the young age of 39. She is buried in Riverview Cemetery next to Sully. Ken, their oldest son, farms acreage on the Kollar Farm in Kangley to this day.

Gladys (Durdan) Palaschak (1927 – 2002)
Gladys married Dick Palaschak in 1948 and later rented a farm near Kinsman, then moved to a farm on Richard's Road where they actively farmed there into the 1990s. Dick and Gladys raised six children: Douglas, Jerome, Gregory, Mary Jane, Teresa, and Julia. Greg, their youngest son, farms that land to this day. Gladys died in 2002 and is buried in Saint Patrick's Cemetery in Ransom, Illinois, next to Dick. They attended Saint Patrick's church for 54 years.

Nancy (Durdan) Shields (1936 – 1995)
Nancy married Leland Shields of Grand Ridge in 1958. Lee and Nancy moved to Granville Illinois where Lee invested in, and operated the Helmer-Shields Funeral Home. They raised one child: Elizabeth. Nancy died in 1995 and is buried in Riverview Cemetery, Streator Illinois, next to her parents and sister.

Esther (Durdan) Sparks (1937 -)
Esther married Harold Sparks of Streator Illinois in 1960. Harold worked for United Parcel Service (UPS) in Peru Illinois and later started his own Vacuum Cleaner business. They raised three children in Peru: Anthony, Christine, and Jeff.

Joyce (Durdan) Blakemore (1939 – 1970)
Joyce married Dale Blakemore of Streator Illinois in 1960 during a double wedding ceremony with her sister Esther. Dale was a Streator firefighter and eventually became Fire Chief. They raised two children in Streator: Andrew and Brenda. Joyce died in 1970 at the young age of 31. She is buried in Saint Mary's Cemetery, Streator, Illinois near her daughter, Brenda.

The Farms
Andy purchased an additional 280 acre farm, just north of their existing property, in 1949. After Mabel died in 1962, and Andy became seriously ill and could no longer work, he agreed to have his farm machinery auctioned off and rented out the farmland. He died in 1964.

The Durdan sisters rented both farms, they maintained the books, purchased seed, and sold grain until the farmland was eventually sold in 1974. Esther told this story about how the farmhouse was cleaned out prior to renting out the property:

"As you know, Mother died in 1962 and Dad in 1964. We cleaned out the house, divided up everything, and everyone took what they needed or wanted. When we got all done after working several days, we stood in the living room, and Gladys had all of us hold hands right there and we all said prayers together."

- Esther (Durdan) Sparks, 2006

About the Author

Jeff Sparks is the son of Harold Sparks and Esther (Durdan) Sparks. Jeff and his wife of 21 years, Wendi, live in Palm Bay, Florida.

Jeff was born and raised in Peru, Illinois. After graduating from LaSalle-Peru Township High School in 1983, Jeff joined the United States Navy, completed Basic Training at Great Lakes in Chicago, Illinois, and volunteered for submarine service. Jeff graduated from Basic Submarine School in New London, Connecticut and was assigned to his first submarine, USS Benjamin Franklin (SSBN 640). There he qualified in submarines and extended his enlistment to attend radioman "A" and "C" schools. While attending "C" school in Groton, Connecticut, Jeff met his future wife, Wendi Lucas. Jeff, Radioman Second Class Petty Officer, was assigned to the USS Pargo (SSN 650), which was in Bremerton, Washington during an overhaul. It was there where Jeff and Wendi were married in a chapel on the Navy Base in Bremerton.

After completing an overhaul in the shipyard and sea trials, the USS Pargo made it's trek down the Pacific Coast, through the Panama Canal, and up the East Coast to be home-ported in New London, Connecticut. Jeff completed many North Atlantic and Mediterranean deployments while serving onboard the Pargo, was honorably discharged from active duty service in 1989, and joined the Navy Reserve. Jeff and Wendi settled in Groton, Connecticut, where Jeff attended night college and earned his degree in Electrical Engineering from the University of New Haven, in New Haven, Connecticut.

Jeff and Wendi relocated to Palm Bay, Florida to be closer to Wendi's parents. Jeff works at Harris Corporation where he specializes in System Integration and Test of Navy Communications Systems.

As a member of Naval Reserve, Jeff came up through the ranks, selected as Chief Petty Officer in 1997, and later commissioned as

Ensign in the Limited Duty Officer program in 1998. Jeff is currently a Lieutenant Commander supporting the United States Southern Command in Miami, Florida. Jeff was mobilized to active duty for Operation Enduring Freedom/Noble Eagle in 2001 in response to the attacks of 9/11 and served at the United States Central Command Headquarters in Tampa, Florida.

Through encouragement from Wendi, Jeff decided to write a book in honor of his grandfather, Andrew Durdan. The purpose of the book is threefold: 1) honor the family, 2) provide the reader with a sense of day-to-day life on a farm in this bygone era, and 3) and to document one year in the life of this family in the unbelievable year of 1945.

Comments from the Author

I hope you enjoyed reading this book as much as I enjoyed writing it. Since Grandpa Durdan died one year before I was born, I was not fortunate enough to get to spend time with him. After reading his 1945 diary and writing this book, I feel as if I know him well.

If you would like to send comments or request a copy of this book, please write to:

Jeff Sparks
P.O. Box 110493
Palm Bay FL 32911